SADDLE UP!

A Guide to Planning the Perfect Horseback Vacation

By Ute Haker

John Muir Publications
Santa Fe, New Mexico

John Muir Publications, P.O. Box 613, Santa Fe, New Mexico 87504
Copyright © 1997 by Ute Haker
Cover and maps © 1997 by John Muir Publications
All rights reserved.

Printed in the United States of America.
First edition. First printing January 1997.

Library of Congress Cataloging-in-Publication Data
Haker, Ute.
      Saddle up! : a guide to planning the perfect horseback vacation / by Ute Haker.
          p.   cm.
   Includes index.
   ISBN 1-56261-295-6
   1. Trail riding—United States—Guidebooks. 2. Trail riding—Guidebooks.
3. Trails—United States—Guidebooks. 4. Trails—Guidebooks. 5. United States—
Guidebooks. I. Title
   SF309.255.H35   1997
   798.2'3—dc21

Editors: Rob Crisell, Dianna Delling, Nancy Gillan
Production: Marie J.T. Vigil, Nikki Rooker
Graphics Coordination: Tom Gaukel
Design: Marie J.T. Vigil
Cover Design: Suzanne Rush
Typesetter: Melissa Tandysh
Maps: Michael Bain
Illustrators: William Rotsaert, Diane Rigoli
Cover photo: Donnie Sexton
Printer: Publishers Press
Back cover photos: top—San Juan Mountains Association
                      middle—Yellowstone National Park
                      bottom—EQUUS★USA

Distributed to the book trade by
Publishers Group West
Emeryville, California

To the memory
of my mother, Irmgard Quasthoff Haker,
who taught me to love nature and wild things,
and of my father, Heinz Haker,
who told a thousand-and-one stories from around the world

Acknowledgments

I am deeply grateful to:

The horses, companies, government agencies, and individuals worldwide who help equestrian vacationers have the time of their lives; John Muir Publications for making *Saddle Up!* possible; everyone who contributed photos or information to the book; Mary Hill, who lent her geology and wildlife library and was a joy to brainstorm with; Cecil Dawkins, writer par excellence, who kindly edited the initial manuscript; my sister, Anke Haker, for bringing the love of horses into our family, and for being a great friend and riding companion; Kim Switzer, who introduced me to many of *Saddle Up!*'s North American areas in the early 1970s; Alicia Butler, who taught me science and opened a whole new world; the travel professionals at Westwind, Journeys Unlimited, Wings, and Santa Fé World for showing me how to help people get around the planet; my dog, Jess, for taking me on daily walks and keeping me sane; and my cats, Dini and Grace, who helped type.

CONTENTS

CATCHING THE SPIRIT!

D o you long to see the Earth's wild places, to follow trails blazed by great explorers and pioneers? Do you enjoy discovering unusual places or seeing the world from a different perspective? Do you like to visit wild creatures on their own turf, or bask in the silence and beauty of the backcountry? If your answer to these questions is yes, then you'll want to consider a riding vacation.

Some of the world's most remarkable places and most engaging journeys can be yours on horseback. You can see parts of national parks most visitors don't know even exist, or ramble through wildernesses larger than some countries. You can ride with the Navajos through the sun-baked buttes and mesas of Monument Valley, or ride down the Nile and camp in the shadows of the pyramids. You can ride a cowhorse on an exciting cattle drive. Whatever your wish might be, there is undoubtedly a horseback riding vacation to fit your dreams.

Horses take you where cars can't go, to places you could never see unless you hike or ride. If you hike, you have to carry your own food and gear, and

Iceland. Diethard Franz/EQUUS•USA

you can go only as far as your legs will carry you. On a horse, you climb easily into the high mountains and descend into deep canyons. You also have your own equine friend—a companion for the entire trip.

Riding vacations are for everyone. People who have never been on a horse can go. Senior citizens, disabled people, and kids can go. Even people who don't want to ride can come along. A children's horseback holiday with parents or grandparents is a childhood highlight. Hikers in the golden years appreciate horse outings when hiking over long distances has become troublesome.

You can bring your own horse or hire a friendly mount. You're only asked to be kind to the horse, be in good condition, and weigh less than 225 pounds. If you're a first-timer, you'll be shown the basics before the ride, and riding guides will keep an eye on you out on the trail. The cost is no higher than for other vacations, and often much less.

Nonriders can stay at a ranch (dude or cattle) and take advantage of everything else: hiking, relaxing in a shady spot with a good book, playing horseshoes or volleyball, lounging around a swimming pool, watching or helping with ranch chores, fishing, river rafting, or square dancing. Luxurious riding resorts may have saunas and whirlpools, jogging trails, fitness centers, tennis courts, and perhaps their own golf course. Or, if you prefer the excitement of being on the move and camping out at night, you can join a wagon train and travel on wheels while the riders accompany you on horseback.

Whatever your delight, this book will introduce you to the many and varied possibilities for outdoor vacations you'll treasure for the rest of your life.

So grab your hat, saddle up, and get ready to ride!

1
RIDING VACATIONS FOR EVERYONE

A rgentine gauchos, Texas cowboys, North African Berbers—what do they have in common with each other? Their lives revolve around their horses, both as working partners and as friends. But any traveler with a spirit of adventure can enjoy a worldwide network of horse-related vacations. *Saddle Up!* presents the 17 varied types of riding vacations that have evolved over the years, each with its own identity, flavor, and devoted followers.

Riding vacations fall into two groups: **Nature Adventures** and **Cowboy Adventures**. Nature adventures emphasize the natural beauty of the world around you. You will enjoy the spectacular scenery on cowboy adventures, as well, but you will also join the traditional life of the American cowboy.

Bringing your own mount is not required on these vacations. Horses and equipment are furnished by the professional horse outfitters, stables, ranches, and riding resorts offering the vacations, and at surprisingly reasonable costs. The cost of all-inclusive riding vacations averages from $100 to $200 per person per day, including horse, saddle and tack, riding guides (wranglers), meals, camping gear where necessary (except, perhaps, your own sleeping bag), and often even airport transfers and taxes. Gratuities for the riding staff are the only additional costs.

In the following pages you will find descriptions of the many different kinds of riding vacations. Chapter 7, The Best Places to Ride: North America, recommends spectacular areas with horse trails and lists U.S. and Canadian providers to contact for these vacations. More detailed outfitter information, including addresses and telephone numbers, price codes, types of vacations, and minimum riding skills required, is given in the Outfitter Directory, Chapter 9. Other recommended riding regions not discussed in the chapters are listed in Chapter 10, Additional U.S. Public Lands with Horse Trails.

Riding vacations aren't limited to North America. Chapter 8, The Best Places to Ride: Worldwide, lists riding vacations from Andalusia and Greece to Kenya and Siberia.

Nature Adventures

Day Rides

If you've never taken a riding vacation and want to ease into the experience, day rides are the best way to start. Hourly, half-day, and full-day rides can take you into spectacular country. The riding possibilities are endless: along deserted beaches where waves crash and seagulls circle overhead; across vast arid stretches; through thick forests; or into steep canyons, rolling foothills, or mountains fragrant with pine.

Day rides are usually arranged on short notice—a day or two before the ride is time enough to arrive at a destination, get oriented, and see how the weather is holding up. Wherever you are, in North America or abroad, simply check the local telephone book under Riding Stables or Horseback Riding, or ask the tour desk at your hotel or resort.

After day rides have introduced you to the pleasures of horse travel, you're ready for the rest of this book. All the other riding vacations last overnight, several days, or weeks.

Day riding is spending the day with a group of friends: laughing, talking, taking in the sights, whether in the American Rockies or anywhere on this planet.

Diethard Franz/EQUUS•USA

Wilderness Expeditions

Throughout history people have wondered what was over the mountain, beyond the forest, or farther along the river. The hardiest souls left familiar surroundings to find out. When they returned with tales of adventure, others wanted to go, and so some explorers became guides.

During North America's Western expansion, American guides were the eyes, ears, and provisioners of those venturing into unsettled territory. The guides knew the wilderness and how to survive in it, and they knew Native American ways. From the Indians they learned to "read sign"—to find meaning in broken twigs and bent blades of grass. From a pile of dung they could tell whether Indian horses or wild mustangs had crossed the trail, and that knowledge sometimes meant the difference between life and death. Guides dressed wounds and ministered to the sick, and they knew edible from poisonous plants and how to behave around wild animals. For his expeditions in the West, even the "Pathfinder" John Charles Frémont (1813–1890) valued his guides. "Scouts are indispensable," he said, "from the time of leaving the frontiers of Missouri until we return."

Today's professional horse outfitters are our modern guides, and they continue the same traditions. They open the backcountry to people who never considered wilderness expeditions, making them comfortable and safe in unfamiliar territory. They guide, protect, and inform—about horses, local history, and the natural areas you ride through.

Some horse outfitters offer wilderness expeditions as brief as one night, but most travelers prefer nothing less than a week. Each wilderness day shows you more of the land and its wildlife, and allows you to reach deeper levels of relaxation. Since you'll leave towns far behind, you'll usually overnight in tents.

Pack Trips

On pack trips, pack animals (horses or mules) carry the gear and supplies. Wherever four-wheel-drive roads go into the backcountry, the gear can be moved by vehicles, but—especially in North America—that is the exception.

Pack trips usually start early, say 7:00 a.m. or 8:00 a.m., so you'll arrive in the town closest to the ride the previous afternoon, with time to explore the area and spend the night at a local motel. In the evening some outfitters provide a welcome dinner or an orientation meeting at a local restaurant.

The next morning the outfitter may pick you up at your motel, or you'll meet at a rendezvous spot, perhaps at the outfitter's ranch, where you can park your car. If you arranged a private pack trip, your friends and family are the only guests; if not, this is where you'll meet the other riders. At the trailhead, you'll meet your horse. While the wranglers load your gear onto the pack animals, you fill your horse's saddlebags with whatever you'll need for the day,

A Pecos Wilderness pack string heads out on the trail, carrying all the food and gear needed for a week.

then walk around to take your first photographs. The excitement grows, and you'll be itching to climb aboard. Finally, you're off: you mount, adjust your stirrups, receive whatever instruction is necessary, and hit the trail.

Soon you're heading into unknown territory. One wrangler rides in front, leading the pack animals. Guest riders follow the pack string, with a second wrangler bringing up the rear. If there are two routes to the day's destination, one wrangler may take the pack string on the shorter trail while you and the other wrangler take the trail that's more scenic or offers freedom to ride faster if you wish.

By the time you stop for photographs or to stretch your legs, you've come to trust your horse and have settled into a comfortable routine. By noon, when you stop for a picnic by a stream, you've forgotten everything but the gentle rhythm of your horse's gait and the breathtaking scenery around you.

Your guide will tell you about the trail's history. Perhaps it once led wildlife to the nearest water source or over a mountain. Native Americans may have followed it to hunt, trade, or visit relatives. Perhaps European explorers—conquistadors seeking gold or missionaries seeking converts—used this very trail.

When you stop at the day's end, the wranglers tend to the horses and set up camp while you wander around and get your bearings. You may want to help with the chores or set up your tent. As the sun descends and the wranglers cook, your group drifts together for appetizers. At dinner the group circles around a campfire, plates in hand, swapping stories as daylight fades. More, bigger, and brighter stars than you've ever seen appear in the immense sky. At bedtime the wranglers furnish hot water for washing up. Listening to an owl hoot, you lie in your warm sleeping bag and wonder why life is not always this simple and good.

The smell of coffee wakes you the next morning, and again there's hot water for washing up. After breakfast, on a progressive pack trip, you'll pack up and ride to another destination. On a base camp ride, you'll take day rides from camp. And so the days pass, riding, exploring, relaxing, and taking it all in. You may see elk or bighorn sheep, or eagles wheeling across the sky. Perhaps you find coyote or mountain-lion tracks, or see a bear foraging in the distance. You'll ask questions, reflect, and smile a lot, until finally, sadly, the last day arrives. In late afternoon back at the trailhead, you'll dismount reluctantly. It's time to say farewell. Your group exchanges addresses and promises to send especially good photographs or perhaps meet again for another ride. After a night at the motel, you'll leave, catching a last glimpse of the countryside you've come to love—and swearing you'll return.

For areas and outfitters, see the Best Places to Ride: North America and Best Places to Ride: Worldwide chapters.

Drop Camps

Drop camps (pack trips out of a base camp arranged just for your group) are great escapes. They're also popular for special occasions—small family reunions, birthdays, anniversaries, graduations—or as bases for hiking clubs, corporate brainstorming, or team-building projects. Spiritual retreats or natural healing seminars often take place at drop camps, as well as photography workshops and all kinds of field trips.

Most horse outfitters will work with you in a number of ways: simply transporting you and your gear into the wilderness—the original meaning of the term "drop camp"; furnishing some or all of the camping gear and food; and/or doing the cooking and camp set-up. The complete package, including food preparation, camp set-up, and daily guidance, is the equivalent of a private base camp pack trip.

The price varies according to what you arrange, but all options place you in natural areas for a memorable vacation. If your trip is a true drop camp, the outfitter and animals leave after delivering you to the destination. Then your group can spend its days hiking, fishing, or just relaxing. On a prearranged date the outfitter will return and pack you out, or you can hike out on your own.

For areas and outfitters, see the Best Places to Ride: North America and Best Places to Ride: Worldwide chapters.

Pack-Supported Hiking

If you'd like to hike into natural areas without carrying your gear, professional horse outfitters will provide pack horses or mules. Outfitters will also deliver your gear to your wilderness campsite for days on your own, and can supply all of the camping gear and even the food. You can also purchase a complete package that includes food preparation, camp set-up, and daily guides—the equivalent of a professional pack trip minus the horse. Even then you can spend as little or as much time as you want with the outfitter. If you're feeling sociable, you can benefit from the outfitter's knowledge of the terrain, wildlife, and local history. If you prefer privacy, the outfitter can ride ahead with the gear and have the camp ready and waiting for you at the end of your hike.

Pack-supported hiking is usually arranged on a custom basis for groups of at least four. Divided by the participants, the already reasonable cost is a bargain. If you have fewer than four people, you may find a scheduled horse trip open to hikers.

For areas and outfitters, see the Best Places to Ride: North America and Best Places to Ride: Worldwide chapters.

Horse/Raft Combos

If you've ever enjoyed the excitement of a whitewater rafting trip, you may be tempted to combine two outings on one trip. In regions where suitable rivers exist and where rafting companies operate, horse outfitters work with the river companies. Not even horses can take you into some sheer-walled canyons, such as parts of Hell's Canyon in Oregon and Idaho. Here the only access is by water, so at a suitable bend in the river your horse outfitter will turn you and your gear over to the river guides. In Montana's

U.S. HORSE/RAFT COMBOS

Arizona: Arizona River Runners
Colorado: Adventure Specialists
Montana: Glacier Raft Company
New Mexico: New Mexico Outdoors
Oregon: Outback Ranch Outfitters
Texas: Lajitas Stables
Utah: Adrift Adventures, Hondoo Rivers & Trails, Western River Expeditions, World Wide River Expeditions

Bob Marshall Wilderness, for example, it's a pleasure to enter the wilderness from the east, spend several days riding, then leave the horses and take a raft to come out on the west. Elsewhere, horseback and rafting may be entirely independent but can be combined by scheduling one after the other, perhaps with a day's rest in between. One of the world's ultimate journeys is to ride at the Grand Canyon (see Best Places to Ride: North America), then spend a week or so whitewater rafting through the canyon.

Horseback Wildlife Safaris

All wilderness expeditions include ample wildlife-viewing, but wildlife safaris are specifically designed for it. As few as four people can arrange custom trips, allowing friends, families, or small wildlife- and bird-watching groups to travel into remote areas. Overseas, African safaris on horseback (see Best Places to Ride: Worldwide) introduce you to elephants, lions, leopards, giraffes, zebra, antelope, hippopotami, rhinoceri, water buffalo, and wildebeest. You can arrange pack trips, drop camps, pack-supported hiking, and horse/raft combos with a wildlife focus. For custom trips in North America, see Best Places to Ride: North America.

U.S. HORSEBACK WILDLIFE SAFARIS

Bighorn Sheep: Utah—Hondoo Rivers & Trails
Buffalo (Bison): Utah—Hondoo Rivers & Trails
Elk: Utah—Hondoo Rivers & Trails
Mustangs: California—Frontier Pack Train, Rock Creek Pack Station. Utah—Hondoo Rivers & Trails

Wagon Trains

In 1961, to celebrate Kansas' Centennial, a number of Kansas ranchers traveled to Topeka, the capital, in covered wagons. Along the way, to the ranchers' surprise, people kept stopping them for pictures and handshakes and requests to ride along. The idea of modern-day wagon trains caught fire, and now vacationers can relive history or simply explore the countryside the old-fashioned way. Wagon trains are ideal for families and groups with mixed riding skills. Riders are furnished horses to ride alongside or go off on short excursions,

Wagon trains enable riders and nonriders to travel together.

while nonriders enjoy traveling by wagon. Come evening, the wagons circle around a campfire just as they used to, and the participants gather for good stories and good food.

For anyone accustomed to modern comforts it is difficult to imagine the hardships the American settlers endured to pursue their dreams of opportunity and freedom. Distances now covered in a few hours by car, or minutes by airplane, meant whole weeks of backbreaking, agonizing work and setbacks. The journeys brought the risk of harm or death through hunger, thirst, exhaustion, or ambushes by Native Americans or bandits. People hung on for dear life and kept going. Some made it, some did not, and many in the process lost children, spouses, lovers, and friends.

Today, the 2,170-mile (3,495-km) Oregon National Historic Trail is a road and trail route approximating the famous Oregon Trail. It crosses six states and has some 300 miles of discernible wagon ruts and 125 historic sites. The trail was the major route to the Northwest for fur traders, missionaries, gold seekers, and settlers. From 1841 until 1861 an estimated 300,000 emigrants followed it on a laborious trek that took five months. Sections of the California Trail branched off the Oregon Trail for those heading to the gold land. From April 1860 until October 1861, the Pony Express horseback mail service also followed portions of the Oregon Trail. In southern Wyoming you can follow segments of all of these trails by wagon train.

****

U.S. WAGON TRAINS

California: Red's Meadow Pack Station
Montana: Big Sky Overland Cruises
Wyoming: Great Divide Tours, Trails West,
Wagons West

****

Dude Ranches and Riding Resorts

In 1872 Yellowstone became the world's first national park. Easterners wanted to see this treasure and the rest of the West, yet few places existed where visitors could stay. The travelers soon realized that their best lodging choices were livestock ranches. Those who knew people on the ranches tried to inveigle invitations. Those who did not aimed to make acquaintances.

The Westerners obliged, and with friendliness and hospitality they opened their doors to friends and strangers who came in need of bed and board. Without their generosity most Western visits would have been impossible. The ranchers were good hosts, and the guests enjoyed the lifestyle.

In 1882 a guest from Buffalo, New York, had such a good time at the Eaton Ranch, a successful hay- and horse-ranch in North Dakota's badlands, that he didn't want to leave. He begged the Eatons to let him stay and insisted on paying for the privilege. This was the first time a ranch was known to accept money for its hospitality. Word got around and people flocked to the Eatons'. Here guests could pay to spend whole summers and not feel awkward, and they kept coming. Now in the guest-ranch business, the Eatons moved in 1904 to a beautiful spot west of Sheridan, Wyoming, at the base of the Big Horn Mountains. The three Eaton brothers divided responsibilities. Alden ran the ranch's day-to-day operations, Willis handled the overall management, and Howard organized pack and hunting trips into the surrounding country and sightseeing excursions into Yellowstone National Park. Yellowstone's Eaton Trail is named for Howard.

James Norris "Dick" Randall founded the OTO, Montana's first guest ranch, in the 1880s. One of his early neighbors was Martha Jane Canary— "Calamity" Jane. Dick later recalled that the term "dude" was first coined in Yellowstone around 1886. Male visitors from the East were called "dudes," female visitors "dudines," and children "dudettes." Ranches that took in paying guests became known as "dude ranches."

When World War I broke out in 1914, Europe was a poor vacation choice. Many Easterners came west instead, an incentive for additional guest ranches. Some visitors came for health reasons. Other clients were "remittance men," usually relatives of wealthy Eastern or European families, sent west because they were a real or imagined disgrace to their clan. Regular remittance kept them away from home.

The Northern Pacific Railroad helped the early ranches. With the 1883 completion of the railroad into Yellowstone, the Northern Pacific sold 19,000 to 51,000 long-distance tickets every summer. Visitors were picked up at the station in four- and six-horse stagecoaches and stayed in park hotels financed by railroad mortgages. When the first motorcars arrived at Yellowstone in 1915, the Northern Pacific was the loser. To continue drawing railroad patrons west, the railroad supported guest ranches, and the number of new ranches kept increasing. In 1925 alone the dude-ranch business increased nearly 40 percent. Initially the dude ranches centered around Yellowstone National Park in Montana and Wyoming; in the 1940s they spread to most western states.

Some of these original ranches still receive guests. Now, as then, they offer good horses and Western hospitality. When you arrive, you'll smell fresh-baked pies from the ranch kitchen and feel at home. Stories abound of guests who cry and children who hide when it's time to leave, and of generations of guests returning year after year. Yet no two ranches are alike. Mountain ranches usually take horseback riding guests only in summer; the desert ranches in the southern parts of Texas, Arizona, or California are best in spring and fall. Some are fancy, others plain. Some offer a lot of riding each day, some only a few hours. Some have riding arenas and provide different levels of instruction; others just give a few basic tips. Some offer activities besides riding—relaxing in swimming pools and hot tubs, enjoying lawn games, sightseeing excursions, river-rafting, or tennis—while others don't. Some provide evening programs such as nature lectures or square dancing. Some organize children's programs, others let families create their own. Some ranches take only a few guests at a time, some accommodate 50 or 100 or more. Whatever your preference, there's a ranch to suit you.

A dude ranch may once have been a cattle ranch, but the few that still run full cattle operations often keep them separate from the guests. Most have become complete guest businesses dedicated to showing visitors the surrounding natural area on horseback.

Some riding resorts' amenities may be similar to those at dude ranches, while at others the offerings take off from there. The most luxurious resorts have heated indoor pools, saunas, fitness rooms, jogging trails, indoor tennis courts, and sometimes even private championship golf courses. All have their own stables and are excellent choices for riders traveling with luxury-minded nonriders. However, most resorts aren't prepared for guests who wish to ride a great deal, so be sure to ask about riding opportunities.

Since there are so many dude ranches and riding resorts to choose from, I recommend that you either work through EQUUS★USA (see page 245), specialists in North American riding vacations, or find suitable dude ranch or riding resort addresses in *Gene Kilgore's Ranch Vacations* (Santa Fe, N.M.: John Muir Publications, 1997).

Inn Rides

Inn rides are a real treat, combining long hours in the saddle with overnights at country inns. On some rides you settle into an inn and take day rides from there. On others you'll ride from one inn to the next, your luggage transported by car. Noontime finds you beside a lake or stream, enjoying a gourmet saddlebag lunch. In the evening the inn pampers you with fine dining. Inn rides match good riding with romance, as growing numbers of honeymoon couples have discovered.

Some, but not all, inn rides require at least medium riding skills and are a good choice for skilled riders seeking a challenge. Some in the U.S., and many overseas, use English saddles and tack. Most international equestrian vacations are inn rides, but the term "inn" may be an understatement. On some overseas rides you stay at top-of-the-line private estates or even palaces and fairy-tale castles. See Best Places to Ride: Worldwide for an overview of tempting journeys abroad.

U.S. INN RIDES

California: Adventures on Horseback, California's Redwood Coast Riding Vacation
Florida: Royal Palms Tours
New Mexico: New Mexico Outdoors
Vermont: Firefly Ranch, Kedron Valley Stables, Mountain Top Inn
West Virginia: Swift Level

Instructional Riding Vacations

All equestrian vacations give riding tips as they are needed. But not all vacation choices have riding arenas for formal lessons, nor do most hire trained riding instructors. The wranglers are excellent riders, but not necessarily

California's Redwood Coast Riding Vacations: By day, you'll canter on beautiful beaches. At night, romantic inns pamper you with elegant meals, hot tubs, and entertainment.

California's Redwood Coast Riding Vacations: Next morning it's on to magnificent redwood forests. Each day brings a new adventure!

teachers. Instructional vacations fill the gap. Here you learn in an intense, daily fashion without distractions. What might take weeks to learn during short lessons at home can often be grasped within days on a vacation program. All you have to do is pack your suitcase and go. A week later you'll be a much more accomplished rider.

If you're a beginning rider, you have many riding disciplines to consider. Ask yourself what you want to do with your skills as you become more expert, then talk to hometown riding stables and take a few try-out lessons that show you the possibilities. Whatever discipline you choose, you will be richly rewarded. You'll spend more time with horses, and the better

U.S. INSTRUCTIONAL RIDING PACKAGES: WESTERN SADDLE

California: Adventures on Horseback, California's Redwood Coast Riding Vacation, Pavoreal Guest Ranch
Colorado: Colorado Trails Ranch, Lost Valley Ranch
Utah: All 'Round Ranch
Vermont: Mountain Top Inn

ENGLISH SADDLE

California: Adventures on Horseback, California's Redwood Coast Riding VacationPavoreal Guest Ranch,
Colorado: Fox Equestrian
Vermont: Kedron Valley Stables, Mountain Top Inn

rider you are, the more you'll enjoy riding. You'll have a greater understanding of your equine companions, and you'll know what to expect in different riding situations. As your training advances, you'll be able to stay in the saddle longer, ride faster if you wish, perhaps even learn to jump obstacles. You will handle more highly trained horses, and suddenly you'll be taking riding vacations you never dreamed possible.

The companies listed above offer week-long packages that include lodging and meals. Europe also offers outstanding instruction programs in English riding. For a few European examples, see Best Places to Ride: Worldwide. All instruction programs include time to relax and sightsee.

Fox Equestrian, Colorado: The majestic Rocky Mountains provide a spectacular setting for the United States' only cross-country jumping resort.

Fox Equestrian, Colorado: Two hundred fifty fine cross-country jumps range from 18 inches to 3½ feet.

Cowboy Adventures

Cattle Drives

Early settlers coming west looked with disgust at the American grasslands that stretched from western Texas north to Canada. They saw only laborious travel through the huge wasteland of dry grass, brown in late summer and often taller than the pioneers. They didn't realize that these waving grasses—which nourished millions of roaming buffalo (bison) and antelope—were extraordinarily high in protein, particularly the grasslands of the northern, wetter regions. Discovery of the value of the Great Plains came slowly, but when it did, investors realized there was money to be made. Young steers could be bought inexpensively in Texas and Mexico, moved to the prairie, grazed there for a season, and sold at immense profit. Far enough north to have potent grass but far enough south to have a reasonably long summer season, the lands that are now the Dakotas, eastern Wyoming, and eastern Montana were favored destinations. And the only way to get the cattle to the grass was by cattle drives.

The American cowboy came on the scene in the early 1800s, when settlers pushing west into today's Texas discovered the long-established Spanish and Mexican ranches. The newcomers quickly copied the methods of the *vaqueros* (Spanish for "cowboys"), who had mastered both the handling of the cattle from a horse's back and the tools of the trade: rope, saddle, spurs, and branding iron. When Texas won its independence in 1836, Texans took over the land and saw the commercial possibilities in the plains' herds of ownerless longhorn cattle and wild mustangs. By the time Texas joined the Union in 1845, the Texas cowboys and their open-range livestock-grazing were already being duplicated elsewhere in the West. When the Civil War ended in 1865, markets had increased in the growing industrial cities of the North, and cowboys found work as far north as Canada and as far west as California.

As many as 5 million head of cattle were driven north on the hoof from Texas. The long drive to such railheads as Abilene or Dodge City was an annual event. Each cowboy had several horses: one for "cutting" cattle out of the herd, another for general transportation, a third for night riding. At night the cowhands took turns watching for animal predators and cattle thieves, and all dreaded that something might frighten the herd into stampeding. The watch sang softly to keep the herd calm. Striking a match for a smoke was strictly forbidden; it risked startling the herd. Anyone caught doing it was fired on the spot. If the nightmare happened and the cattle stampeded, the entire crew was called out. The hands jumped on their horses and raced in the dark to get ahead of the frightened animals. If a horse tripped and fell, both rider and horse were often trampled to death. Reaching the front of the

On cattle drives, the herd is moved slowly enough to graze and put on weight. The pace is set by a lead bovine, usually a big, gentle animal who is a natural leader.

herd, the riders shot their pistols to slow them and turn them around. But the work was not over. After the herd was finally calm, strays lost during the stampede had to be found. A stampede could mean staying in the saddle for 24 hours.

The expansion of the railroad, and the increasing use of barbed wire to confine cattle on ranches decreased the need for cowhands, and today the wild adventures of the great cattle drives are past. But because on large ranches tens of thousands of acres are untouched by road, some ranches still move herds by old-fashioned cattle drives to fresh, green summer pastures in the spring and back to the ranch in the fall. A few of these ranches invite guests to come along, and if you've ever dreamed of being a real cowhand, here's your chance. Shouting "Yee-haw!" and heading out with the herd, your city worries and responsibilities quickly fade away. Ahead are wonderful days in the saddle filled with spectacular scenery, the whooping of cowboys, and the bawling of hundreds of animals slowly making their way across the landscape.

Cattle drives usually take only a few guests, depending on the number of cowhands and cattle involved. You can choose simply to ride along or, if you're a medium rider, to participate as much as you like. Covering 50 to 75 miles takes about a week. The actual distance you ride will be much greater, though, if you work the cattle and ride out to look for strays. At night everyone sleeps in tents or, occasionally, rustic cow camps.

At the end of the drive you'll feel a sense of accomplishment, and rightly so. Toughened by a week of long hours in the saddle, braving whatever the herd and the weather hold in store; your mind sharpened by new realities; your disposition mellowed by the wide-open spaces and friendships with good horses and good people—you were part of a job well done.

U.S. CATTLE DRIVES

California: Spanish Springs Ranch
Colorado: Broken Skull Cattle Company,
  MW Ranch
Wyoming: Cheyenne River Ranch,
  Great Divide Tours, Schively Ranch,
  Two Creek Ranch

Cattle Drives with Wagon Trains

In 1989, on the 100th anniversary of Montana's statehood, Montana ranchers organized the Montana Centennial Cattle Drive. Riders went by horse, nonriders by covered wagon, and everyone had fun moving cattle by day and enjoying cowboy poets and country singers at night. Several groups of Montana ranchers now arrange similar events a few times each summer. For a week, guests of mixed riding ability enjoy beautiful scenery, practice roping and cattle skills, ride to their heart's content or move along in the wagons, camp out at night, and gain a new appreciation for Big Sky cattle ranching. At the week's end guests show off their new Western skills by competing in informal rodeos they'll long remember. The final night, the group gathers to dance the two-step before farewells in the morning.

U.S. CATTLE DRIVES
WITH WAGON TRAINS

Montana (Billings): Half Moon Enterprises,
  Powder River Wagon Trains & Cattle Drives
Montana (Bozeman): Montana High Country
  Cattle Drive

Cattle Roundups

When the range was still open, with no fences from Texas to Canada, cattle roamed the Great Plains from end to end and line riders at outlying cow camps kept track of the animals. Each spring a roundup gathered mother cows and their newborn calves. A captain chosen by the ranches directed the affair, and each ranch sent a group of cowhands and horses.

U.S. CATTLE ROUNDUPS

California: Rock Creek Pack Station, Spanish Springs Ranch
Colorado: Southfork Outfitters
New Mexico: N Bar Ranch, New Mexico Outdoors
Texas: Encinitos Ranch
Utah: Bar Ten Ranch, Hondoo Rivers & Trails
Wyoming: Cheyenne River Ranch, Great Divide Tours, High Island Ranch, Two Creek Ranch

---

The roundup captain sent cowboys off in pairs to search for cattle. The cook, meanwhile, drove the chuck wagon to a designated spot and set up camp. By mid-afternoon the cowboys herded the cattle in and held them until all riders arrived. The best ropers gathered the calves while the rest of the crew worked in pairs, throwing the calves and holding them down for branding, castrating, and earmarking. As the ropers dragged the calves to the branding fire, they called out the brand of the mother cow the calf had been following. In cases of disputed ownership, the roundup captain settled the matter. It was up to the cowhands to see that their home ranches got fair treatment.

On modern ranches, cattle are still rounded up for moves from pasture to pasture, for branding, or for vaccinations, and some ranches invite guests to participate. The distances are less than in the old days; many roundups can be accomplished by day rides from the ranch. The better rider you are, the better your chance to join the action, but even beginners and nonriders enjoy staying at the ranch during these special times.

Gabriele Roselius/N Bar Ranch

N Bar Ranch, New Mexico: Pushing strays toward the misty Mogollon Mountains

N Bar Ranch

N Bar Ranch, New Mexico: There are 31,200 acres to roam on the ranch, not counting the adjacent Gila Wilderness.

Southfork Outfitters, Colorado: A roundup guest brings mother cows and calves to the corral.

Southfork Outfitters, Colorado: Cowboy work in the spring and fall, Weminuche Wilderness pack trips in the summer

Horse Drives

A running horse is an awesome sight. Neck arching, muscles playing under firm flesh, tail flying, the horse is a symbol of everything free and wild. When a whole herd explodes around you and the ground trembles under thundering hooves, your pulse quickens and you can't resist chasing after them to be part of the sun, wind, and speed. The feeling is electric and irresistible.

In the spring some ranches move their horses to a summer ranch for work, then back to the winter ranch in the fall. Horse outfitters offering high-country wilderness expeditions move herds to their summer mountain pack stations and down again in the fall. Other outfitters run several horse drives a season to keep their horses fit between less challenging rides.

Several ranches and outfitters invite you to join their horse drives. You need at least some riding experience to come along, but to participate fully you should be an expert rider. Overnights are in tents along the way.

U.S. HORSE DRIVES

California: Bedell Pack Trains, Frontier Pack Train, Red's Meadow Pack Station, Rock Creek Pack Station, Spanish Springs Ranch
Wyoming: Great Divide Tours

Cattle Ranches

The sudden swarm of gold hunters in the 1850s greatly expanded the American West's market for beef. From a few scattered cows around fur-trading posts or along the Oregon Trail, newcomers began building cattle herds. From all over the country, and even the world, people entered the cattle-ranching business (see sidebar).

Today, some cattle ranches in the American West take in paying guests to supplement the ranch income and to mingle with travelers from around the world. These are still primarily cattle operations, and here you can become a temporary part of a working ranch team. You'll visit beautiful country and get a sense of the people and the land that have had such profound influence in shaping the American character and the national experience.

EARLY CATTLE RANCHERS

Richard Grant, a Scotsman of Falstaffian proportions who had once worked for the Hudson's Bay Company, bought foot-worn livestock along emigrant trails in Wyoming and drove his herds into Montana's sheltered western valleys. The animals thrived and, trailed back in the spring, were sold to new waves of travelers. Visitors to Montana's Deer Lodge Valley commented on the herds of Richard's son John in 1862. "He does not winter feed," said one, "but lets them graze thro' the winter. . . . We never saw larger, better, or fatter cattle anywhere."

Missourian D.A.G. Floweree, "Flurry" to his friends, had hunted gold in California when he was 17. Legend says that later he was a member of an ill-fated filibustering expedition to Nicaragua in the 1850s and escaped death only with the aid of a lovely señorita.

Robert Ford came out of Missouri as a bullwhacker on the Santa Fe and Oregon Trails, and eventually reached the Deer Lodge Valley as captain of a wagon train. He won the government contract to provide hay for Cow Island's cavalry and bought cattle with his earnings.

In 1866 Nelson Story led the pioneering cattle drive from Texas to Montana. He had done well in the Alder Gulch gold diggings in Montana, invested in a herd of 600 Texas longhorns, and trailed the cattle north from Texas over the Bozeman Trail to a ranch near Livingston, Montana. Indian troubles sealed off this particular route for some time, but the movement of Texas cattle onto lush northern grasslands became an integral part of the expanding open-range cattle industry.

No large investment was needed. Under the Homestead Act of 1862 it was easy to acquire a free nucleus of 160 acres. With careful selection and an eye for a steady supply of water, aspiring ranchers could graze their animals on public domain land all around them. But in the long run, few cattle companies showed consistent returns. Eastern and overseas capital often pulled out if profits failed to materialize quickly enough, and rail costs were high and shipping facilities poor. Market prices fluctuated according to consumer demand. Overgrazing became a problem, and disease, icy winters, and summer droughts killed whole herds.

EQUUS•USA

Ranch guests Tom and Mike bring up the rear while cowhand Cody veers off to ride the flank.

Some ranches ask each evening what you would like to do the next day—ride out with the cowhands for cattle work, nature ride, hike or fish or picnic—while others simply integrate guests into whatever cattle work needs doing. You can watch or participate in the work. You will be expected only to enjoy yourself, but if you'd like a taste of the life of the cowhand, you're welcome to put on your blue jeans and your boots, and jump in. All cattle ranches offer unlimited riding—you can ride as much or as little as you want, or not at all. By the end of the day you'll feel pleasantly spent and filled with memories. Most cattle ranches only take a few guests at a time, and evenings are spent talking quietly around the fireplace or retiring early. But if there's a rodeo or square dance nearby, hosts and guests pile into the ranch pickups and head out.

Again, with so many cattle ranches to choose from, I recommend you either work through EQUUS★USA (see page 245), specialists in North American riding vacations, or find suitable ranches in *Gene Kilgore's Ranch Vacations*.

Cow Camps

When cattle ranches move their cattle in the spring to remote summer pastures, the cowhands take turns looking after the herds from rustic line camps.

A few ranches invite you not only to visit the West but also to live it. Each day you ride out with the cowboys to tend to various chores. In spring it's rounding up cattle for branding and dehorning; toward fall, herds must be moved closer to the ranch. The months in between are for mending fences and chasing down strays. You stay close to the herds, right in the middle of things. Day's end brings stunning sunsets and gentle evenings. You'll sit by the campfire with your new friends, recharging for tomorrow's adventures.

U.S. COW CAMPS

Colorado: Broken Spoke Ranch, Everett Ranch
New Mexico: Half Moon Cattle Company, New Mexico Outdoors
Utah: Dalton Gang Adventures
Wyoming: Sanford Ranches, TX Ranch

2
PLANNING YOUR
RIDING VACATION

All vacations begin with the questions what, where, when, and how long. As you read this book, make notes on how you answer those questions and which geographic areas appeal to you. The Riding Vacation Overview Table on the following pages will help you. It lists stationary vs. progressive vacations, amounts of riding involved in different vacations, and an "accommodation comfort scale."

What? Which type of riding vacation interests you? Do you prefer a nature vacation, or experiencing the life of the American cowboy? Would you like to be on the move (progressive rides), or stay in one place and ride from there (stationary rides)? Do you want to ride a little, a lot, or not at all? Are rustic accommodations acceptable, or do you prefer luxury? In addition to the Overview Table, see this chapter's sections on vacations for riders with varying abilities.

Where? Which country or state interests you most? Which region, national park, or designated wilderness? To help you decide, read Chapters 7 and 8, Best Places to Ride: North America and Best Places to Ride: Worldwide, and Chapter 10, Additional U.S. Public Lands with Horse Trails.

When? What month or exact dates do you want to ride? Does that match the riding season of your favored location? Mountain treks are best in high summer, desert treks in spring and fall. Desert ranches and riding resorts are great destinations for sunny winter riding. To help you decide, look for the Travel Tips boxes at the end of each section in Chapter 7, Best Places to Ride: North America.

How Long? Are you looking for a three-day weekend nearby, or do you have enough time to make long-distance travel worthwhile? How long a vacation can you afford? Chapter 8 (Best Places to Ride: Worldwide) and the Outfitter Directory, Chapter 9 include price codes. One week is an ideal minimum.

Nonriders

If you are a nonrider, see the Overview Table's Vacations with Nonrider Options. On wagon trains, and cattle drives with wagon trains, you'll move with the riders. During the other vacations you'll hike, fish, sightsee, and relax while the riders are off with the horses.

RIDING VACATION OVERVIEW

PROGRESSIVE VS. STATIONARY

Progressive Riding Vacations
Nature Adventures
Progressive Pack Trips
Progressive Pack-Supported
  Hiking
Horse/Raft Combos
Progressive Wildlife Safaris
Progressive Inn Rides
Wagon Trains

Stationary Riding Vacations
Nature Adventures
Base Camp Pack Trips
Drop Camps
Base Camp Pack-Supported
  Hiking
Base Camp Wildlife Safaris
Stationary Inn Rides
Dude Ranches
Riding Resorts
Instructional Riding Vacations

Cowboy Adventures
Cattle Drives
Cattle Drives with Wagon Trains
Horse Drives

Cowboy Adventures
Cattle Roundups
Cattle Ranches
Cow Camps

RIDING AMOUNT

Vacations with Nonrider Options

Nature Adventures
Pack-Supported Hiking
Inn Rides
Wagon Trains
Dude Ranches
Riding Resorts
Instructional Riding Vacations

Cowboy Adventures
Cattle Drives with Wagon Trains
Cattle Roundups
Cattle Ranches

Vacations with Choice of Riding Amount

Nature Adventures
Base Camp Pack Trips
Drop Camps
Horse/Raft Combos
Base Camp Wildlife Safaris
Stationary Inn Rides
Wagon Trains
Dude Ranches
Riding Resorts
Instructional Riding Vacations

Cowboy Adventures
Cattle Drives with Wagon
   Train
Cattle Roundups
Cattle Ranches
Cow Camps

Vacations Requiring Lots of Riding

Nature Adventures
Progressive Pack Trips
Progressive Wildlife Safaris
Progressive Inn Rides

Cowboy Adventures
Cattle Drives
Horse Drives

ACCOMMODATION COMFORT SCALE

Most Rustic: Progressive Wilderness Expeditions, Cattle Drives, Horse Drives
Rustic: Stationary Wilderness Expeditions, Wagon Trains, Cattle Drives with Wagon Trains, Cow Camps
Less Rustic to Comfortable: Cattle Roundups, Cattle Ranches
Comfortable to Luxurious: Inn Rides, Dude Ranches, Instructional Riding Vacations
Luxurious to Very Luxurious: Riding Resorts

Novices and Beginners

If you are a first-time rider, or it's been a while, check "Vacations with Choice of Riding Amount" in the Overview Table, pages 28–29. Here you can ride as much or as little you want, or even skip a day if you need a break. On "Vacations Requiring Lots of Riding" it's often difficult to ride less than a full day, and many trips have few or no layover days.

Consult the Questions to Ask Outfitters section under Selecting Your Outfitter, below, and the Minimum Skill category in the Outfitter Directory (Chapter 9). All vacation providers listed in this book specialize in matching riders with horses and trail difficulty. For a perfect fit, be honest about your riding ability.

Skilled Riders

Advanced beginners can trot and gallop for short distances and are comfortable in all terrain. Medium riders can trot and gallop for a long time, can post at the trot, and can take minor jumps such as logs and small ditches. Experts can handle spirited horses, lots of fast riding, and jumping fences.

If you're an expert rider, pick any vacation you like. If you're looking for challenge, consult the Questions to Ask Outfitters under Selecting Your Outfitter, below, and the Divides Groups by Skill category in the Outfitter Directory (Chapter 9). Some dates are reserved for skilled riders; other dates are divided by skill for parts of the ride.

Any time you have a few like-minded friends, you can arrange custom trips with outfitters to suit your skill. Instructional vacations are automatically divided by skill.

Riding with Children

The sooner you introduce your children to horses, the more years they'll have to enjoy them. Most riding vacations accept children when accompanied and supervised by at least one adult. The Children's Minimum Age category in the Outfitter Directory lists each vacation provider's age policy. The type of vacation you choose depends on your children's riding skills. See the Nonriders, Novices, Beginners, and Skilled Riders sections, above.

During their prime season, some dude ranches and riding resorts offer specially designed children's programs that give families time together as well as apart. To find horseback camps for unaccompanied children, contact your local recreation department and youth organizations, or the tourism departments of other states.

Scotland's Argyll ride shows you a kaleidoscope of lochs, mountains, castles, and ancient settlements.

Scheduled or Custom Dates?

Riding vacations used to be arranged purely on a custom basis. If you had four riders, you were in business. Modern outfitters realize that nowadays people often travel alone or in twos, and that the magic number of four is hard to achieve. To work with these new travel patterns, outfitters offer scheduled rides that allow individual riders to come together on a given date. Joining other riders is an excellent way to meet like-minded travelers and make new friends. Common group sizes are six to 12 guests, rarely more than 15.

In addition to scheduled rides, most outfitters still offer custom trips. Groups of at least four people can request a private trip—usually at no extra cost—or allow the outfitter to add additional guests. If you are fewer than four, you can join an ongoing party or pay a surcharge for a private trip.

Selecting Your Outfitter

Professional outfitters — wilderness outfitters, riding stables, ranches, and riding resorts —make riding vacations possible for you. Outfitters are not remote corporations. They are people who enjoy horses, the great outdoors,

and making new friends. They are young or old, short or tall, male or female. Some have extensive college educations; others a lifetime of hands-on experience. Many are born into the lifestyle; others are horse-knowledgeable refugees from suburbia. Some work by themselves with the help of a few hired wranglers; others are organized into family partnerships or small horse-centered businesses

Vacation providers are listed in Chapters 1 (Riding Vacations for Everyone), 7 (Best Places to Ride: North America), and 8 (Best Places to Ride: Worldwide). Check the Outfitter Directory for detailed information about the North American providers. As you read about the companies that interest you, note their differences and select two or three who meet your criteria.

Most U.S. states demand that a person wishing to outfit and guide have a state license and a permit for riding through private or public land. To be prudent, make sure that whomever you hire is properly licensed and has a clean safety record. Illegal outfitters don't like to draw attention to their operation and are often hesitant to call for help when a client becomes sick, injured, or lost.

Call your selected companies to form a personal impression. Request a brochure and a list of references. Call former guests; ask what they liked best and least, and whether they would travel with the outfitter again. If you still can't decide, or you want someone else to make the arrangements, call EQUUS★USA at (800) 982-6861 or (505) 982-6861, or fax them at (505) 984-8119. A ride consultant will ask you several important questions, call you back with specific information, and handle all reservations.

Questions to Ask Outfitters

- Which of your scheduled or custom dates have space available?
- What are your rates? Are they all-inclusive?
- What do your rates exclude—i.e., airport transfers, taxes, gratuities? What do these generally cost?
- Do you have special prices for groups, families, children, seniors, or corporations?
- Is there a surcharge for singles requesting their own tent or room?
- Do you have off-season rates?
- On camping trips, do I need to bring my own sleeping bag and insulating pad? Can I rent them from you? At what price?
- On wagon trains, what is the price for riders? For nonriders?
- Is this particular ride suitable for children? Do you offer other rides that are better for them? Do you furnish child-size saddles?
- Is this ride challenging? If so, in what way: terrain, long hours in the saddle, pace?

- What is the shortest ride you recommend? What is the longest?
- Can you send me a rough schedule of what happens each day?
- What time do we meet the first day? When do we get back on the last?
- How long do we ride each day? Can I ride more if I want?
- Will I have opportunities to trot and gallop if I want?
- Is this particular ride progressive or stationary?
- On progressive rides, how many nights do we stay at each site? (Layover days allow more exploring. It's also more relaxing if you don't have to pack up every morning and unpack every night.)
- On base camp rides, how many hours is it to camp? On the last day, do we return the same way or by different route?
- How many hours of cattle work are there each day? Do some dates have more cattle work than others? Will there be any nature riding?
- Do you ride cavalry style (50 minutes on the horse, 10 minutes off—considered by many the ideal)?
- How do you handle special requests: special diets, allergies, fear of heights?
- Should I buy a fishing license before I arrive? Do you furnish fishing gear?
- Are you licensed by your state as a professional outfitter? Do you carry all proper permits for riding into this area?
- What is the weather usually like that time of year?
- Is there anything else I should be aware of?

Bringing Your Own Horse

With the increase of urbanization, horse trails near towns are quickly disappearing. If you're an experienced rider with wilderness skills, you have a choice when you explore backcountry. You can either engage a guide or, with proper preparation, go it on your own. If you plan to ride on public land, it is essential that you contact the stewardship agencies shown throughout *Saddle Up!* for wilderness permits, specific trail information, and instructions for horse use. If you cross private land on your trip, obtain permission and instructions from the owners beforehand. The backcountry is wild and no place for the unprepared. If you're unsure, the safest and easiest way to enjoy the land is with experienced help.

If you lack wilderness skills, sign up with a horse outfitter who allows visiting horses (see the Outfitter Directory), or participate in a riding club's guided outings. Call the head wrangler to discuss whether your horse is up to the task. Long days in rough terrain, at high altitudes, or in extreme temperatures may put your horse at risk. Also, horses live in hierarchies. While the horses rearrange the pecking order, yours may get bitten or kicked. It's good to be aware of the dangers. Sometimes it's wiser to leave your horse at home and depend on a different mount while traveling.

Making Your Reservations

All riding vacations must be booked early. Small guest numbers and short riding seasons spell high demand. I recommend making reservations at least six months ahead to get the date you want, but some dates are filled a year or more in advance.

Decide how much additional time you want to spend in the area. Riding vacations can easily be combined with sightseeing days or multiple-day activities such as river-rafting. Don't focus your vacation too narrowly; allow at least a few extra days before or after the ride to get to know the wider region. Rental cars don't cost much, especially on a per-person basis when shared by several people. Day rides, guided walks, or hourly rafting trips can be added short-notice once you are on location.

SAMPLE ITINERARY

1. Before Ride:
Sunday, August 1—Morning flight to Durango, Colorado. Hotel (1 night).

2. Ride:
(Base Camp Pack Trip, Weminuche Wilderness, 6 days of riding)
Monday, August 2—Outfitter picks us up at hotel. First day riding, camping.
Tuesday through Friday—Full days of riding from base camp.
Saturday, August 7—Ride ends in afternoon. Outfitter returns us to same hotel (2 nights).

3. After Ride:
Sunday, August 8—Narrow-gauge train to Silverton, round trip.
Monday, August 9—Pick up rental car, drive to Mesa Verde National Park. Hotel (1 night).
Tuesday, August 10—Drive to Moab, Utah. Hotel (3 nights).
Wednesday, August 11—Sightseeing: Arches National Park, Dead Horse Point, etc.
Thursday, August 12—Sightseeing: Jeep tour/river float Canyonlands National Park. Evening: Sunset horseback ride, Arches National Park.
Friday, August 13—Drive via La Sal Mountains to Ouray, Colorado. Hotel (1 night).
Saturday, August 14—Drive to Durango, return rental car, afternoon flight home.

Allow plenty of time to get to the ride start. A missed plane, lost luggage, car trouble, or driving all night are unfortunate ways to begin your vacation. If you plan to drive, scout your route by map and allow plenty of time.

Put all your ideas and interests together in a day-by-day itinerary. First write down the riding dates you favor, then fill in the rest. With the itinerary in hand, make your reservations. If you'd like someone else to place them for you, call EQUUS★USA at (800) 982-6861 or (505) 982-6861, or fax your itinerary to (505) 984-8119. A ride consultant will call you with your confirmation and will mail a trip packet complete with directions.

Getting Ready

After making your reservations, start focusing on what's ahead. The more leisurely this phase is, the more excitement you'll build and the more relaxed and mentally prepared you'll be for your trip. Browse your local library and bookstores for books on the area you'll visit. Look for historical accounts and biographies of the area's well-known citizens, and spend quiet evenings reading. If you are traveling abroad, borrow library cassettes to get a feeling for the country's language. Pack well in advance. Start putting

How about putting some of this stuff on one of the other mules?

Donnie Sexton/Travel Montana

things in a special closet to see what you have or still need to buy. Set aside a pleasant Saturday to shop for clothes or gear.

You don't need to be an athlete to pleasure-ride, but you must be fit enough to be comfortable in the saddle and stay healthy during your vacation. If you don't have a regular exercise program, begin stretching and walking every day. Vary the routine by increasing the speed and adding uphill stretches. Walk and stretch while on vacation to continue feeling your best.

Regardless of which type of riding vacation you select, make a list of the riding or horse care skills you might like to learn. You can watch the wranglers bridle and saddle your horse, for example, or ask them how to improve your riding seat. Review the list now and then to see how you are doing. For inspiration, find horseback riding books in your library and bookstores.

Finally, make sure you read Chapter 6, Trail and Wilderness Essentials—it's important information.

Suggested Packing List

Nighttimes can be chilly, even in the hot summer desert. In the mountains it can snow or hail in July. If you are well prepared, inclement weather won't spoil your trip. Plan to dress in light layers so you can shed them as the day warms and add them as it cools.

Clothes

- Comfortable jeans or riding pants (ideally without noticeable inseam, to avoid chafing).
- 1 pair riding boots or riding sneakers (with heel, comfortable off the horse).
- 1 pair tennis shoes or light hiking boots for when you're afoot.
- 1 broad-brimmed hat with chin strap (against sun and rain). A riding safety helmet is highly recommended.
- 1 pair riding gloves (to prevent scratches and sunburn, also good for changes in weather).
- Long-sleeved blouses or shirts (important against sunburn).
- Sweater or sweatshirt.
- 1 warm jacket (extra warm for fall and winter), 1 light one (windbreaker).
- 1–2 bandanas to protect nose and mouth in case of heavy trail dust.
- T-shirts, underwear, socks (include warm socks, just in case).
- Swimsuit, shorts, light sandals for when not riding.
- Pajamas or nighttime T-shirt.
- Rain jacket, rain pants, plastic hat cover, rain overshoes.
- 1 pair long johns, wool cap, warm gloves or mittens (just in case).

- Cotton leggings or bicycling pants to wear under your trousers (a precaution against chafing).
- Chaps. Not necessary, but they do protect pants while riding through underbrush.

General Gear

- Sunglasses, sunscreen, lip protectant, insect repellent, cloth handkerchiefs.
- Toiletries (biodegradable soap and shampoo). It's best to bring only unscented products: mosquitoes, flies, and other biting insects are attracted by scented items, as are bears.
- Comb, small mirror, personal items, vitamins, medication.
- Laundry bag for soiled clothing.
- Flashlight and extra batteries.
- Camera and extra battery, at least 2 rolls of film per day, lightweight binoculars.
- Prescription glasses (contacts don't like trail dust).
- For periods off the horse: playing cards, small musical instrument, photos from home to share with fellow riders, notebook and pen.
- For traveling with small children: favorite toy or stuffed animal, bedtime stories, own notebook, colored pencils, coloring book.
- Airline tickets, traveler's checks, credit cards, cash, maps, travel books (paperback).
- If traveling outside the country: passports, electrical adapters.

Day Needs

As you pack, set aside the items you'll need on day rides. Bring a fanny pack if your outfitter doesn't supply saddle bags. Your jacket and rain gear can be strapped to the saddle. If your group will be divided by riding skill, or takes a different route than the pack animals or support vehicles, make sure you won't get separated from your lunch.

- Lunch, snacks, water canteen, camera and extra film, binoculars, small plastic bags for trash.
- Jacket, sweatshirt, rain gear, hat, riding gloves, bandana.
- Sunglasses, sunscreen, lip protectant, insect repellent, roll of toilet paper (white, unscented).

Camping Gear

If you'll camp on your riding vacation and your gear will be carried by pack animals, keep your luggage minimal. Some outfitters request everything

Don't forget your swimsuit, whether joining this group in Iceland or riding in North America.

packed in one or two duffel bags rather than a suitcase. Some furnish the duffel bags; others ask you to bring your own. Some accept soft travel bags instead of duffels. Do not overstuff the bags and do keep them within the outfitter's weight and size limit. Line each one with a large trash bag for waterproofing. Mark all pieces with name tags.

Feel free to bring some of your own gear even on all-inclusive trips, but let the outfitter know ahead of time. Camping stores and mail-order catalogs carry wonderfully small, lightweight tents and ultrawarm, lightweight sleeping bags and insulating pads. (Instead of an insulating pad, a self-inflating air mattress is worth the price if you'll use it often.) Having a few things of your own quickly creates a "homey" feeling even in the wilderness.

Unless you are certain the outfitter has tents with waterproof floors, bring a lightweight groundsheet. Pack a small washbowl to take into the privacy of your tent, as well as small towels and washcloths. Bring your own solar shower if you like. Your sandals will come in handy inside the tent and while bathing. A clean pillowcase stuffed with your jacket makes a good pillow.

Successful Traveling

More than any other leisure time, vacations—whole blocks of time—enable you to escape daily routines and feel completely free. You'll have time to think about what is important to you, to reawaken long-lost desires and talents. While engaged in your inward journey, you are confronted with the world around you. The farther you travel, the more exotic the world is likely to seem. People look different, dress differently, speak different languages. They set different priorities for themselves, enjoy different foods, and their houses and towns follow different architectural ideals. Each day, try not to drive yourself too hard, not to see too much in too short a time. Instead, set aside portions of the day to process new information. Talk to your travel companions and organize your impressions in a journal or letters home. Sit quietly by yourself and appreciate the local customs for the color, variety, and perspectives they add to your life. Underneath we are all humans, all trying to find the best solutions for our particular place and time in the world. Venture forth and return home a richer and more accomplished person.

3
HORSES, HORSES

"A horse! a horse! my kingdom for a horse!"
William Shakespeare (1564—1616),
Richard III, Act V

About 70 million years ago *Eohippus*, the dawn horse, the modern horse's ancestor, lived in North America and Europe when the two continents were still connected and covered by tropical forests. The first dawn horse fossil ever found was discovered in Kent, England, in 1839. Because the skull was small and the teeth did not resemble horse teeth, British naturalist Sir Richard Owen thought the dawn horse was related to the pig. He recognized its relationship to the modern horse only a few years later when a more complete specimen was discovered.

The size of a cat to a medium-size dog, the dawn horse looked more like a present-day deer than your powerful mount. In contrast to the modern horse's one toe per foot, the dawn horse's front feet had four toes each; its hind feet, three. Then, as now, a protective hoof covered each toe. Its teeth were relatively short, much like our own, indicating a fairly soft diet of fruit and leaves.

When the North American continent drifted west about 65 million years ago, the newly formed North Atlantic Ocean divided the dawn horse population, and from then on, North American horses and their European relatives evolved independently. The European dawn horse, unable to cope with its environment, became extinct about 30 million years ago. The North American dawn horse gradually increased in size. Longer teeth allowed it to eat grasses and other fibrous plants that quickly wear down shorter teeth, and it was able to live in the cooler grasslands that replaced the tropical forests. Over time it gave rise to *Orohippus, Protohippus, Hipparion*, and, finally, *Equus caballus*, our modern horse.

About 2 million years ago the world's climate grew colder, and ice sheets formed over vast areas of North America and Eurasia. At the end of the Great Ice Age, around 8000 B.C., dense woodlands in North America spread in regions that had been tundra and grass. Seeking new grazing grounds, the horses migrated via then-existing land bridges to the grassy plains of Eurasia, some even reaching Africa. By 6000 B.C. they had disappeared from the Western Hemisphere. Only fossils are left to prove their existence.

Humans first tamed prehistoric horses several thousand years ago in Central Asia and caught an increasing number of wild horses for domestication. As more people and livestock moved into the prehistoric horses' lands, the remaining wild herds lost access to grazing and water sources. Other wild horses were slaughtered for meat. The only prehistoric horses surviving into modern times are sturdy, yellow-brown animals named Przewalski's horse for the Russian explorer Nicolai Mikhailovich Przhevalsky, who saw them during his expeditions in the 1880s.

For centuries large herds of Przewalski's horse roamed the Eurasian plains. Gradually their habitat was pushed back until they lived only on the arid, semidesert plains near the Altai Mountains that form the boundaries between Mongolia, China, and Siberia. In 1968 they were sighted in their natural habitat for the last time, and probably no longer exist in the wild. The descendants of 31 survivors live in zoos around the world. All other wild horses today are feral horses—descendants of once-domesticated stock.

The horse you ride today is descended from a long line of domesticated horses. After birth, it was on its feet and suckling within half an hour. It was toothless, but its central two incisors cut through its gums after 10 days. By 6 to 9 months the foal had a full set of milk teeth. At 5 to 6 years it had permanent teeth, and if your horse is less than 10 years old, its age can be judged by its teeth. As a yearling, your horse was still leggy and uncoordinated.

Taking care of your horse in France

Diethard Franz/EQUUS•USA

Its rump was noticeably higher than the withers, but as it grew older, its frame filled out and the two points came into line. The last areas to reach maturity were the epiphyses, the "growth plates" on the long bones of the legs. Until these close, the legs are unable to sustain hard work, particularly under weight. When the horse was between 2 and 2½ years of age the plate at the end of the radius, just above the knee, closed.

If your horse is a mare, she reached puberty at 15–24 months, but domestic mares are not bred until age 2 or 3, and 4 is more acceptable. In spring, mares become sexually interested and, unless mated, continue to come into heat (estrus) at monthly intervals until the end of summer. Males are often sexually capable as yearlings, but are not bred before age 3 to 4. Many males are gelded (castrated) to make them more docile riding horses. Although your horse can live 30 years or more, it reaches the peak of its powers between ages 5 and 10. An older horse's joints grow puffy as its circulation slows, and the effects of work show clearly. Old horses often "stand over at the knee," hollows develop over their eyes, and their backs may sway. With age, the teeth are worn, chewing is harder, and the digestive process is sluggish.

When your horse neighs with a friendly greeting, its ears are alert and upright, its mouth slightly open. Ears strained forward usually indicate fear. Watch a group of horses and you may see signs of submission—ears down, while the mouth makes nibbling movements. Horses at ease engage in mutual grooming, standing beside one another and nibbling at the neck or the base of the tail. Ears pressed back and mouth open is a threat gesture. Horses' calls vary from a soft nickering of recognition to a loud whinny that alerts the herd to danger.

Walking into a horse barn is like entering a special world, no matter how often you've done it. The smell of hay, the muted light filtering in, the sound of sleeping horses. Then curious heads pop out of each stall, wondering what's new or whether you are bringing goodies. When you stand close to a horse, touching it, brushing its fur, the smell of its coat reminds you of the great outdoors, of sunshine and wind and the freedom.

Many early human cultures centered on horses. Horses were interred beside their masters in the graves of Scythian kings and in the tombs of Pharaohs. Greek mythology created the centaur, the symbol of oneness of horse and rider. A beautiful, well-trained horse was a status symbol in ancient Greece. The names of famous horses are inseparably linked to those of their famous riders: Bucephalus, Alexander the Great's charger; Incitatus, made a senator by the Roman emperor Caligula; El Morzillo, Cortéz' favorite horse, of whom contemporary Native Americans erected a statue; Roan Barbery, the stallion of Richard II mentioned by Shakespeare; Copenhagen, the Duke of Wellington's horse, who was buried with military honors.

From the time the first human climbed on a horse and managed to stay there, horses have given riders power and speed. Nomadic tribes of central Asia were riding horses by at least 2000 B.C. Horses were probably raced early in history. The first recorded races were between chariots, preceding ridden races by centuries. Ridden racing, the "Sport of Kings," has long been part of the sporting scene but owes its modern form to the creation of the Thoroughbred in seventeenth- and eighteenth-century England.

Most modern horse sports originated in the military. The Greek general Xenophon (ca. 430–355 B.C.) first described specific movements and a progression of training. The formal and highly skilled modern dressage tests originated in European cavalries in the 1800s. Show jumping developed in Italian cavalry training. Eventing, which involves three phases (dressage, a steeplechase, and show jumping), evolved from the old "Military," a test for officers and their horses. Endurance riding also has a military precedent.

A rider communicates with a horse in several ways: through the voice, the hands by way of reins and bit, the legs and heels, and the shifting of the rider's weight. Whips, spurs, and devices such as special nosebands or special reins are artificial aids that can be used by experienced riders. The style of riding—the saddle, length of stirrup, and the rider's seat—changes with the purpose for which the horse is ridden.

In the English riding style, the rider *direct reins* by holding a rein in each hand. In Western riding, the rider *neck reins* by holding both reins in one hand. The Western style was developed to free one hand for the cowboy to swing a rope, the fur trapper to carry a rifle in the crook of his arm, and the packer to lead a string of pack animals. A horse trained in direct reining responds to the gentlest movement on the sides of its mouth, a horse trained in neck reining to the gentlest movement on the sides of its neck.

For millennia, horses were ridden bareback or simply with a cloth or blanket. The leather saddle, developed between 300 B.C. and A.D. 100 on the Asian steppes, made it easier for the rider to stay aboard. The Sarmatians, a tribe of Asian nomads near the Black Sea, built the first saddle on a wooden frame. Modern saddles use the same pattern, though usually made from strips of laminated wood reinforced with metal plates. Saddles were greatly improved in medieval Europe, especially in France, and became an indispensable ingredient in knightly shock combat.

Modern saddles are divided into two main types. The Western saddle evolved from the saddles brought to America by the Spanish and was later adapted by the American cowboy. It has a high horn on the pommel, used to secure a lariat. A large cantle (the higher rear part of a saddle) provides a firm seat for cattle-roping. The Western saddle is comfortable for long journeys, and all of the cowboy's gear can be fastened to it. The English saddle, lighter and flatter, was designed for sport and recreation.

In the wild, natural selection determines evolution. The dawn horse's long-legged foals ran faster and escaped enemies better than its short-legged siblings. They survived longer, mated more because of their longer lives, and thus produced more offspring. Generations later, no short-leggeds were left. The change in their environment favored foals born with teeth shaped for eating grass. Those who needed soft plants died out when tropical forests gave way to grasslands, and only the grass-eating horses survived to continue the species.

As the domestication of horses spread across Eurasia, owners began to practice artificial selection on their horses. A filly (female foal) born bigger and stronger than other fillies was bred with the biggest and strongest stallions. Generations of such selection produced very large horses, and other desired traits were bred for as well. Two general groups of horses emerged: the light, fast, spirited horses called *hotblooded* for their origin in hotter, southerly climates (typified by the modern Arabian), and the heavier, slower, calmer horses called *coldblooded* for their origin in colder, northerly temperature zones (typified by the Belgian). The Arabian breed is said to have stemmed from five mares given by his followers to Muhammed, who lived from about A.D. 570 to 632. Later breeding strategies resulted in *warmbloods* (typified by Thoroughbreds)—intermediate horses who combine characteristics of both hotbloods and coldbloods. *Purebred* horses are born of parents of the same breed and exhibit typical characteristics. When we speak of horse *types*, we classify horses by their use. For example, a *saddle horse* may be any horse used for pleasure riding, whether a purebred or a mixture between two breeds (*crossbreed*).

Although breed societies place emphasis on correct conformation and size, color is the prime consideration for "color breeds"—Palominos, Appaloosas, American Pintos, and Paints. All of the spotted colorings come from strains once relatively common in Spanish Barbs and Andalusians but extinct in modern Spanish horses.

White markings on a horse's face, muzzle, or legs can be used for identification and are carefully recorded by breed societies. Whorls, or "cowlicks," are permanent, irregular settings of coat hairs that also help in identification. On some horses a dark stripe extends along the spine; it's almost always found with a dun coat. The dun coloring and dorsal stripe were characteristic of primitive horses like Przewalski's horse, and are seen in some stock descended from them.

People often brand their horses for identification. Normally only one mark is made, but occasionally several brands are used, each having a different meaning, including the name of the breed. Lipizzaners, for example, have four brands: the stud, ancestral, foal, and the traditional brand, a simple L.

Horses were essential to farming through the 1800s. Farms depended on them, from preparing the land through sowing, cultivating, harvesting, and subsequent delivery of crops to the consumer. In the U.S., huge harvesters were drawn by 40-horse teams, and for over a century railroad horses moved freight and rolling stock to and from railheads. Horses pulled freight barges along European and American canals, drawing loads of 60 to 70 tons.

Between 1900 and 1910 over 5,000 breeders of the huge Percherons operated in the U.S. In towns and cities, lighter breeds drew buses, cabs, and

POINTS OF A HORSE

poll
forelock
forehead
face
bridge of nose
nostril
muzzle
upper lip
lower lip
under lip
cheek
crest
throat latch
chin groove
neck
point of shoulder
chest
elbow
arm
withers
shoulder
girth
forearm
knee
cannon
back
barrel
loin
abdomen
rump
point of hip
ankle
fetlock joint
hoof
flank
dock
buttock
thigh
stifle
gaskin
chestnut
pastern
hock
coronet

A horse's height (measured to the highest point of its shoulders, or "withers") is often expressed in "hands." One hand equals about 4 inches (10 cm).

delivery wagons. Mining companies used ponies underground and larger horses aboveground.

The first horses to return to the Western hemisphere were beautiful Spanish Barbs and Andalusians who accompanied sixteenth-century Spanish conquistadors in their quest for gold. Carried in slings on the decks of sailing ships, many horses died during storms at sea. More were thrown overboard if the voyage took longer than expected and drinking water ran low or to lighten the ship so it would respond to the smallest breeze. Because stallions were favored, mares were sacrificed first. One stretch of the Atlantic Ocean 30 degrees north and south of the equator was notorious for insufficient winds, causing delays and hardships. The Spanish called the stretch the Mares' Gulf; today it is known as the Horse Latitudes.

In the Old World, noblemen and royalty favored Spanish Barbs and Andalusians. In the New World they laid the foundation for new breeds, and the indelible mark of Spanish blood is still apparent. The many horses that broke away during and after Spanish rule were called *mustangs*, after the Spanish *mesteno* ("ownerless" or "belonging to everyone and no one"). Their freedom became a symbol of the American West.

One stallion and his harem of two to eight mares, their foals, and various young mustangs make up a mustang herd. The herd wanders and grazes its territory, tolerating other herds only on its outskirts. Occasionally herds unite to ward off predator attacks. An older female leads the herd away while the stallions challenge the aggressors. If trapped, the mares and stallions form a tight circle, with the foals inside. The stallions snap their teeth and snort wildly, pawing the ground and raising clouds of dust.

A mustang mother and her newborn stay in a hidden birth location for 2 or 3 days until the foal is strong enough to join the herd. A little over a year later, the herd's fillies join other herds when they first become sexually interested, although they are unlikely to mate for another year. The stallion drives colts (male foals) from the herd when they are 1 to 3 years of age. Too young to attract females, the colts form colt herds for several years, occasionally challenging the stallions, until at about age 6 they win mares of their own.

Two to 5 million mustangs roamed the western U.S. in the late 1700s. As settlers cultivated the land, mustangs were killed by the thousands. Others survived, domesticated by Native Americans or trained as cow horses on ranches. The Cheyenne thought sacred mustangs—spotted on the head and chest— would bring them victory in battle. The greatest destruction of mustangs took place in the 1900s, when huge numbers were captured for use in the Boer War and World War I, or caught and killed for pet food and fertilizer. By the mid-1960s only 18,000 to 34,000 wild mustangs were left in remote areas with sparse vegetation, and by the early 1970s there were less than 10,000. Laws passed in 1971 made it a federal offense to harass or kill mustangs. Today, wild horse reserves protect some of the remaining herds.

Having interbred with many types of horses, mustangs have no uniform body type or color. In the hardships of today's limited habitat they remain small, usually no more than 14 hands (56 inches, or 140 cm), with a sturdy build and wiry frame. Daily life centers around food. The mustangs must contend with the scarcity and low nutritional value of the coarse grasses, sagebrush, and juniper available to them. With their tough teeth and strong jaws they tear at the vegetation in their inhospitable surroundings and survive on a diet that wouldn't sustain domestic horses. Often the lead mare heads the search for food while the stallion guards the rear. He usually feeds first and then protects the herd. If necessary the animals go without food or water for days; they clear clogged water holes by digging, and break open the ice on frozen springs.

Much time has passed since our human ancestors first realized that horses could be tamed. Today, when life seems to be spinning out of control at an increasing rate, horses allow you to immerse yourself in a slower way of seeing the world. During some riding vacations you may come upon wild mustangs. Perhaps at this moment, as you gaze from your domestic horse at its wild cousins, you'll fully appreciate your horse's remarkable history and its willingness to carry you wherever you wish.

4
NATURE DETECTIVES

"To see a world in a grain of sand,
And a heaven in a wild flower,
Hold infinity in the palm of your hand,
And eternity in an hour."
William Blake (1757–1827)

Your riding vacation is an excellent time to develop nature hobbies or deepen your naturalist skills. Your interest may be as mild as taking a few photographs, or so strong you'll travel far to see unusual phenomena and species.

Before your vacation, decide which books or accessories to take. Field guides are books that enable you to identify animals, plants, and geological features. Along with your plant field guide, bring a magnifying glass. Look closely at plants' leaves, fruit, bark, overall shape, and location. To identify animals, take a wildlife field guide and good pair of binoculars. If you visit different parts of the U.S. at different seasons you'll see many of North America's 850 bird species. Watch for land birds in the morning and late afternoon, ducks and geese all day, shorebirds at ebb tide, and nightjars and owls at night. A bird's size and shape, particularly the shape of the bill, help you determine its family. Additional details—color patterns, behavior, song, habitat, and range—point you to the species. Range maps in field guides show which birds are resident, which are migratory.

North America is home to some 290 species of land mammals and 40 of marine mammals. Land mammals are active mostly at dawn, dusk, and night. During the day, watch for tracks and scat; study the track pictures in your field guide. Bare patches on tree trunks may have been caused by deer or elk cleaning velvet off new antler growth. Claw marks might be a sign of a mountain lion or bear. Beach walking, tide-pooling, snorkeling, and scuba diving show you the wealth of ocean life.

Insects are by far the world's most numerous animals: over 100,000 species live in North America alone. You'll see insects that live in social groups—ants and bees, for instance—and creatures that undergo amazing metamorphoses—butterflies, moths, and beetles. Fortunately, the number of pesky insects is relatively small. Living in North America are close to 300 species of reptiles (turtles, lizards, snakes, and crocodilians) and almost 200 species of amphibians (frogs, toads, salamanders). Field guides to rocks and minerals, and guidebooks to the geological history of particular areas, help you identify the processes that formed the landscape around you.

Recording your experiences adds pleasure to your riding vacation and gives you lasting mementos. If you've not used it for a while, reacquaint yourself with your camera. Wide-angle lenses are great for landscapes. For wildlife photos take a 90- to 135-mm telephoto lens or a zoom. Higher focal lengths capture additional detail, but without a tripod you'll need a very steady hand or a shoulder brace. Pack a macro lens for plants and insects. A flash attachment allows nighttime shots to 20 feet and eliminates close-up daytime shadows. A medium-speed film should handle most situations you're likely to encounter. For more professional images, bring 100 ASA film for full sun, 200 ASA for sunny to partially cloudy conditions, and 400 or 1000 ASA for dusk and for dark areas, such as forests. Video cameras capture wildlife sounds and behavior.

You might like to stop at animal-viewing sites on your way to your riding vacation. The Watchable Wildlife Program of various government and private organizations marks U.S. viewing sites accessible by car or short trail. In addition, the U.S. has more than 450 national wildlife refuges. The Bureau of Land Management (BLM) oversees 270 mustang and burro areas in ten states

White-breasted nuthatch

U.S. National Park Service

U.S. National Park Service

Female grizzly with cubs

and is developing viewing sites. The Wild Horse and Burro Act of 1971 declared these animals living symbols of the historic and pioneer spirit of the West, and an integral part of the natural system of the public lands.

Interest your children in nature. Buy them their own binoculars that little fingers can focus, and teach them to use field guides and maps. Focus the kids' attention on something specific. There is always a drama unfolding, if you look and listen carefully. Open-air, wire-encased bug jars allow children to catch insects, observe them for a while, then set them free unharmed. If you see a salamander, you can lie on your belly and watch it climb over rocks and dive into a stream.

5
TRAIL CHOICES

"Far trails await me; valleys vast and still,
Vistas undreamed-of, canyon-guarded streams,
Lowland and range, fair meadow, flower-girt hill,
Forests enchanted, filled with magic dreams."
Henry Herbert Knibbs (1874–1945)

Before railroads and highways, people traveled by foot, horseback, or wagon on routes that began as wildlife trails and became Native American tracks, followed later by European explorers and missionaries. Many original trails still exist, others were added more recently as recreational trails or more direct routes to scenic wonders. Many are on public land and open to everyone, including horseback riders.

The trails offer riding for every taste. Some are level, some steep. Some are extremely narrow, others generously wide. Many are highly panoramic, others were blazed with little eye for beauty. Some are short, others long. Some are best on a one-way trek, others offer loop routes so you end up where you started. Some are heavily used, others offer a more isolated experience. *Saddle Up!* lists some of the world's most outstanding riding areas in Chapters 7 (Best Places to Ride: North America) and 8 (Best Places to Ride: Worldwide), and in Additional U.S. Public Lands with Horse Trails, Chapter 10.

Traveling with professional horse outfitters gives you their expertise in selecting the best trail for the vacation you want. You won't need to worry about trail conditions, directions, the best stream crossings, where to camp, wilderness safety, and food and water. All that is handled by the outfitter. You can concentrate on what you came to do: ride through beautiful landscapes and admire the wildlife and plants who live there.

Trail choices depend on the time of year. In the northern hemisphere, high-country trails are snow-free only in July and August; you are limited to lower trails the rest of the time. Desert trails are ideal in spring and fall.

How much time you have determines what you'll see. Day rides and short overnights are great for sampling an area but merely tease your appetite. A week gives you a very different vacation.

If you ride 15 miles a day—which many riders consider a lot, especially in mountainous terrain—you'll cover 75 miles in five days. Most national parks and designated wilderness areas have extensive trail systems much longer than that. Depending on how steep and rocky the trail is, allow about 3 miles per hour when riding with pack animals, 5 miles per hour without. Add time for rest stops and lunch. The faster you ride, the less detail you'll see. Stationary wilderness camps allow you intimate knowledge of an area. On progressive treks, you'll encounter some of your most rewarding nature experiences on layover days when unexpected animals pass near your camp.

Each year, the stewardship agencies decide which trails to open for use. Trailhead, trail, and campsite conditions are vital considerations, as are fire danger and the availability of water. For horse, mule, and llama users, grazing areas are taken into account. Professional horse outfitters build the approved routes into each season's offerings. But things change: a tree falls on a trail and has not yet been cleared, summer weather is late and a mountain pass is snowpacked even in July, a rock slide closes a canyon.

Different government agencies practice different sign philosophies. Signs on some trails are carefully maintained, on others they are not or were never installed. Some agencies believe in returning the land completely to the wild, so signs are removed or not replaced. If you are traveling without professional help, you'll need topographic maps and a compass. Before entering your planned trail, be sure to obtain trail updates from the nearest ranger station.

Regardless of who will guide your ride, be sure to read Chapter 6, Trail and Wilderness Essentials.

Wilderness expeditions take you through backcountry normally seen only by hikers.

Scott Rowed/Travel Alberta

6
TRAIL AND WILDERNESS ESSENTIALS

Trail Courtesy

Whether riding for an hour or trekking for weeks, leave no trace of your visit. Horses and mules are big animals whose hooves damage the landscape wherever they go. Keep your groups small to minimize impact. When riding cross-country, spread out wide to avoid creating new trails, and guide your horse along wash bottoms and other areas where harm to the vegetation and soil is minimal. Be aware that cross-country riding is not permitted on many public lands because of the inherent problems. When following designated trails, don't ride next to fellow riders or take shortcuts, and always ride in the center of the trail. Rain carves hoofprints into gullies and widens and deteriorates the path. Prevent your horse from skirting puddles and minor obstacles. Remove the obstacles or ride over them.

Preserve the land for the wildlife and plants who live there, and for future travelers. Seashells and driftwood are used by wildlife for all sorts of purposes and need to stay in place. Leave eggs in their nests and rocks where they lie. Don't uproot plants, pick flowers, or collect seeds. Don't litter—and for good measure, pick up trash others left behind. Refuse is not only unsightly but dangerous to animals. They may eat what is poison to them or become tangled in plastic bags, fishing line, or rope. Discarded glass can cut wildlife and, heated by the sun, may start devastating wildfires.

Keep your group together to avoid getting lost. If you get separated, wait for the others to catch up. Do not blaze trees, hang ribbons, or gather rock piles to mark a path for others to follow. Leave radios and electronic equipment at home, and keep your voices low.

Never visit a camp, scenic overlook, or historical or archaeological site on horseback. Tie your horse well away, ideally in a rocky area or thicket where no one is likely to camp. Choose a tree at least 8 inches in diameter. To minimize harming the bark, wrap the lead rope around the trunk twice before you tie the knot. Tend your horse often to make sure it does not trample tree roots. For longer stops, tie your horse to a high line between two sturdy trees, protecting the tree bark with "tree saver" straps.

While visiting the site, don't touch, take, or leave anything. Always stay on footpaths. Seemingly unimportant mounds may contain future finds.

Backcountry high in the Austrian Alps

Climbing on roofs or walls can destroy in seconds what has stood for centuries.

The backcountry has no toilet facilities. Create your own latrine at least 75 paces (200 feet) from the nearest camp, trail, and water sources (lakes, streams, springs). Use a stick or tiny trowel to dig a "cat hole," 6 to 8 inches deep. Discard the waste and used toilet paper in the hole, then close it with the dug-up soil. Cover the area with a rock to prevent wildlife from disturbing the site. Tampons and feminine sanitary napkins do not decompose readily. Place them in plastic bags and pack them out.

Because horses may kick tailgaters, maintain a horse's length from the horse ahead. Exercise caution when approaching other trail users. Call out "Horses," if you are coming up behind. Yield the right-of-way when possible. If hikers seem unsure what to do, offer instructions to permit safe passage. Suggest that the hikers move to the lower side of the trail. If your horse shies, it's likely to do so uphill. Also, a backpack changes a person's shape. Keep talking to the hikers to help your horse recognize them as people. Thank them as you pass. If you speak to hikers for any length of time, dismount to place yourself on equal footing. If two groups of riders meet, the uphill string has the right-of-way in the morning, the downhill string in the afternoon. If meeting on the level, the longer string has the right-of-way.

Many guides will ask you not to let your horse graze during a ride. Ask whether this is because of grazing restrictions or because it would slow the pace. If grazing is the concern, your horse will have to wait till feeding time in camp. If pace is the problem, allow your horse to nibble only during stops.

When riding in treacherous terrain, don't be ashamed to get off and lead your horse. If your group does not follow the cavalry style of riding—50 minutes on the horses, 10 minutes off—feel free to request it. Halt your horse while other riders are mounting or dismounting, and never initiate faster riding without reaching a consensus with every member of your group. When riding uphill, lean forward to minimize your weight on your horse's kidneys.

Trail maintenance is a way to say "thank you" for the privilege of using public trails. Since horses can carry an ax, shovel, and even a saw, riders are better equipped than hikers to do the work. Also keep in mind that in backcountry emergencies your horse may be called upon to carry injured parties to safety.

Wilderness Safety

Never infringe on the comfort range of wild animals. Use your binoculars to observe them from a distance, your telephoto or zoom lens to take photos or video coverage. If an animal is aware of you, you are too close. Do not approach young animals. Even if they seem alone or lost, the mother will likely appear as soon as you leave. Ride away calmly or move around in a huge circle. Be quiet when you want to see wildlife. Talk, sing, clap your hands, wear bells, or shake pebbles in a can when you do not. Always watch where you place your fingers and feet.

Don't feed wild creatures. They can become aggressive to get what they want, and kick, butt, gore, or bite. Scavenging animals search campsites for edibles, particularly at night. Use bear-proof storage lockers when available. When not, hang all food in trees well away from where you sleep. Choose a spindly branch that cannot support a bear's weight, at least 12 feet off the ground and 5 feet from the trunk. In treeless areas, prop cooking pans against your food storage to make noise if animals try to get in. Never cook in your tent and never keep food, toothpaste, or scented products in it. Do not wear perfume or hair spray. Don't sleep in clothes you wore while cooking. To be on the safe side, women should avoid bear country during menstrual periods.

During lightning storms, quickly leave mountain peaks and other high places. Avoid metal objects and tall points, such as a single tree or rock. Stay away from overhangs, cliffs, and shallow caves. If you are wearing rubber-soled shoes, squat as low as possible, with only your shoes touching the ground. Alternatively, lie down or take cover in a ditch or head-high bushes. Deep woods are statistically safe (except near the tallest trees), as are low and deep rock shelters. Stay several feet from the walls, and well back from the entrance. Storms can cause flash floods. Camp away from dry streambeds and avoid getting caught in narrow canyons.

A minor illness can become serious at high elevations. Ride to a lower altitude while you still can. Always travel in groups of three or more, at least one of whom knows wilderness survival and basic first aid. In case of a serious accident, one person stays with the victim, the other rides for help.

Even crystal-clear mountain water can harbor microbes that may not harm the local outfitter but may quickly spoil your trip. Use only properly boiled or chemically treated water for drinking and brushing your teeth. Do not immerse your head while swimming, or splash water into your mouth or nose.

Smoking can cause backcountry fires. Since hot ash or sparks may fall off without your noticing, do not smoke while riding. Light up only during rest stops and only when it's not windy so you can be sure no ash or spark will escape. Place all ash, butts, and matches in a covered travel ashtray, not into nature.

Wildlife-Viewing Tips

Find out how the species you are seeking spends its days. Check your field guide for life history and preferred habitats. When does the animal eat, nap, bathe, drink? Consider the weather. After a rain, for instance, many creatures emerge to feed on displaced insects. Take note of the season to find out whether the animal is shopping for a mate, preparing a nest or den, getting ready to migrate, or fattening for winter. Spend time at known wildlife areas: drinking sites, ledges overlooking open areas, trail intersections. The border between two habitats is ideal for seeing residents of both areas.

Most animals see, hear, and smell you long before you catch their drift. They size you up and, depending how far away you are and how you behave, they decide whether to stay, defend themselves, or flee. Give nests and dens a wide berth. Although you mean well, your visit may lead a predator to the young or cause the parents to abandon them. Do not use taped recordings to lure elusive species into the open. Animals desert their territories if subjected to it.

Wear natural colors and unscented lotions, and remove glasses that glint. Walk softly and avoid snapping twigs. Try not to throw a shadow and remember, your reflection may be seen in water. Move like molasses: slow, smooth, and steady.

Crouch behind boulders or vegetation to hide or break up your contour. Breathe deeply and open all your senses. Use your peripheral vision rather than constantly turning your head. Switch your attention periodically. Focus on the foreground for a while, then change to the wider view. Look above and below you.

Watch for out-of-place motions and shapes: horizontal patterns in a mostly vertical forest, a vertical shape on a tree branch. Heed your instincts. If the hair on the back of your neck stands up—a vestige of the days when we had fur—an animal may be near. Cup your hands around the backs of your ears to amplify sounds. A sudden silence may indicate a predator passing through the area. If you would like to see the predator, stay in hiding. If you are nervous, stand up, calm yourself, and be noisy.

Wilderness Camping

Wherever you are, it's somebody's home. Rather than disturb new areas, choose already established sites that are at least 75 paces (200 feet) from trails, historical and archaeological sites, and the nearest lakes, streams, and springs. Confine the horses and mules in a dry area a distance away from your camp, also at least 75 paces (200 feet) from waters, trails, and sites.

Place your kitchen site in the most resilient location. Rock outcrops withstand heavy use and often afford a view. In bear country, locate the kitchen at least 100 feet downwind of sleeping areas. Traffic between the kitchen, tents, and horse area creates trails. To minimize impact, stay on established paths.

Backcountry high in the Rockies

Mark Nohl/New Mexico Department of Tourism

Do not dig trenches or build camp structures. If temporary structures are erected, dismantle them completely before leaving. Don't cut trees or drive nails into them. Even dead trees are part of the wilderness beauty and are homes for chipmunks, pine squirrels, owls, weasels, bluebirds, and woodpeckers. Do not block wildlife access to water and trails.

Since campfires pollute the air, burn the underlying soil, deplete wood sources, and cause fire danger, use a camping stove to cook. If you must use a campfire, keep it small and in an existing fire ring. Collect only small pieces of dead and fallen wood, and do not build a fire on windy days when sparks may fly. Never leave the fire unattended.

Soapy water and fish don't mix. You'll have wonderful opportunities to swim in beautiful lakes, hot springs, and streams, but never use soaps, shampoos, or products of any kind in them. To wash—whether it's yourself, dishes, or laundry—carry water at least 75 paces (200 feet) away from natural waters and trails, and even then use only unscented, biodegradable cleansers.

Different outfitters favor different latrine systems, but for small groups, keep a shovel at an assigned spot near camp, with a roll of toilet paper on the grip. If the shovel is gone, someone is in the woods. Women go to the left of camp, men to the right. Follow the "cat hole" method described under Trail Courtesy.

When you leave, remove all evidence of your stay and that of previous visitors. Pack out everything you brought in. Don't leave anything and don't bury trash. If you used a campfire, burn only small amounts of paper, food scraps, and bacon grease. If previous campers established more than one fire ring, dismantle the surplus and leave only one. Return the excess rocks to outlying areas. Scatter unused firewood and livestock manure, then rake the camp and livestock site with a tree branch. Close holes caused by trampling hooves. Drown your campfire. When the coals are cold to the touch, remove all trash that did not burn. Using a sack or cloth, carry the ashes several hundred feet from camp and scatter them out of view. When you swing into the saddle, take a last look. If you left nothing to mark your visit, you did right. You are taking only memories and leaving only hoofprints.

BEST PLACES TO RIDE:
NORTH AMERICA

BRITISH
COLUMBIA

Jasper
National Park

Calgary •

North Cascades
National Park

ALBERTA   SASKATCHEWAN   MANITOBA

Seattle

WA

Mt. Ranier
National Park

Bob Marshall Wilderness

• Great Falls

ND

Portland

Crater Lake
National Park

OR

MT

SD

Yellowstone
National Park

ID

WY

Lassen Volcanic
National Park

Cheyenne ★

NE

San
Francisco

★
Salt Lake City

NV

UT

Denver ★

CO

KS

Capitol
Reef
National
Park

Yosemite
National
Park

Las
Vegas

Weminuche
Wilderness

CA

Los
Angeles

Sequoia &
Kings Canyon
National Parks

Grand Canyon
National Park

Pecos Wilderness

• Albuquerque

Pacific Coast Trail

AZ

NM

OK

★
Phoenix

Gila Wilderness

Superstition
Wilderness

Monument Valley
Navajo Tribal Park

• El Paso

TX

7
BEST PLACES TO RIDE: NORTH AMERICA

This section introduces you to some of North America's most spectacular national parks and designated wilderness areas you can explore by horse. Horseback wilderness expeditions take you the farthest into these treasures, but inn rides, wagon trains, cattle drives, day rides, and the other riding vacations may also take you near them, or at least enable you to ride in them for a while. Or you can stay at a dude ranch, riding resort, cattle ranch, or cow camp, then day-ride from there. Some ranches offer horseback wilderness expeditions, and a popular option is to visit the ranch for a week, then take its expeditions for further exploration.

All horse outfitters listed in the Travel Tips boxes at the end of each chapter offer wilderness expeditions. Their addresses, telephone numbers, and other pertinent information are given in the Outfitter Directory, including price codes, minimum riding skills needed, and which outfitters allow you to bring your own horse.

These pages give you an overview of what is special about each area, what is interesting to see and know. Then, to give you a closer feeling for the land, each chapter highlights one or two noteworthy trails. Be aware, however, that these descriptions are not step-by-step trail guides. They should not be used in lieu of either traveling with professional outfitters or following topographic maps and current trail instructions from the stewardship agencies listed in the Travel Tips boxes.

The described regions are vast and the horseback rides usually stay away from heavily traveled areas and roads. Your ride may not necessarily include everything described here, so you may want to spend a few extra days before or after your horseback trek to sightsee by car. Addresses to contact for additional information are listed in Travel Tips. The details of your vacation will evolve once you decide where and when you wish to travel and for how long.

PACIFIC COAST STATES

Mount Rainier. Washington Department of Tourism

THE PACIFIC CREST NATIONAL SCENIC TRAIL

"The lava first wreathed into curious forms when it flowed down there, then, in later times, weathered into fantastic shapes—walls, battlements, pinnacles shooting up hundreds of feet, more forms than can be described."
William H. Brewer (1828–1910)

Riding to Your Heart's Content

In 1921 forester Benton MacKaye realized that though many trails still crisscrossed much of North America, others were being lost to urbanization, and none allowed the long-distance foot or horse travel of our forebears. He envisioned a greenway stretching from Maine to Georgia, hugging the crest of the Appalachian Mountains. In 1925 the Appalachian Trail Conference formed to develop and maintain this trail. Congress passed the National Trails System Act in 1968, providing federal assistance to the Appalachian Trail and recognizing the need for other long-distance pathways. The Appalachian and the Pacific Crest became the first national scenic trails.

Except for 18 miles open to horseback riders in Smoky Mountains National Park, the Appalachian Trail permits only hikers. But on the Pacific Crest Trail, 2,638 spectacular miles (4,245 km) between Canada and Mexico offer you the horseback adventure of a lifetime. The trail cuts through three U.S. states, seven national parks, 33 designated wilderness areas, 24 national forests, five state parks, four Bureau of Land Management regions, one national monument, and one national recreation area. Averaging 15 miles per day, the trip would take you 176 days without layovers, delays, or side trips.

Because of the trail's length and the varied elevations and weather conditions, you'll need to ride it in segments. But on the next pages let's ignore the logistics and ride all of it right now from north to south. We'll concentrate on the national parks to highlight the trail's natural splendors.

Riding South

When you mount your horse at the trailhead in Canada's Manning Provincial Park in British Columbia, you're in the 700-mile-long Cascade Mountain Range that stretches from Canada's Mount Garibaldi to

California's Lassen Peak in Lassen Volcanic National Park. You get to know Manning Provincial Park, then cross the border into the U.S. Cascades and ride their entire length.

Seen between the ears of your mount, the beauty of the pine-needle-strewn trail with its checkerboard patches of glittering sunlight and dark shade is unforgettable. Squirrels flit across the trail, occasionally a black bear or coyote walks along it, golden eagles soar overhead. In these northern stretches you may spot grizzly bears, mountain goats, moose, or even gray wolves. White-tailed ptarmigans live here, and in winter bald eagles congregate along the rivers to catch salmon.

Variations in temperature, rainfall, and snow determine the kinds of trees found along different segments of the Pacific Crest Trail, and at different elevations. On the Cascades' lower slopes the forests are bathed by moist ocean winds, and the low western slopes are the wettest. Thriving on the moisture, old-man's beard lichen hangs from trees, making the forest a fairyland. The Cascades frog, whose habitat is only in the Cascades and the nearby Olympic Mountains, lives at elevations between 3,000 and 9,000 feet. Occasionally you'll see one along streams as high as timberline. As you climb, giant Douglas firs, Sitka spruce, and Western pines tower over you. The Douglas squirrel (also called chickaree), a western cousin of the red squirrel, prefers the higher fir forests. In the fall the squirrel stores up

Great scenery and the freedom to explore it

Chuck Coleman/Oregon Department of Tourism

to 160 unopened Douglas fir cones in a place damp enough to keep them from opening until the squirrel is ready to eat the seeds.

Higher yet the forest changes to predominantly silver fir. Timberline is about 5,600 feet in Washington, about 10,000 feet farther along the trail in California. Just below timberline, Engelmann spruce, whitebark pine, and subalpine fir dominate. Above timberline are rich meadows. There, on the bleak, windswept tundra, small plants hug the ground to evade winter winds. Alpine flowers bloom in profusion and marmots and pikas keep a watchful eye on you and your horse. Mule deer are comfortable at almost all elevations.

Except for the most northern Canadian section, the entire Cascade Range consists of volcanic rock. All of its well-known peaks are volcanoes—including Mount Baker, Glacier Peak, Mount Rainier, Mount Adams, Mount St. Helens, Mount Hood, Mount Shasta, and Lassen Peak. The volcanoes, neatly arrayed in stately single file down the coast, are part of the Pacific "Ring of Fire" that arcs from here to South America, across to Indonesia and Japan, and back to Alaska. The ring includes three-fourths of the world's active volcanoes. During the last 4,000 years Cascade volcanoes have erupted at least once per century, and future eruptions are certain.

The Cascade volcanoes are so high and the surrounding country so low that the highest summits dominate the land in every direction, making them the largest freestanding objects in the lower 48 states. Many Cascade peaks are high enough to support alpine glaciers. You'll see more U.S. glaciers here than anywhere outside Alaska. In the winter these mountains are among the world's snowiest places. Below the glaciers your horse takes you alongside crystal-clear mountain lakes, some fed by the glaciers, others formed when lava blocked a stream's flow.

North Cascades National Park

From Washington's beautiful Pasayten Wilderness your horse takes you into the southeastern corner of North Cascades National Park. Established in 1968 to protect a portion of the northern Cascades, it consists of two units separated by Ross Lake National Recreation Area. Lake Chelan Recreation Area forms the southern tip of the complex. In 1988 Congress designated 93 percent of the total 684,000-acre (276,808-ha) area as the Stephen Mather Wilderness to provide additional protection. The northern park unit borders Canada and includes Mount Shuksan and the Picket Range. The southern part boasts the Eldorado high country and the Stehekin River valley, one of the finest glacier-carved canyons in the Cascades. The park encompasses 318 glaciers, and offers some of the best mountaineering in the U.S.

The Cascades have long been sacred to Native Americans. The first non-Indians to see them close-up were fur trappers and hunters, and you'll be as amazed as they were by the spectacular alpine landscapes. Prospectors

Sawtooth Outfitters

Sawtooth Outfitters, Washington: Riding the PCT's Kennedy Ridge, with Glacier Peak towering behind

Sawtooth Outfitters

Sawtooth Outfitters, Washington: Twenty miles into the PCT's Sawtooth Wilderness, with Finney Ridge and Skookumpuss Mountain in the background

and fortune-seekers were lured by gold, and hardy souls settled in the mountains to sell food and equipment. The mid-1800s saw the beginning of timber harvests. The abundance of water from snowfields and glaciers spurred hydroelectric projects. Protective legislation for the northern Cascades' natural environment was first introduced in 1916, but a critical need for action did not become obvious until the 1950s. In his book *The Wild Cascades*, Harvey Manning recalls that as recently as 1948, he and other outdoor people felt that "the wilderness was inexhaustible, and if one valley was logged, or two or three or a dozen, we could always escape to what seemed uncountable valleys remaining." A growing number of bulldozers, chain saws, and logging trucks changed everything.

Each morning in the backcountry is exhilarating and full of promise. The sun bursts over the ridge, moves up the west wall of the valley, and brushes your camp as you finish breakfast. Your group takes down its tents, someone does the dishes, someone else packs the pots and pans. The rest straighten the camp to make it look like no one has been there. When you lead your horse back to the trail, the sun has gained strength. You settle back in the saddle. There's more great country ahead, and your vacation's end is a long time away—long enough to pretend these wonderful days will go on forever.

By noon your horse, belly heaving from the morning climb, drinks from a river born of glaciers and snowpacks. Next to its hoof you notice a perfect counterpoint to the mountain grandeur, a tiny blue flower no more than a fraction of an inch above the ground. After lunch the journey continues, snaking slowly up the next ravine, then zigzagging carefully down—a whole new vista of Cascades majesty ahead. The height, the shapes, and the aura of enormous power never end. Now your horse takes you past rockbound lakes, some still frozen in August. By late afternoon your group finds an excellent spot for the night's camp in a sheltered valley below a sheer-walled, flat-topped ridge that protrudes from the jumbled heights of a colossal peak. You slide off your horse and sink into grass so invitingly soft, it's tempting to lay down your sleeping bag. But you choose more level, higher ground and set up your tent. When the sun's last rays comb the forest and dance on the cliff, dinner is cooking and another day is coming to a perfect end.

Mount Rainier National Park

You have ridden a little more than half the length of Washington state when you reach the eastern border of 235,612-acre (95,352-ha) Mount Rainier National Park in the middle Cascades. About 29,000 acres of unmelting ice and snow sit atop Mount Rainier, at 14,410 feet the highest Cascade peak. It rises higher from its base than any other U.S. summit south of Alaska, and in clear weather it's visible for hundreds of miles. Here you can study glaciers in the more intimate setting of a single-peak system. Forty-one glaciers blanket the mountain, 25 of them important enough to be named. Emmons Glacier, about 4½ miles long and 1 mile wide on the northeast flank, is the largest glacier in overall size in the lower 48 states. Six-mile-long Carbon Glacier on the mountain's northern face is the longest U.S. glacier south of Alaska. Ninety-three miles of the park's more than 300 miles of trails make up Wonderland Trail, which completely circles the mountain.

Mount Rainier's summit is indented by two geologically youthful craters, still hot enough to keep the crater rims free of snow and generate scores of steam vents and fumaroles (holes that release hot gases and vapor). In one of the crater's bowls lies a lake created by steam that melted ice beneath the summit ice cap, 14,000 feet above sea level. When Mount Rainier was born it had the smooth, contoured slopes of the typical volcanic cone—such as Japan's Mount Fujiyama—but today its sides are crenulated by deep canyons and sharp ridges that were carved by the erosional forces of mountain streams, glaciers, and wind.

Glaciers are formed in regions where the amount of snowfall exceeds the rate of melting. New snow falls on top of old snow, adding weight and compressing the layers into solid ice. Gravity pulls glaciers from higher to lower elevations, the speed varying with the glacier's weight, the slope's steepness, and the surrounding air temperature. As glaciers move—faster at the center than along the edges—they rip the terrain, leaving in their wake ragged walls and smooth, polished surfaces. In the valleys where they came to rest you'll ride among glacial moraines—the deposits of torn-away rocks and boulders, sand, and dust.

From Mount Rainier National Park you'll point your horse toward the Mount Adams Wilderness. Mount St. Helens, lying to the west, erupted violently on May 18, 1980. The explosion blew off the upper 1,300 feet of the peak and left a 2,500-feet-deep crater. Hot volcanic debris shot out the side of the mountain, mixed with melted snow and ice, killing everything within 154 square miles. A cloud of hot ash, catapulted nearly 13 miles into the sky, was carried around the world by winds.

Near the Columbia River the Pacific Crest Trail crosses the Oregon National Historic Trail (see Wagon Trains section of Chapter 1), and the Lewis & Clark National Historic Trail (see Lewis and Clark Expedition sidebar). Once you cross the Columbia River, you're in Oregon. On the Columbia River's Bridge of the Gods, the elevation drops to 140 feet, the lowest point along the Pacific Crest Trail. As the river sliced through the land's volcanic flows it exposed the Cascades' interior.

Crater Lake National Park

The Cascade crest now guides you through Oregon, always in sight of such volcanoes as spectacular Mount Hood, at 11,245 feet Oregon's highest peak

LEWIS AND CLARK EXPEDITION

In 1803, shortly before the Louisiana Purchase, President Thomas Jefferson (1743–1826) commissioned Captain Meriwether Lewis (1774–1809) and Lieutenant William Clark (1770–1838) to undertake the first U.S. overland expedition to the Pacific Coast and back. Theirs is the story of the ultimate horse/raft combo. It took 2 years and 4 months, covered over 8,000 miles, and changed the country.

The Lewis and Clark expedition climbed into their boats on May 14, 1804, near St. Louis, Missouri, and started up the Missouri River. By November they had managed the slow upstream ascent to present Bismarck, North Dakota, where they wintered with the Mandan Sioux. In the spring they employed French-Canadian fur trader Toussaint Charbonneau as a guide and continued the journey in two boats and six dugout canoes. Charbonneau brought along his 17-year-old Native American wife, Sacajawea (Sacagawea), and on Sacajawea's back their infant son, Jean-Baptiste.

The presence on the expedition of this gentle Shoshone girl and her child often helped allay the suspicions of other Indian tribes, and she also served as an interpreter. In April 1805 the group entered what is now Montana. Their journals are full of the wildness of the land and of strange plants and animals. Lewis shot at a "tiger kind" (probably a mountain lion), was chased by a grizzly, and found a large rattlesnake near his bed.

They ran out of navigable river beyond present-day Three Forks, Montana, and wandered about the Rocky Mountains, cutting through ravines, skirting snowfields, running short of rations. On August 13, 1805, the group came upon a Shoshone camp and discovered that the leader was Sacajawea's long-lost brother. They stayed with the Shoshones for two weeks and purchased horses. Riding across Lolo Pass the expedition entered today's Idaho and continued to the headwaters of the Clearwater River. Here they built new canoes and set off downstream to the Snake River, then down the Columbia River to the Pacific Ocean, their goal. The following March they began their return trip to St. Louis, arriving on September 23, 1806, amid much celebration.

and birthplace of five large rivers. In southern Oregon you reach Crater Lake National Park. About 6,600 years ago an ancient volcano, Mount Mazama, once a 12,000-foot peak in the Cascade Range, threw out 42 cubic miles of material. According to the Klamath Indians, from his throne on Mazama's summit the Chief of the Below World warred with the Chief of the Above World, who stood on top of Mount Shasta 100 miles to the south. For seven days, the legend goes, explosions blackened the sky and fires and ash destroyed the forests and the Indians' villages, and Mazama caved in upon itself.

For many years scientists thought the area was the shattered base of a mountain that had exploded, but geological evidence later confirmed the Native American story handed down by word of mouth for 6,600 years. Mount Mazama had erupted, then imploded into the vast chamber that previously contained its lava. Indian artifacts found in nearby areas have been covered with ash and pumice from Mount Mazama's eruptions.

The immense caldera left by Mazama's collapse gradually filled with rain and snow to form Crater Lake. Almost 2,000 feet at its deepest point, Crater Lake is the deepest lake in the U.S. and the second deepest in the Western Hemisphere, exceeded only by Canada's Great Slave Lake. Yet the lake barely reaches halfway up the caldera's highest cliffs. From the cliffs the entire lake, 6 miles wide and 20 miles in circumference, offers a spectacle hard to match. Surrounding the deep, brilliant blue lake are sharply contrasting green forests of pines, fir, and hemlock. Continued volcanic activity on the caldera's floor formed three small cinder cones, but only one, 2,600-foot Wizard Island, rises high enough above the lake to be seen.

The 183,180-acre (74,131-ha) Crater Lake National Park also offers other displays of volcanism. Giant lava spikes poke up from the canyons of Wheeler and Annie Creeks, the solidified cores of gas vents now exposed by erosion. Several volcanic dikes—pathways of molten rock that welled up through cracks and then hardened—were left in the caldera when surrounding material eroded away. Lava flows can be seen in valleys, and the Pumice Desert, which you are now crossing, is a broad stretch of upland with packed lava dust up to 200 feet deep below your horse's hooves.

Riding into the Golden State

From Crater Lake your trek takes you into the Sky Lakes Wilderness, Rogue River National Forest, Winema National Forest, and public land administered by the Bureau of Land Management. You'll cross the northernmost arm of the California National Historic Trail, then you'll enter California in the Siskiyou Mountains. While you're still in the coastal fog belt, before the Pacific Crest Trail turns inland after the Russian Wilderness, be on the lookout for the mighty coast redwoods, the tallest living things on Earth. Some of today's coast redwoods are more than 2,000 years old.

Fossil remains show that similar giant conifers grew 160 million years ago, and that the trees took on today's redwood characteristics about 20 million years back. Before the Great Ice Age, redwoods covered what are now Europe, Asia, and North America, but most of the trees died when the glaciers melted. After the Ice Age three redwood species remained, two now found only in California: the coast redwoods on the Pacific Coast between Big Sur and the Oregon border, and the sierra redwoods, or giant sequoias, along the Sierra Nevada's western slopes (see Sequoia & Kings Canyon National Parks section). The third species, the dawn redwood, is deciduous and now grows only in China.

High in the redwood forest ravens and crows squabble loudly, and are joined by the Steller's jay looking for handouts that can be begged, borrowed, or stolen from human and animal passersby. Banana slugs dine on dead leaves and debris that cover the redwood forest floor. The Roosevelt elk

SETON-WATCHING

As you travel along the Pacific Crest Trail, get off your horse every so often, walk to a quiet spot, and make the land your own. Sit very, very still until you meld with your surroundings. This is sometimes called Seton-watching, after naturalist Ernest Thompson Seton, who practiced it to perfection. While you sit, try to "see" with all your senses: feel the warm sun, listen to the wind, inhale the aroma of the grasses, flowers, and trees. The results are astounding. You'll be at peace, and animals will forget you are there and go back to what they were doing. Birds will land on your head, mice will walk over your shoes. A beaver once climbed out of a pond and curled up in a woman's lap while she was Seton-watching.

Of all wildlife, birds are the least fearful of humans. In your presence they'll fly about, squabble, perform mating dances, eat, build nests, and throw back their heads and sing amazingly. Bring your binoculars — It won't hurt your Seton-watching to lift them gently once in a while.

that once ranged throughout North America is now found mainly in the national parks along the Pacific Coast. Predatory martens hunt at night for chipmunks and birds asleep in redwood branches.

At the edge of the redwood groves are mixed forests of evergreen and deciduous trees and scented azaleas. Poison oak builds thickets beneath redwood trunks and vine maple spreads along the ground. Many kinds of mushroom and other fungi grow in the shade, and a wide variety of ferns flourish. In spring the redwood sorrel sports pinkish-purple blooms, and during spring and early summer the forest floor is covered with the delicate white-to-dusty-pink blossoms of trillium, a member of the lily family.

Lassen Volcanic National Park

Riding into 106,372-acre (43,048-ha) Lassen Volcanic National Park you'll come to the end of the Cascade Range. From the tiniest mud pots, bubbling away in hidden hollows; to fumaroles, hot springs, cinder cones, lava plugs, and lava flows; to the crater of 10,457-foot Lassen Peak, the park is a showcase of volcanic activity. Lassen Peak began life as a vent on the northern flank of a volcano called Mount Tehama, which geologists believe was 2 miles high and over 11 miles wide at its base. Tehama eventually collapsed and

Lassen Peak, the southermost of the Cascade summits. As you continue south on the Pacific Crest Trail, the Sierra Nevada awaits you.

Lassen National Park

eroded, but ruins of its caldera flanks are the park's Brokeoff Mountain, Mount Diller, Pilot Pinnacle, and Mount Conard. What is now the park's Sulphur Works was probably Tehama's main vent.

In May 1914 Lassen Peak began a 7-year cycle of sporadic volcanic explosions, the most violent in 1915, when the peak shot a giant mushroom cloud 7 miles into the air and profoundly altered the landscape. The area was designated a national park in 1916 because of its volcanic significance. Until the 1980 Mount St. Helens eruption, Lassen Peak was famous for having had the most recent eruption in the contiguous 48 states. Today Lassen National Park serves as a recovery model for Mount St. Helens' wildlife and vegetation.

Lassen National Park boasts more than 50 mountain lakes, dense forests, and rich vegetation and wildlife, and lies at the crossroads of three great biological provinces: the Cascades to the north, the Sierra Nevada to the south, and the Great Basin Desert to the east. The park is home to some 779 plant species (nearby Mount Shasta has only 485 species). About 14 Cascadian species reach their southern limit here; about 24 Sierran species, their northern range.

More than 200 species of birds have been identified in the park. Many are neotropical migrants—such as warblers, vireos, and tanagers—who breed at Lassen in the summer, then winter in Mexico or Central and South America. Recent studies have shown that Lassen's numbers of neotropical visitors are declining, partly because of the expanding range of the brown-headed cowbird, or buffalo bird, that once lived with the large buffalo herds on the American plains. When an increasing human population farmed, ranched, and cleared forests, the cowbird spread rapidly throughout the lower 48 states. A nest parasite, it neither builds its own nest nor cares for its young. Female cowbirds lay their eggs in the nests of other birds, often resulting in the death of the host young who cannot successfully compete with the larger cowbird chicks for food.

Riding through the Lassen area you'll be on the ancient meeting ground of four Native American groups: the Atsugewi, Yana, Yahi, and Maidu. You'll camp where the groups camped in the warmer months for hunting and gathering, before wintering elsewhere. The tribes' combined population is estimated to have been 4,000 people in 1776, but by 1950 they had dwindled to 350. In 1911, in Oroville, California, a Yahi Indian appeared who had never mixed with whites before and whose tribe by then was thought extinct. Ishi, which means "I am a man," was the last Stone Age survivor in the U.S. He spent his remaining days sharing his knowledge at the University of California Museum in Berkeley, actually living in a museum exhibit, and died in 1921.

As you leave Lassen, the 400-mile length of the majestic Sierra Nevada Range stretches before you. The Sierra Nevada is North America's longest continuous mountain range and rises higher above the adjacent landscape than any other range in the lower 48 states. About 11,000 vertical feet separate the floor of Owens Valley on the east and the top of 14,494-foot Mount Whitney, the highest U.S. peak outside Alaska. With an average width of 60 to 80 miles, the Sierra Nevada covers more area than the European Alps.

Lake Tahoe and Beyond

As you approach Lake Tahoe, your horse takes you near the Donner Memorial. For many years the arid Great Basin to your east thwarted overland travel to California. In the summer of 1846 the unfortunate Donner party was only the tenth group of settlers to make the journey. From what is now Salt Lake City, Utah, they followed the Humboldt River and broke a new trail through the Wasatch Mountains, then attempted to cross Donner Pass when winter weather was already upon them. That winter was one of the harshest in the history of the Sierra Nevada, with snow depths of over 20 feet. Freezing and starving, the party urgently built rough cabins and took shelter as best they could. During the long months the families ran out of food and were unable to hunt in the deep snow. Some survived on the bodies of comrades who had succumbed to the hardships. Forty-seven people lived through the ordeal, 42 did not.

Near the southern end of Lake Tahoe you'll ride across the Pony Express National Historic Trail. From April 1860 until October 1861 the Pony Express was a horseback mail service that, though brief, sparked the nation's admiration. Between St. Joseph, Missouri, and Sacramento, California, the mounted carriers relayed across 1,800 miles in 10 days. Way stations every 15 miles broke the journey. The riders had 2 minutes to switch saddlebags to a fresh mount and be on their way. They sped at a full gallop day and night, through good weather and bad, over rugged terrain, and often through hostile Indian land. Expert riders willing to risk death were asked to apply for the job. Orphans were preferred. William F. ("Buffalo Bill") Cody and "Pony Bob" Haslam rode for the company and added to its fame. When the transcontinental telegraph system was completed, the Pony Express ceased.

The High Sierra

Farther south on the Pacific Crest Trail you'll ride through breathtaking Yosemite National Park (see the Yosemite section in this chapter), then enter the Ansel Adams Wilderness. The trail descends into timber and reaches Rush Creek Forks, and later the meadows and ponds of Island Pass—a haven for fairy shrimp and mountain frogs. The island-dotted surface of Thousand Island Lake reflects the imposing facade of Banner Peak and the sharply etched mass of Mount Ritter. You'll pass colorful Emerald Lake and the east shore of dramatic Ruby Lake, and ascend steeply to the outlet of Garnet Lake. On the rocky ridge above Garnet Lake you'll have excellent views of the lake itself, Mount Ritter, Banner Peak, and Mount Davis. You'll descend

1,000 feet to Shadow Creek and continue to beautiful Shadow Lake, a true mountain gem.

The route passes through some of the highest botanical displays in North America. With a natural curiosity, you'll become familiar with an extraordinary variety of wildflowers. Elegant alpine lilies grow in protected places. Gentian's tubular blue flowers blossom at elevations as high as 10,000 feet. Sulphur flower and paintbrush transform open ridges and sunny slopes into gardens of scarlet and yellow. But few are as striking as the penstemon, whose small magenta trumpets cluster in granite clefts and produce some of the most dazzling Sierra displays. One moment you're in an open, breezy pass amid barren rock, the next minute you're in a soft vale of ferns. About three dozen fern species grow in the Sierra Nevada, some widespread but so small and hidden they are frequently overlooked.

As the Pacific Crest Trail approaches Devils Postpile National Monument, the jagged, knife-edged Minarets dominate the skyline to your right, products of volcanic activity 150 million years ago. Look for Mammoth Mountain on your left, an ancient volcano with barren upper slopes that erupted about 400,000 years ago. (On a busy winter day Mammoth entertains up to 20,000 skiers.) Plan to visit the national monument's stunningly beautiful lava formations. A little less than 100,000 years ago, dark, molten basalt sizzled through Mammoth Pass and oozed down the canyon. Here the liquid cooled, solidified, contracted, and cracked into three- to seven-sided vertical columns—the

A view of the eastern Sierra Nevada from the White Mountains. Imagine yourself riding across the Sierran heights.

Jeff Gnass/California Department of Tourism

"devil's postpile." Glaciers later scraped the columns' tops, leaving the beautiful surface of glacial polish you admire today.

Back on the Pacific Crest Trail you ride past Kings Creek Trail, down a steep hillside to a wooden bridge over the Middle Fork. From here to Mount Whitney is one of the most up-and-down parts of the entire Pacific Crest Trail. Again and again the trail rises above treeline to 10,000 or more feet, only to cross a pass or ridge and descend on the other side to a meadow, creek, or canyon, then repeat the process. While your body absorbs the elevation change, your mind is busy taking in a thousand sights. Polished granite walls, dramatic gorges, and glacier-gouged basins engulf you and your horse, diminishing you to insignificance. Minutes later you emerge at lofty heights, feeling larger than life and on top of the world.

Under heavy cover of red fir you cross Crater Creek, a favorite of black bears, and enter the John Muir Wilderness, leaving the Ansel Adams Wilderness behind. Where a trail comes in from Mammoth Pass, burrowing Belding's ground squirrels keep the soil loose, and lodgepole pines invade the grasses along the Upper Crater Meadow's edge. A long, gentle climb takes you to fine views of the Thumb to the northeast. Soon your horse crosses a low divide and drops toward Deer Creek on a dry, south-facing slope covered with sagebrush, Indian paintbrush, manzanita, and gooseberry. You glimpse the vast Cascade Valley and the Silver Divide beyond.

After Purple Lake your horse climbs over a ridge to deep-blue Lake Virginia and drops steeply to Tully Hole, a well-flowered grassland where the McGee Pass Trail departs toward the east. You follow Fish Creek for a mile, then ascend through hemlock-and-fir forest to timberline at Squaw Lake and continue past treeline to 10,900-foot Silver Pass. You approach timberline again at Marie Lake and gently ascend barren, 10,900-foot Selden Pass. Coming down you skirt small Heart Lake, then wind between the beautiful Sally Keyes Lakes. You enter Kings Canyon National Park and cross the San Joaquin River several times. Your horse ascends steeply into marvelous Evolution Valley (see Sequoia & Kings Canyon National Parks section).

You exit the southern Sierra beyond the Domeland Wilderness, briefly enter the Mojave Desert, and ride through the mountains, national forests, and wilderness areas east of Los Angeles. As you leave the San Bernardino National Forest, the Pacific Crest Trail crosses the Juan Bautista de Anza National Historic Trail. In 1775 a group of 30 Spanish families, a dozen soldiers, and 1000 cattle, horses, and mules left Mexico under the leadership of Colonel Juan Bautista de Anza to establish an overland route to California and protect San Francisco Bay from claims by the Russians and British. For three months the party traversed the deserts of the Southwest. It took another three months to reach the northern bay.

Your own journey ends 50 miles southeast of San Diego, near the settlement of Campo, at the California–Mexico border.

TRAVEL TIPS
Pacific Coast States

Prime Horseback Season: High elevations: Mid-July through August. Southernmost desert: March–May and October–November.

Horse Outfitters: Washington: Early Winters, North Cascade Outfitters, Sawtooth Outfitters. Oregon: Outdoor Adventures Plus. California:Bedell Pack Trains, Frontier Pack Train, Glacier Pack Train, Pine Creek Pack Station, RainbowPack Station, Red's Meadow Pack Station,Rock Creek Pack Station.

Trail Information: Pacific Crest Trail Association,5325 Elkhorn Blvd., Suite 256, Sacramento, CA 95842; (800) 817-2243. National Trails System Branch, National Park Service (782), P.O. Box 37127, Washington, DC 20013-7127; (202) 343-3780.

Stewardship Agencies: Canada: Manning Provincial Park, Box 3, Manning Park, British Columbia, Canada VOX1RO; (604) 840-8836.
United States: USDA Forest Service, Pacific Northwest Region, 333 SW First Avenue, P.O. Box 3623, Portland, OR 97208; (503) 326-2971. USDA Forest Service, Pacific Southwest Region, 630 Sansome Street, San Francisco, CA 94111; (415) 705-2874.
Bureau of Land Management, Medford District Office, 3040 Biddle Road, Medford, OR 97504; (503) 770-2200. Bureau of Land Management, California State Office, PublicRoom, 2800 Cottage Way, Sacramento, CA 95825; (916) 978-4754.

General Tourist Information: Washington Department of Tourism, (800) 544-1800; Oregon Department of Tourism, (800) 547-7842; California Department of Tourism, (800) 862-2543

SEQUOIA & KINGS CANYON NATIONAL PARKS

"Who can picture, in language, or on canvas,
all the sublime depths of wonder
that flow to the soul in thrilling and intense surprise,
when the eye looks upon these great marvels?"

Joseph Mason Hutchings (1820–1902)

The Big Trees

In total volume of living mass the sierra redwood, or giant sequoia, is the largest living thing on Earth. Seventy-five groves of these gargantuan trees remain on this planet, all located on the moist, unglaciated ridges of the Sierra Nevada's west slope. Some groves contain only a few trees, others several thousand. The largest groves and the biggest individuals are protected in Sequoia National Park and adjacent Kings Canyon National Park. At Red Mountain Grove in Kings Canyon National Park, you stand among 15,800 giant sequoias with base diameters greater than a foot. Sequoia National Park's Giant Forest Grove surrounds you with 8,400 such trees, including the champion of all: the General Sherman giant sequoia, the largest living individual on Earth. It has a base diameter over 36 feet, stands 275 feet tall, and is estimated to be between 2,300 and 2,700 years old. It takes 20 people with outstretched arms to encircle the tree's trunk. The Giant Forest Grove is home to four of the world's five biggest individuals.

The giant trees were probably first seen by Europeans in the Yosemite region in 1833, by members of the Joseph Walker party, but it was not until 1852, when bear hunter A. T. Dowd chased a wounded grizzly into a grove north of Yosemite, that the world heard of them. Dowd couldn't believe his eyes. No tree could possibly be that big. Forgetting the bear, he raced back to camp and told what his companions called his "big trees" story. He persuaded them to go to the grove only after pretending he needed help to cart the bear. The story of the mammoth trees spread quickly, and visitors hurried to the new wonder.

In 1858 Native Americans led rancher Dale Tharp up twisting trails in Sequoia's Giant Forest to show him the trees. In one of the many lush forest meadows the rancher later made a summer cabin in the huge hollow trunk of a fallen sequoia. Here, before the park was established, he and his family

The General Grant giant sequoia is as tall as an average 26-story building; its base diameter exceeds the width of many city streets.

grazed stock. Conservationist John Muir came upon the sequoia cabin some years later while hiking with his mule, Brownie. Muir, who named the Giant Forest, described Tharp's log as a "noble den . . . likely to outlast the most durable stone castle, and commanding views of garden and grove grander far than the richest king ever enjoyed."

To loggers, the trees were a marvelous discovery, and the forest soon echoed with the sound of falling giants. Other entrepreneurs, whom John Muir called "laborious vandals," came up with wild schemes. One stripped the bark off a live sequoia and displayed it in New York as the "Tree Mastodon: A Mountain Of Wood." Another built a two-lane bowling alley atop a fallen giant. The stump of a third tree was smoothed off and roofed over to use as a ballroom for up to 48 dancers. It became a theatrical stage, and later housed the press and staff of a short-lived newspaper.

Sequoia, the world's second-oldest national park, was established on September 25, 1890. A week later Congress increased its acreage. Some proponents of national park protection in the Sierra Nevada sought to preserve water supplies for irrigation, others protested unwise logging practices. Preserving land as habitat for living things or for scenic, scientific, educational, spiritual, recreational, and heritage values was then an infant idea.

In 1893 a Sierra Forest grant set aside more lands, and in 1926 Kern Canyon was added to Sequoia. Kings Canyon National Park, established in 1940, includes the former General Grant National Park, created in 1890 to protect the lovely Grant Grove of sequoia trees. The outstanding giant here is the General Grant tree, the world's third-largest living individual. The General Grant is widely known as the nation's Christmas Tree, and Christmas observances are held at its foot each year. In 1978 Congress added Mineral King Valley to Sequoia National Park.

Riding the Backcountry

Sequoia and Kings Canyon National Parks have been administered jointly since 1943. Extending from the foothills of California's Great Valley on the west to the crest of the Sierra Nevada on the east, they protect a chunk of wild Sierra Nevada larger than Yosemite National Park, including Mount Whitney, North America's highest point outside Alaska. Palisade Crest in Kings Canyon National Park and the Mount Whitney group in Sequoia each boast six mountains over 14,000 feet.

More than 90 percent of the 863,710 combined acres (349,535 ha) are backcountry, accessible only by foot and horse. Hundreds of miles of trail reach into all corners of the two parks and can be accessed from all park boundaries. The lowest elevations begin around 1,500 feet. Up to 3,000–4,000-foot elevations, the summers are hot and dry and the winters usually free of snow. Here you ride through drought-resistant chaparral. As you ride higher you'll follow the moist air from the Pacific Ocean, forced up when it meets the Sierra Nevada. The rising air cools and releases its moisture as rain or snow, most of it in the giant sequoia belt between 5,000 and 8,000 feet. None of the parks' few roads go higher than 7,800 feet. East of the Sierra Nevada, in its rain shadow, lies the semiarid Great Basin.

You may not see many birds in the sequoia forests in the daytime, but at dawn the chorus is magical. The warble of purple finches, the triple notes of western tanagers, the melodic arch of a black-headed grosbeak, and the trill of Oregon juncos combine in a mystic melody. The big trees are resistant to decay and rot, so not many birds search them for insects, but pileated woodpeckers march up and down nearby tree trunks, their hammering resounding through the forest. Nuthatches busily feed insects to their children, safely hidden in an evergreen stump.

Any time of day you may see Douglas squirrels clip off sequoia cones, as many as 13 in 10 seconds, and drop them to the forest floor. When they've harvested enough, they cart the cones off to their caches in hollow logs and

NAMING GIANTS

For many years the sierra redwood and the coast redwood shared the scientific classification *Sequoia*, named by botanist Stephan Endlicher in honor of the Cherokee leader Sequoyah (1760–1843), who invented the first Native American alphabet. The son of a Cherokee mother and a British trader, Sequoyah never learned to speak, read, or write English. Around 1809 he began developing a system of writing to help the Cherokees maintain their identity. By 1821 he had perfected 86 symbols that covered all Cherokee speech. Cherokees throughout the nation adopted the system and published books and newspapers. Scientifically the sierra redwood now is called *Sequoiadendron giganteum* and the coast redwood *Sequoia sempervirens*. The General Sherman tree was discovered in August 1879 by James Wolverton, who named it for General William Tecumseh Sherman (1820–1891), under whom he had served in the Civil War.

crevices, often near creeks. They plan to eat the cones throughout the winter, but their harvest is so abundant and the cones hidden in such good places that many seeds sprout, renewing the forest.

You'll ride through a variety of pine forests—sugar, Jeffrey, ponderosa, and lodgepole—and through stands of red and white fir and incense cedar. Quaking aspens rim moist meadows and dot the higher slopes. You're likely to see mule deer and, with luck, you may spot a black bear browsing in the forest. In winter the mule deer drift to lower elevations, but the bear simply goes to sleep in a sheltered spot among the rocks or in a hollow log. Though rarely seen, mountain lions hunt the mule deer, weeding out the old or diseased animals. Higher yet, the parks offer magnificent lakes and streams, forests and meadows, and farther up, a wonderworld of bare granite.

Kern Canyon in southern Sequoia is 6,000 feet deep, and several other canyons in the two parks exceed 4,000 feet. Outside the park, along the Kings Canyon Highway, just downstream from the confluence of the Middle and South Forks of Kings River, Kings Canyon plunges some 8,200 vertical feet from Spanish Mountain's peak to the river. No other canyon in North America is this deep, not even the Snake River's Hells Canyon in Idaho.

Kings Canyon National Park's Cloud Canyon, with Whaleback Mountain in the background

Sequoia & Kings Canyon National Parks

OLDER THAN TIME

While the General Sherman is the world's biggest tree, the world's oldest is a bristlecone pine called Methuselah. It is 4,600 years old and lives at 10,000 feet in California's Ancient Bristlecone Pine Forest east of the Sierra Nevada near Big Pine. If you are riding into Sequoia and Kings Canyon National Parks from the east, you might pay homage to these ancient beings. The world's oldest tree ever recorded was a bristlecone pine designated WPN-114, which grew at 10,750 feet on the northeast face of the Sierra Nevada's Wheeler Ridge, west of Bishop, California. Studies in 1963 and 1964 estimated it to be about 4,900 years old. Vandals cut it down with a chain saw.

Pacific Crest National Scenic Trail

From Yosemite National Park the Pacific Crest Trail coincides with the most famous of all Sierra Nevada trails, the John Muir Trail. Riding south on the combined trails, you'll enter Kings Canyon National Park near Evolution Valley at an elevation of 9,650 feet. From here to the end of the John Muir Trail at the summit of Mount Whitney, 97 miles of some of the world's finest high mountain riding lie before you. Averaging 15 miles a day, the journey will take you seven glorious days.

In the summer of 1895 Theodore S. Solomons hiked from Yosemite, visiting alpine regions virtually untraveled by non-Indians. At the head of Evolution Valley he climbed a lofty, granite-rimmed basin and was enthralled by the alpine vistas before him. "As I photographed and sketched," wrote Solomons, "I felt that here was a fraternity of Titans that in their naming should bear in common an august significance. And I could think of none more fitting to confer upon them than the great evolutionists." He called the peaks Darwin, Huxley, Wallace, Spencer, Haeckel, and Fiske.

You'll ride through Evolution Valley's lush meadows sprinkled with bright wildflowers, then cross and recross a small creek and climb southward. As you top 10,000 feet the forest thins, and you'll see whitebark pines, harbingers of approaching timberline. Faraway peaks are outlined sharply and seem deceptively close. Snow patches from last winter's storms lie in sheltered nooks. At the north end of sparkling blue Evolution Lake the scenery is breathtaking. Mounts Mendel and Darwin are on your left, the Hermit on your right, and the steepled rooftops of Mounts Spencer and Huxley dead ahead. Clusters of wildflowers live around the lake— Indian paintbrush, yellow buttercup, white aster—and yellow monkey flowers line gurgling streams.

Your horse lumbers up steep switchbacks, each hoof-thud sending tiny explosions of granite dust onto leaves of trailside plants. At the top of 11,955-foot Muir Pass a circular stone hut was erected in 1931 to honor John Muir. You are now standing on Goddard Divide, which separates the San Joaquin and Kings River watersheds. Not a single tree frames the mountain views, and there is nothing between you and the sky. Near the head of Le Conte Canyon you'll drop into a delightful emerald-green valley, the massive buttress of Black Giant looming high as a backdrop. At Big Pete Meadow, your horse follows the forested edge, then takes you south. The Yosemite-like grandeur of Le Conte Canyon comes into full view, Langille Peaks soaring to your right. When you round the steep west shore of a lake at 12,248 feet, the trail hugs barren canyon walls and switchbacks skyward to a narrow notch in the Kings–Kern Divide. This is 13,180-foot Forester Pass, the highest point on the entire Pacific Crest Trail. The views are stunning. To the north and east are Mounts Pinchot, Keith, and Bradley, and Junction, Center, and University Peaks. Mount Stanford and Caltech Peak tower to the west, and to the south are Kaweah Peaks Ridge, the Red Spur, Picket Guard Peak, and Kern Point. You are entering Sequoia National Park.

On the immense slope of Tawny Point, you'll ride among foxtail pine, a species found mainly in the high southern Sierra. The spectacular panorama you'll see as you approach the Bighorn Plateau is one of the Sierra's finest. From the plateau's summit you'll see for the first time the terminus of the John Muir Trail: Mount Whitney. After Wright Creek you cross the Wallace Lake Trail. Downhill it connects with the High Sierra Trail descending to the Giant Forest. You continue on the Pacific Crest–John Muir Trail, and near Crabtree Ranger Station the broad back of Mount Whitney reappears. Your horse takes you past the avalanche-scarred north face of Mount Hitchcock, its lower portions smoothed by glaciers.

Below Discovery Pinnacle it's time to say good-bye. The John Muir Trail veers off to the left, beginning a 2-mile ascent of Mount Whitney, the end of its journey from Yosemite National Park. The Pacific Crest Trail continues south to Mexico.

TRAVEL TIPS
Sequoia & Kings Canyon National Parks

Prime Horseback Season: July and August

Horse Outfitters: Eastern Sequoia and Kings: Bedell Pack
Trains, Glacier Pack Train, Pine
Creek Pack Station, Rainbow Pack Station, Rock Creek
Pack Station. Western Sequoia and Kings: Bedell Pack
Trains

Stewardship Agency: Sequoia & Kings Canyon National
Parks, Three Rivers, CA 93271; (209) 565-3134

General Tourist Information: California Department of
Tourism, (800) 862-2543

YOSEMITE NATIONAL PARK

*"These beautiful days must enrich all my life. They do not exist as mere pictures . . .
but they saturate themselves into every part of the body and live always."*

John Muir (1838–1914)

Granite Grandeur

At 747,956 acres (302,964 ha), Yosemite National Park is a national treasure
larger than Rhode Island and offers you magnificent Sierra Nevada peaks,
majestic granite domes, steep-walled canyons, luxuriant forests, and silvery
waterfalls. Yosemite Valley, the park's most famous feature, is flanked by
sheer granite monoliths greater than the rock of Gibraltar and by Yosemite
Falls, a waterfall eight times the height of Niagara. At Yosemite Falls' highest
section, Upper Yosemite Falls, the waters fall free for 1,430 feet, then plunge
675 feet over Middle Falls and onto Lower Falls for a final 320 feet.
Altogether, Yosemite Falls descends a magnificent 2,425 feet, making it the
world's second-highest waterfall.

Yosemite National Park has 37 species of trees. The giant sequoia is the
most notable, and you can visit three major groves. The Mariposa Grove
near the southern entrance is the largest and holds the Fallen Wawona
Tunnel Tree and the Grizzly Giant. The Tunnel Tree became famous in
1881 when a passage was cut through its base. For the next 88 years people
drove right through the tree—first in stagecoaches and later in automo-
biles—until, uprooted, it toppled in 1969. You can still see it just as it fell.
The Grizzly Giant, Yosemite's largest and oldest sequoia, is 35 feet in diameter, 210 feet high, and about 2,000 years old.

Tall in the Saddle

Unless otherwise posted within the park, all of Yosemite's 840 miles of designated trails are open to horse use. Inside Yosemite Valley horse trails are
marked as bridle paths. Park elevations range from 2,000 feet at El Portal to
13,114 feet on top of Mount Lyell, Yosemite's highest summit. If you ride
quietly, you may encounter some of the park's more than 240 species of birds,
80 species of mammals, 24 species of amphibians and reptiles, and 10 species
of fish. Watch for the rare peregrine falcon and for the dipper (water ouzel),
a curious land bird that nests behind waterfalls and walks underwater to feed

on aquatic insects. At dusk you may hear the hoot-hoot of a northern pygmy owl or see flying squirrels gliding silently from tree to tree. With luck you'll see black bears and raccoons, and the park's five species of chipmunks. Although the name Yosemite comes from a Native American word meaning "grizzly bear," no grizzlies are left in the park.

Many of Yosemite's animals stay within a particular park area year-round; others migrate north or south, lower or higher depending on the season. Spring thaw works its way upslope from mid-May to mid-July, and the mule deer follow the retreating snow line into the high country. Near their burrows you may see yellow-bellied marmots sitting upright on lookout boulders. The pika, a tiny relative of the rabbit, lives among the rocks of the high peaks, making little haystacks in the fall for its winter fodder. An Arctic species, it migrated here during the Great Ice Age and was marooned when the glaciers melted. Mountain lions and bobcats are rarely seen, as are porcupines, coyotes, and gray foxes. In open country and forest clearings, great gray owls hunt rodents at night.

John Muir Trail

The John Muir is the most famous trail in Yosemite, and indeed the entire Sierra Nevada. From Yosemite Valley it climbs to the Tuolumne River's 8,800-foot-high Tuolumne Meadows—the largest subalpine meadow in the High Sierra—and is joined by the Pacific Crest Trail. Together the two trails make their spectacular way along the Sierra's crest and connect Yosemite with Kings Canyon and Sequoia National Parks via the Ansel Adams Wilderness, Devils Postpile National Monument, and the John Muir Wilderness. About 180 miles southeast of Tuolumne Meadows, the two trails divide and the John Muir Trail climbs steeply to its magnificent end atop Sequoia's Mount Whitney—the highest point in the U.S. outside of Alaska.

The trail begins at Yosemite Valley's 4,035-foot-high Happy Isles as an asphalt ribbon climbing the wall of the Merced River Canyon. Switchbacks take you near viewpoints overlooking Vernal and Nevada Falls and the great granite domes above them. About 300 yards before Nevada Fall the Panorama Trail departs southward, bound for Glacier Point and one of the world's most awe-inspiring vistas. From here, 3,200 feet above the valley floor, you'll see the park's high country in the distance, Half Dome nearby, Vernal and Nevada Falls below you, and Yosemite Falls across the valley.

Back on the John Muir Trail, from the lip of Nevada Fall you'll see Glacier Point high ahead, Liberty Cap on the right, and below, the Merced River descending in cascades and pools, finally disappearing over Vernal Fall. Nevada Fall drops 594 feet in a fantastic display, its waters striking granite ledges, ricocheting out in plumes of spray. Other falls in Yosemite drop greater distances, but none has as much water as the Nevada. Its thunderous

Ascending Nevada Fall Trail, with Yosemite Falls in the distance

roar serenades you for miles. Your horse catches its breath as it strolls into forested Little Yosemite Valley. Near the river, guide your horse left, away from the stream. Riding through mixed conifers you reach the trail to Half Dome, an incredible 4-mile round trip that should not be missed.

On the John Muir Trail once again, your horse crosses Sunrise Creek, fords the stream, and carries you up, then down, to the lower end of Long Meadow and below the Sunrise High Sierra Camp. At the upper lobe of Long Meadow the trail turns northeast and ascends the slopes below Columbia Finger. Inspiring panoramas of the park's southeast section abound before the trail descends gently to the flower-filled swale at the south side of 9,730-foot Cathedral Pass. In the stillness, birds sing cheerily, gray squirrels with long bushy tails scamper about, and wildflowers and butterflies add their color to the scene. Your horse takes you past the southeast shore of shallow Upper Cathedral Lake. As along most of Yosemite's lakes and waterways, you may see signs of black bears, or perhaps the bears themselves. Talk or sing to alert them of your presence. A long, gentle ascent levels off on the west slope of Cathedral Peak. On the shady north slope the trail drops through several small meadows rimmed with mountain hemlock. The descent continues and 23 miles from Happy Isles your horse brings you to Tuolumne Meadows.

With James W. Marshall's discovery in January 1848 at John Sutter's sawmill northwest of Yosemite, the cry of "Gold!" exploded on the local population. From San Francisco to Los Angeles people left their fields, houses, and businesses and rushed to the Sierra. Soldiers deserted their posts and sailors, their ships. Conflict with Native Americans was inevitable, and the Mariposa Battalion was organized to subdue the Indians. In March 1851 the battalion entered Yosemite Valley in pursuit of Native Americans. From that moment on, word about the valley's scenic beauty and natural wealth spread and private attempts to exploit it were soon underway.

By 1860 logging and overgrazing were destroying the incomparable valley. Concerned citizens saw the dangers and appealed to Congress, and in 1864 the valley became the first area in the world to be officially protected. Congress and President Lincoln granted the valley and the Mariposa Grove to the State of California, on condition that "the premises shall be held for public use, resort, all recreation . . . for all time."

John Muir, a native of Scotland who had emigrated to the U.S. with his family in 1849 at the age of 11, first saw Yosemite Valley in 1868. He was the first to attribute the spectacular scenery to glacial erosion. Concerned that the Sierra's high-country meadows, which had not been included in the state grant, were also endangered by overgrazing, he launched a passionate campaign for their protection. On October 1, 1890, Yosemite became the nation's third national park, encompassing not only the state lands but also a sizable area around it. Military units headquartered in Wawona administered the park while the State of California continued to govern the areas covered

BLACK BEARS

While searching for food, female black bears range as much as 35 square miles; males have territories up to 200 square miles. Females do not share their area, but those of males may overlap. The animals are most active at night, but forage some during the day, particularly when they are feeding heavily to prepare for winter. As cold weather approaches, the bears search for protected spots. Although their body temperatures drop, and their respiration and metabolic rates slow, bears are not true hibernators; they remain semiconscious the entire winter. When they emerge from their dens in May they are extremely hungry. They tear bark from trees to eat the cambium layer just beneath the surface, rip into rotting logs to look for small insects and grubs, and climb trees to raid bird nests for eggs. They tear open beehives, eat such mammals as porcupines (carefully), and hunt fish in streams and rivers.

Black bears mate in June and July, but females become pregnant only every few years. In January or February two to three cubs are born. The mother usually awakens during birth, cleans her newborn, and goes back to sleep. The tiny cubs, naked and blind, spend the winter in the den, kept close and warm by their mother. The mother's fat gives her enough energy to stay alive and maintain muscle mass. By May the cubs' eyes are open and their coats are grown. Though weaned at 6 to 8 months of age, they still spend the second winter with the mother. The following spring or summer they become independent. Sometimes the cubs stay together for a few months after separating from their mother, and at times even den together that first winter.

Aside from the polar bears of the Arctic, North America has two species of bears—black and brown —though color is an unreliable guide. Brown bears range from pale gold to dark brown or even almost black. The "black" in black bears can range from ebony to cinnamon, and both of these extremes may be born in the same litter. Bears share a common ancestry with dogs, but about 18 million years ago their skulls became massive, their teeth blunt and heavy, their legs stocky, and their tails reduced to mere stubs.

by the original land grant. In 1892 John Muir helped found the Sierra Club to aid in securing federal administration for the entire Yosemite region.

In 1903 President Theodore Roosevelt spent three days in the park with John Muir. The first night they camped among the valley's giant sequoia trees and listened to the sounds of the forest and the waterfalls. "It was like lying in a great solemn cathedral," Roosevelt wrote, "far vaster and more beautiful than any built by the hand of man." In 1906 California returned the original grant lands to the federal government. Civilian park rangers began administering the park in 1914, and two years later Congress created the National Park Service.

Pacific Crest National Scenic Trail

The Pacific Crest Trail cuts across the great park for 70 miles, offering you solitude and a chance to renew a sense of childlike wonder. South of the park, the Pacific Crest Trail takes you high above timberline. Inside the park, you ride below treeline and enjoy a more sheltered vacation, especially in the luxuriant canyon bottoms and valleys. Under the canopy of some of the world's finest forests, only filtered light penetrates, and the heady aroma of pitch is everywhere.

Coming from the north, the Pacific Crest Trail reaches Yosemite from Toiyabe National Forest, crosses 9,550-foot Dorothy Lake Pass, and drops to Dorothy Lake, following Grace Meadow, and the meadows beyond. Tilden Lake lies off to your left; later you'll ride past much smaller, shallow Wilma Lake, 7,930 feet in elevation. Between the lakes you become intimately acquainted with streams that accompany you down canyons and along lush meadows, bathe you in a fine spray, and fill the air with sounds of rushing or trickling water. Rocks beneath the swirling currents create abstract patterns that change from second to second. And then there are the cries and screeches of birds, the movement of wings as they pass by, the tracks and sightings of land animals, the scent of trailside flowers, the outstanding scenery, and always, always the gentle rhythm of your horse.

As you continue, consider a short ride to the long, sandy beach on Benson Lake's north shore—the "Benson Riviera"—for a swim. At the Glen Aulin High Sierra Camp, you reach the Tuolumne River. For an excellent side trek, take the Tuolumne Canyon Trail along the river to California Falls, Le Conte Falls, famous Waterwheel Falls, and eventually to the Grand Canyon of the Tuolumne, one of the deepest canyons on Earth.

Beyond the Tuolumne's Grand Canyon lies Hetch Hetchy Reservoir. Hetch Hetchy, a valley running parallel to Yosemite Valley on its north, was once as beautiful as Yosemite, but the Tuolumne River was dammed to supply water for the city of San Francisco, although less attractive sites could have served the same purpose. John Muir and others fought hard for this remarkable area, but in 1913 the Raker Act was passed, and the valley was lost under the waters of the reservoir. Hetch Hetchy is now nearly filled with sediment and in a few years will no longer be useful.

Back at the Glen Aulin High Sierra Camp, the Pacific Crest Trail is only a few miles from Tuolumne Meadows. You'll ride past White Cascade and Tuolumne Falls, a series of sparkling rapids separated by large pools and wide sheets of water spread out across slightly inclined granite slopes. The trail climbs through several glades brightened by Labrador-tea flowers and corn lilies, then takes you near Little Devils Postpile, a dark basalt plug that was forced up through granite 9 million years ago. Just before Tuolumne Meadows you cross Tioga Road, the highest road across the Sierra Nevada.

Safely on the other side, you join the John Muir Trail coming up from Yosemite Valley and continue on the combined John Muir–Pacific Crest Trail. Look for mountain bluebirds and northern goshawks in the meadows and lodgepole pine forest. You'll cross the Lyell Fork of the Tuolumne River, then ride past Rafferty Creek Trail. Later you enter the Lyell Fork's marvelous canyon. Here your horse takes you along a number of campsites, then climbs steeply to excellent views of Mount Lyell and the large glacier clinging to its north slope. The Pacific Crest Trail swings northeast, then southeast, as it ascends rockily to 11,056-foot Donohue Pass on Yosemite's southern border.

Yosemite Valley's 3,593-foot-high El Capitan is not only stunning but also a great challenge for mountain climbers.

Yosemite National Park

TRAVEL TIPS
Yosemite National Park

Prime Horseback Season: July and August

Horse Outfitters: Frontier Pack Train, Red's Meadow Pack Station, Rock Creek PackStation

Stewardship Agency: Yosemite National Park, P.O. Box 577, Yosemite, CA 95389; general information (209) 372-0200; lodgings (209)-252-4848

General Tourist Information: California Department of Tourism, (800) 862-2543

DESERT STATES

Near Superstition Wilderness. Arizona Department of Tourism

GRAND CANYON NATIONAL PARK

"A gigantic statement for even nature to make, all in one mighty stone word."

John Muir (1838–1914)

The Greatest Visual Shock on Earth

Nothing compares to the Grand Canyon. It is the most magnificent example of erosion anywhere—a chasm 277 miles long, 18 miles wide, and 6,000 feet deep. Peaks, cliffs, buttes, and spires rise from its bottom, where the Colorado River bores ever deeper into the Earth's skin. The colors of the rock change from the morning's gold and yellow and blue to brilliant orange and red at high noon. Evening darkens the mood to magical hues of rose, purple, and gray. No other place shows you as impressive a record of Earth's history. At the river level you walk on rocks more than 2 billion years older than those at the rim. As you travel down you'll have a firsthand view of everything that's happened to our planet. Plant and animal fossils are abundant, from primitive algae in the lower strata to increasingly complex life forms closer to the top, retracing evolution. Ancient seashells lead to fish, ferns, insects, amphibians, reptiles, dinosaurs, and finally to mammals such as prehistoric camels, elephants, and horses.

The North Rim looks down on the 1,200-foot-lower South Rim, 220 miles away by car. With different climate, plants, and animals, the North Rim is another world. Here, about 8,200 feet above sea level, the stately ponderosa pines are at their best, and magnificent spruces and firs tower high above you.

"Do nothing to mar its grandeur," President Theodore Roosevelt said of the canyon. In 1908 he set it aside as a national monument. In 1919, three years after the creation of the National Park Service, about 700,000 acres were upgraded to national park, and further acres were added in 1932 and 1969 as national monuments. In 1975 the monuments were integrated into the park, and today Grand Canyon National Park protects 1,219,000 acres (493,100 ha) of the world's most intricate and complex system of canyons, gorges, and ravines, from Glen Canyon to Lake Mead National Recreation Areas.

Horseback riding is not foremost on the minds of most visitors, yet fine riding not only exists but offers you the world's most spectacular scenery. In addition to hourly rides along both rims, you can choose among four outfitted overnight rides inside the park—two along the North Rim, and two inside the canyon from the South Rim.

WAITING FOR ANOTHER CANYON

The Grand Canyon is the result of a combination of conditions and events so unusual that the probability of their happening again is remote. First, the Colorado Plateau, a vast tableland covering about 831 million acres (336 million ha) in the Four Corners area provides easily erodible rock, miles thick. Second, these deep layers had to be uplifted and exposed by shifts in the Earth's crust. Third, a powerful, swift river had to flow across the land carrying great amounts of sediment to act as abrasives and cut into the bedrock. The Colorado River, the second-longest in the U.S., flows as fast as 20 miles per hour, and on average carries half a million tons of abrasive sand and silt through the canyon every day. Finally, although the land had to rise to make the canyon, its uplift could not be faster than the cutting action of the river, or it would have spilled the Colorado from its path. As the Colorado Plateau began to rise about 5 or 6 million years ago, the river eroded its bed at approximately the same speed as the uplift occurred. Wind, rain, snowmelt, and tributary systems have done the rest, shaping the rock formations that rise between the river-cut layers. Moisture seeps easily into the pores and cracks of desert rock. Working mechanically, the water breaks down the rock structure as it freezes and thaws. Working chemically, the water dissolves soluble rock and weakens harder rock by leaching out soluble materials within it. Yet if it were not for the aridity of the American Southwest, the Grand Canyon would not have been preserved. Slope wash would long ago have eroded and smoothed the canyon walls and removed the stair-step topography and the distinctive sculpturing of the rock.

At times the Colorado Plateau's uplifts caused its rivers and streams to change direction. Shifting back and forth, the waters undercut the canyon walls and, aided by rain, snow, ice, and wind, brought down masses of rock, eventually exposing the original plateau surface in a series of majestic mesas. Over time, further erosion changed some mesas to tall, lonesome buttes, and buttes to elegant rock towers. In Monument Valley, your horse takes you across wide-open landscapes punctuated by mesas, buttes, and towers: the magnificent ghosts of long-ago canyons.

Horse Trekking the North Rim

On the seven-day Red Rock Ride, part of the fun is getting to the Grand Canyon. Day One finds you in Las Vegas, Nevada, packed and ready to go at 5:00 a.m. You'll have time to catch up on sleep while you and fellow riders are whisked by charter bus to Zion National Park. There you'll have your first ride, exploring the great park by horse. Then the bus brings you to Bryce Canyon National Park to camp two nights and ride. On Day Three you'll ride the Box of the Paria, where outlaws, rustlers, and polygamists evaded the law. On the fourth day the bus speeds you across the top of the Arizona Strip—a vast stretch of remote public land overseen by the Bureau of Land Management. You'll end the day with a sunset ride at the North Rim, and will spend three nights here. You board a scenic flight back to Las Vegas on Day Seven, admiring from above the world-famous landscapes you enjoyed.

The Bar Ten Ranch, a cattle ranch 8 miles off the North Rim, arranges four-day pack trips near the rim and on the Arizona Strip. You'll arrive either by scenic flight from Las Vegas or by four-wheel-drive rental car over rough dirt roads. You ride for three unforgettable days, camp two nights, and spend the last night at the ranch. You can extend your stay to day ride from the ranch, work with the cowboys, or descend by helicopter to the river and join an overnight raft trip back to Las Vegas.

Mather Point on the Grand Canyon's South Rim.

Rainer Hackenberg/Arizona Department of Tourism

EUROPEANS ARRIVE

Riding in the Southwest, you may well be following trails used by Spaniards in search of the fabled Seven Cities of Cíbola, reputedly rich in gold and other treasure. In 1540 General Francisco Vásquez de Coronado led a full-scale expedition to locate the cities and plunder them. Two hundred and thirty mounted soldiers, 62 foot soldiers, a number of friars to convert heathens, close to 1,000 Native American servants, and 1,500 horses, mules, and meat animals made their way slowly through what are now Arizona, New Mexico, Texas, Oklahoma, and Kansas. Near today's Gallup, New Mexico, they found six Zuñi Indian pueblos, the villages of ancient Native Americans who had developed irrigation, architecture, and crafts to a high degree. But Coronado found no gold, and he was not interested in ancient civilizations.

In an empty gesture Coronado declared these pueblos six of the golden cities of Cíbola and took possession of them for Spain. He never found the seventh. Some of his men and animals had already perished, and the rest were gaunt, thirsty, and hungry. Disheartened, he sent scouting parties to learn if riches lay farther afield. One of his groups discovered a cluster of Hopi villages atop three mesas in Arizona, the same villages you may visit today. Another group marched east and reached the numerous pueblos of the upper Rio Grande in the vicinity of what is now Santa Fé, New Mexico, but all lacked silver and gold.

A third party, under Don García López de Cárdenas, came upon the Grand Canyon. Cárdenas was not enraptured. His men and horses were parched from their journey across the desert. To them the great abyss merely meant an obstacle to overcome. Try as they might they found no way to reach the Colorado River a mile below. For three days they attempted to descend. Some managed to get about a third of the distance down but no farther. Unbeknownst to them there was human life on the canyon floor. As they still do today, the Havasupai Indians, one of the most isolated people on Earth, were cultivating about 400 acres of flat land. Cárdenas and his men turned back, leaving the Grand Canyon to be unseen by Europeans for another two centuries.

Inside the Canyon: Horsetrail to the Havasupai

Native Americans have lived in the Grand Canyon region for at least 4,000 years. Animal figures made of twigs of willow and cottonwood, the earliest evidence of their presence, were found in caves below the rim. Since the twelfth century the Havasupai, the "People of the Blue-Green Water," have lived in one of the most remote corners of the Grand Canyon. After flowing through the Supai village and watering the tribe's lush farms and orchards through diversion ditches, Havasu Creek makes several spectacular drops over travertine terraces before draining into the canyon. The loveliest of these is Havasu Falls, two separate falls plunging into a blue-green pool. Although the Havasupai Reservation lies within the boundaries of Grand Canyon National Park, it does not fall under park jurisdiction. Helicopter tours sanctioned by the Havasupai tribe, as well as whitewater rafts, take visitors into the valley.

You can also visit the tribe via a horse and foot trail, the Havasupai's link to the outside world. By advance reservation with the Havasupai Tourist Enterprise, tribal horses carry you from Hualapai Hilltop, 55 miles northwest of the South Rim's Grand Canyon Village, to the Havasupai Indian Reservation inside the canyon. To get to the trailhead, turn north about 7 miles east of Peach Springs, Arizona, and continue for 62 miles on a partially paved, all-weather road. The road ends abruptly. From here the horses take you 8 miles down to Supai Village. The tribe maintains two lodges and three campgrounds for overnight guests. Read Stephen Hirst's *Life in a Narrow Place* for an intimate look at the tribe's past and present.

Inside the Canyon: The Classic Mule Ride

For many years Grand Canyon visitors have been intrigued by the overnight mule ride making the seemingly perilous trek from the South Rim to the bottom of the canyon and back again. This is the Grand Canyon's most famous ride, and it is truly one of the world's great adventures. The trail is narrow and serpentine, and many times the mules hang over the edge. But the mules know their business—riders from all over the world have taken this trip and lived to brag about it. One American rider, Ferdinand Rudolph von Grofé (1892–1972), afterwards enthusiastically wrote the *Grand Canyon Suite*, conveying in lovely musical tones the clip-clop of the mules' feet and the swaying of their bodies.

With a coveted advance reservation from Grand Canyon National Park Lodges, you, too, can make the journey. During summer you'll spend one night at Phantom Ranch; from mid-November through March, two nights are possible. Downhill the ride is about 10½ miles (5½ hours), back up 8 miles (4½ hours). You'll meet your mule at the Stone Corral near the head of Bright Angel Trail, just west of Bright Angel Lodge in Grand Canyon Village. Bright Angel Trail is the park's most well-known and popular trail.

Your hair will stand on end as you start switchbacking. "If you fall off," the wranglers tease you, "the scenery's awful purty on the way down." The South Rim's forest gradually changes to stunted piñon and juniper bushes below. Cacti abound. Porcupines are sometimes seen, and gray foxes hunt rock squirrels. The cacomistle, a catlike raccoon that has changed little over the last 10 million years, lives in rock crevices and hunts rodents and lizards by night. You'll pass grayish limestone walls, the floor of an ancient sea. Then the trail enters yellowish sandstone, an earlier age's sand dunes. The layers continue to change color and texture as you descend from stratum to stratum, always moving backward in time.

The enormous distance from top to bottom creates a range of climates, from Arctic-alpine at the top to dry subtropical at the bottom. In this one place you can see animal and plant life indigenous to areas from southern Canada to northern Mexico. Seventy-five species of mammals, 50 species of reptiles and amphibians, 25 species of fish, and more than 300 species of birds live at the Grand Canyon.

You will ride past what geologists call the Great Unconformity. Here, rock layers of vastly different ages are separated only by a thin, distinct surface, signaling a gap of several million years of missing Earth history. Either vast quantities of Earth materials were removed by erosion or there was little or no deposition during those eons. The location of the Great

Bright Angel Trail: The classic mule ride

Rainer Hackenberg/Arizona Department of Tourism

Unconformity may vary and is a good example of the uplifting, sinking, and displacement the Earth's rock layers have experienced. In the greenish Bright Angel Shale you may see fossils of primitive crablike animals.

The great width of the Grand Canyon is a barrier to animals, affecting their evolution. A few million years ago, the Abert squirrel and Kaibab squirrel were one species, but today can no longer interbreed. Both feed on ponderosa pine. When the Colorado cut the canyon deeper than the ponderosa's lifezone, the ponderosa disappeared from the canyon floor and the squirrels no longer had food for a journey across. Thus separated, they evolved differently. Today the South Rim's Abert squirrel has a white belly and a gray tail, while the North Rim's Kaibab squirrel sports a black belly and white tail. Eagles can fly nonstop from rim to rim, but small birds apparently develop acrophobia looking down through a mile of air. They fly down, then over the river, then up again, or elect to stay home.

Once you reach the Inner Gorge—about 1,000 to 1,500 feet above the river—you'll find the walls getting darker as you move down. This is the Precambrian layer, some of the oldest rocks on Earth. You are seeing our planet in its youth, when early sands and mud were squeezed by tremendous pressures into solid schist and intermingled with molten rock that slowly cooled into pink granite. Millions of years later, when the Colorado had almost cut the canyon to its present depth, volcanoes began erupting from vents high on the north flank. One volcano, Vulcans Throne, spewed lava into the canyon, forming a dam about 550 feet high that blocked the river from cutting this canyon section deeper. Eventually the river cut through the barrier and has since lowered the canyon another 50 feet.

You continue to the Colorado, then follow the River Trail. You'll welcome the shade of the canyon's floor, for summer temperatures can reach up to 120 degrees and heat radiated from the rocks keeps the summer's night air a warm 86. Maidenhair ferns, feathery tamarisks, and crimson monkey flowers grow along the river and creeks. Waterfalls spilling over canyon walls nourish gardens of green ferns and mosses that feed the chuckwalla, a 2-foot-long lizard. When frightened, the chuckwalla hides in a rock crevice and gulps air to swell up and wedge itself in so that predators can't pull it out. Flocks of birds feed near the water. A pink subspecies of the Western rattlesnake lives only in the canyon, where its coloring conceals it against the red rocks. It feeds on small mammals and reptiles. Kangaroo rats, pocket mice, and spotted skunks emerge in the cooler temperatures of the night. Scorpions also hunt at night. The mountain lion, lynx, and coyote range throughout the canyon, and mule deer and bighorn sheep eat the sparse vegetation.

A narrow suspension bridge crosses the Colorado River. From the rim you saw the river as a tiny band far below you. Here the bridge under your feet vibrates and you feel the roar of the water and the rumble of boulders grinding and pounding against each other. Yet the river is not what it was. Nowadays two dams have a profound effect on the Colorado. At the upper end of the canyon Glen Canyon Dam, completed in 1963, releases only controlled amounts of river water that are stored in Lake Powell. Below the canyon Hoover Dam, completed in 1936, holds the river in Lake Mead and floods the lower 40 miles of the Grand Canyon when the lake is full. As you look toward Glen Canyon Dam, imagine the river running here all the way from its origin in Rocky Mountain National Park in Colorado. Looking toward Hoover Dam, imagine it plunging to its destination in Mexico's Gulf of California. Altogether the Colorado River is 1,450 miles long, and though the most spectacular, the Grand Canyon is only one of many beautiful canyons the river has carved.

After crossing the suspension bridge, the ride proceeds on the river's north side along Bright Angel Canyon to Phantom Ranch. After a night or two here your mule takes you up the South Kaibab Trail. You'll be back in time for lunch.

TRAVEL TIPS
Grand Canyon National Park

Prime Horseback Season: Along rim: May–September. To bottom of canyon: March–April and October–November.

Horse Outfitters: Along North Rim: Bar Ten Ranch, Red Rock Ride. Inside the Canyon: Grand Canyon National Park Lodges, Havasupai Tourist Enterprise.

Stewardship Agency: Grand Canyon National Park, P.O. Box 129, Grand Canyon, AZ 86023; recorded park information (520) 638-7888. North Rim lodgings (801) 586-7686; South Rim lodgings (520) 638-2401.

General Tourist Information: Arizona Department of Tourism, (800) 842-8257

MONUMENT VALLEY NAVAJO TRIBAL PARK

"In beauty I walk
With beauty before me I walk
With beauty behind me I walk
With beauty above me I walk
With beauty all around me I walk
In beauty it is finished."

Navajo chant

Land of the Sleeping Rainbow

Arizona, Colorado, New Mexico, and Utah meet at Four Corners, the only place in the U.S. where more than three states touch each other. The plaque that marks this spot can be considered the center of the vast Colorado Plateau, one of the most famous landscapes in the world and nearly the size of California. Under a powerful sun and an enormous sky, desert mesas and a myriad of giant canyons stretch to infinity. This is the Navajos' Land of the Sleeping Rainbow. Rocks of all shades—reds, pinks, yellows, browns, grays, whites—are exposed in high cliffs and eroded columns, spires, and natural bridges. Surprisingly, these arid landscapes are rich in wildlife: wild buffalo (bison), mustangs, desert bighorn sheep, and elk. From Four Corners, nine spectacular Colorado Plateau national parks are yours to explore: the Grand Canyon and the Petrified Forest to the southwest; Zion, Bryce Canyon, Capitol Reef, Canyonlands, and Arches to the northwest; and, to the northeast, Mesa Verde's ancient cliff dwellings are tucked in hidden canyons. To the southwest is Chaco Culture National Historical Park, the largest example of ancient Pueblo life. Countless beautiful national monuments and recreation sites lie between the national parks, and Native American reservations and tribal parks accept visitors as well.

In Monument Valley you'll visit world-famous sandstone masterpieces and meet the people who live amid this splendor. Monument Valley belongs to the Navajos and they allow three ways to visit their land: driving your own car along Valley Drive, a 17-mile unpaved loop road that takes in some of the valley's major highlights; joining a guided Valley Drive tour that shows you the valley from the Navajo perspective and includes a stop at a hogan—a traditional Navajo home—for a brief visit with a Navajo family; and horseback riding with

EQUUS•USA

Monument Valley: Riding the freedom of the open spaces

sanctioned outfitters. The horseback rides last from a few hours to several days. Plan at least a week to absorb and experience this beautiful place.

Riding like John Wayne

In 1938 Hollywood was surprised to find there was a real West. Film director John Ford and a young, untried actor named John Wayne drove to Monument Valley to make *Stagecoach* and movie history. Countless movies and commercials followed and you're bound to recognize world-famous settings. But there is much more to see, and the original adventure remains. In the heart of the valley you'll ride along established trails; the rest of the time you ride cross-country, guided only by Navajo instructions and what your group would like to see.

Each day you start from a base camp and fan out from there. The red-orange sandstone cliffs you'll pass are part of the 160-million-year-old Cutler Formation. The monuments are made of 200-million-year-old DeChelly (pronounced deh-SHAY) Sandstone, with the harder and younger Shinarump Formation sitting on top and protecting the lower layers. At the base the softer Organ Rock Shale erodes in stairlike horizontal terraces and forms the sloping foundations. Each monument engages your imagination in a different way. Here the thumblike towers of the East and West Mittens loom above you, there the Three Sisters, Elephant Butte, and Camel Butte. A lonely outpost near the Yei Bi Chei Rocks is called the Totem Pole.

The DeChelly Sandstone is named for the prominent sandstone layer in nearby Canyon de Chelly National Monument, also on the Navajo reservation. If you're curious about what Monument Valley looked like long ago, you'll especially enjoy visiting this younger, beautiful canyon system not as far along in its journey of erosion.

The reddish hues in Monument Valley and on the Colorado Plateau result from iron. Iron oxides produce not only the brick-red hues but also salmon, pink, buff, yellow, brown, and even green or bluish-green. This does not mean, however, that these rocks and sandstones are sources of iron ore. The smallest traces of iron, generally only 1 to 3 percent, are enough to create even the darkest shades of red.

In Mystery Valley, adjacent to Monument Valley and close to the Kayenta highway, the prominent volcanic neck called Agathla Peak (El Capitan) rises 1,225 feet above you. In Navajo, *agathla* means "the place of the scraping of hides." When Agathla's volcano became inactive, its liquid lava interior cooled and solidified. In time the volcano's outer structure eroded until nothing was left but the core. (The absence of surrounding ash or lava suggests it eroded a long time ago.) Four miles beyond, Chaistla Butte stands 400 feet above the desert floor.

Feel the magic of magnificent Monument Valley and take it all in: the generosity of the open land; the dramatic shapes of the monuments; the deep red stone and sand; the cobalt blue sky; and the green shades of sparse desert shrubs. Smell the aroma of the sun-baked Earth, listen to the wind as it comes around a mesa. Imagine the valley in winter and spring, when ice expands the rock fractures, eventually breaking the rocks apart. Watch the summer rains wash the fallen rock debris into streambeds and carry the material north to the San Juan River.

Riding to Meet the Navajos

On today's ride you may come upon a small Navajo girl herding a flock of sheep, her velvet dress shining against the red rock country like a bright purple flower in spring. You wave to her and call a friendly "*Ya-a-tay*," the Navajo greeting, and she smiles shyly. Later you ride past a hogan, perhaps the small shepherd's home. To the side is a brush corral; beyond, a small garden brims with tall yellow and blue corn and ripe melons.

Next to the hogan a proud elderly Navajo woman—the girl's grandmother?—kneels beneath a sun shelter of cottonwood boughs and weaves a Navajo rug of bold geometric design. Her handsome face is turned to her work. As she weaves, she sings a strange, high-pitched chant that climbs up and down, wild and mysterious as the land itself.

NAVAJO TERRITORY

Ironically the Spanish, who in their conquests destroyed many Native American cultures, provided the Navajos with key elements of their identity—horses, sheep, cattle, and the craft of silversmithing. The Navajos and Apaches apparently had tried to befriend the Spanish and later the Mexicans and Americans. But as early as the 1600s both tribes were raiding Spanish missions, and the Apaches may have been partial instigators of the Pueblo Revolt of 1680. The Apaches' and Navajos' warlike reputations succeeded in discouraging the Spanish from seriously penetrating the Southwest. After Mexico achieved independence from Spain in 1821, much of the Southwest was essentially abandoned for more than two decades. In 1848, at the end of the Mexican War, the region became a U.S. territory. Gold-hunters brave enough for the overland journey to California began passing through, and some stayed.

In the 1850s several U.S. forts were built to safeguard settlers. Sporadic fighting between the army and the Apaches and Navajos erupted. In 1863 and 1864 a federal campaign under frontiersman Colonel Christopher ("Kit") Carson killed more than 650 Native Americans, captured almost 9,000, spoiled wells, burned cornfields and peach orchards, and killed horses, cattle, and sheep. In 1865 the Navajos surrendered. They were forced to make what Navajos call "the Long Walk," marching 250 miles from Fort Defiance, southwest of Canyon de Chelly, to Bosque Redondo, 180 miles southeast of Santa Fe, near Fort Sumner. Navajos who resisted were physically abused or shot. Women who gave birth along the way were not allowed to rest. Elderly people and children had a hard time keeping up the pace.

The government had negotiated contracts with non-Indians to provide food to the prisoners. Most suppliers were corrupt and made huge profits, giving the inmates meager portions of spoiled rations. People sickened with digestive problems, and the region's salty water gave them dysentery. In 1868 the Navajos signed a treaty that returned to them one-fourth of their land. In 1958 the Navajo Tribal Council set aside Monument Valley as a 29,817-acre (12,067-ha) tribal park.

The Navajos and Apaches speak Athabaskan languages and probably once were a single group that lived in the Lake Athabasca region in northwestern Canada. Other Native American groups may have reached North America from Asia as long as 30,000 years ago, but theories exist that the Athabaskans may have arrived as recently as A.D. 1233, when fleeing from Genghis Khan.

In the 1400s the Navajos reached what now is the U.S. Southwest, entering the Colorado Plateau from the northeast in present-day northern New Mexico. The Navajos call themselves the Diné, which means "The People," and they probably first established bases in northwestern New Mexico, a region they still call Dinétah, "The Land of the People."

The Navajos' own story of their origins begins with the emergence of all living things through a series of worlds. Some storytellers report the first world to have been black, the second blue, the third yellow. They call the fourth world—the present world—glittering and bright. In most versions, the main reason humans and other creatures move from one world to the next is their inability to get along with one another. When everyone finally arrives in the present world, they find it covered with water. They come to terms with the monster who controls the waters, and the waters withdraw and today's world begins. The sun, moon, and stars appear in the sky, day and night start their daily dance, and the year separates into seasons. Many obstacles and adventures follow in stories of First Man and First Woman, Changing Woman, and Spider Woman. In the end the world becomes safe for the Navajos because they receive help, even from such unlikely creatures as the water bug and worm.

TRAVEL TIPS
Monument Valley Navajo Tribal Park

Prime Horseback Season: Mid-April–mid-June, September–mid-October

Horse Outfitters: Don Donnelly Stables, Ed Black Horseback Tours, Eknel Tours

Stewardship Agency: Monument Valley Navajo Tribal Park, P.O. Box 360289, Monument Valley, UT 84536; (801) 727-3287 or (801) 727-3353

General Tourist Information: Arizona Departmentof Tourism, (800) 842-8257. Utah Department of Tourism, (800) 200-1160

Arizona

SUPERSTITION WILDERNESS

*"The palpable sense of mystery in the desert air breeds fables,
chiefly of lost treasure. Somewhere within its stark borders,
if one believes report, is a hill strewn with nuggets."*

Mary Austin (1868–1934)

Feast or Famine

Arizona's 160,200-acre (64,800-ha) Superstition Wilderness, 40 miles east
of Phoenix, is an ideal spring and fall destination when other parts of the
country lie under snow. You'll discover the rugged desert mountains and
canyons the way the old cowboys and pioneers did: by horse. It is a wonderfully quiet way to see the desert wildlife, Native American ruins, and
abandoned mines and ranches. Few arid lands match the Superstition's
beauty. Sandy or rocky plains are punctuated by dramatic mountains, and
by a rich array of cacti, desert shrubs, and trees adapted to survive in
extreme conditions. After it rains, the dry landscape is miraculously trans-
formed into fields of blooming desert flowers. Mound Mountain is the
Superstition's highest point at 6,265 feet, and Weaver's Needle, a 4,553-
foot weathered volcanic plug, is a well-known landmark.

Dutchman's Trail

Some 180 miles of beautiful trails take you through the Superstition. Let's
ride one of the great loop routes, starting and ending at the Peralta
Trailhead. The loop takes you from desert to ponderosa pine high country,
to Rogers Canyon Cliff Dwellings and the site of the former Reavis Ranch.
Allow six days for this adventure, including one layover day at Reavis Ranch.
The trail is steep, rough, and narrow in places. If you suffer from a fear of
heights, this may not be for you.

On your way to the Peralta Trailhead, if you have time, don't miss walking
the marked native plant trail at Lost Dutchman State Park. It's an excellent
introduction to the desert plants you'll meet on your ride. At the trailhead,
unload your horse and head east on the Dutchman's Trail (U.S. Forest Service
Trail 104), crossing the Peralta Canyon creekbed, winding around small desert
hills, and dropping into Barkley Basin. Settle into your saddle and take stock of
this wide-open land—its moods, colors, and grandeur. A few short weeks from
now it will be too hot to spend much time here.

The desert may seem empty around you, except for the plants and rocks, but don't be fooled—it's a busy place. Early in the morning you may see javelina looking for prickly-pear cacti, their favorite food. An owl may be asleep inside one of the large saguaros, in an old nest-hole pecked by a Gila woodpecker. Watch for roadrunners sprinting across your trail. Mule deer, elk, coyotes, turkey, quail, and a wealth of birds are found throughout the Superstition. Squirrels and rabbits dart around, and the streams are home to bass and trout. With luck you'll see a Mexican raccoon or a kangaroo rat. Kangaroo rats can spend many days underground when it's too hot outside, eating stored seeds and taking in moisture with their breathing. Mountain lions prefer the eastern sections of the wilderness, but occasionally are spotted elsewhere, and the bobcat's range is wide. Bears used to live here but were hunted to extinction.

Sharp ridges rise in the western Superstition, bisected by twisting, turning canyons that challenge your sense of direction. The central and eastern terrains are less radical. "The land of the wood that sinks and rock that floats," the

DESERT PLANTS

All desert plants are either drought evaders or drought resisters. The evaders spend their days as seeds, ready to spring up when it rains. When their big moment arrives they flower quickly, produce another seed crop, and die. The resisters practice various methods of water gathering, moisture storage, or need reduction. Succulents are one of the most prominent resisters, and cacti are the best-known succulents on the American desert. Cacti come in a wide range of sizes, from tiny round ones the size of a thumbnail to the world's largest cacti, the saguaros—many 50 feet tall and 200 years old. The world's tallest saguaro was an armless individual in Cave Creek, Arizona, near Phoenix, which in 1978 measured 78 feet.

Of the world's 1,600 cactus species, only five grow outside the Americas, in Ceylon and South Africa. The Superstition Wilderness is in the Sonoran Desert, which covers portions of the American Southwest and northern Mexico and has the world's greatest abundance of cacti.

A 57-armed Saguaro off the Dutchman's Trail, about an hour from La Barge Canyon

George E. Johnston

Superstition has been called. And it truly is a place of paradoxes and extremes. The wilderness has stands of ironwood, a wood so dense that it sinks, and the mountains are old volcanoes that long ago spat volcanic froth, pumice, a rock that does indeed float. Spanish explorers called the Superstitions *Sierra de Espuma*, "Mountains of Foam." Where the volcanic material is eroded, or was never deposited, your horse's hooves clip-clop on granite at least 570 million years old.

Your horse on your Superstition journey may well be an American Quarter Horse, the most popular horse in North America. The Quarter Horse was first bred in Virginia during the late 1700s by crossing Chickasaw horses descended from wild mustangs with stock imported from Europe. The resulting cross-breed possessed a quick, early burst of speed and was bred especially for the popular "quarter races"—straight sprints over a quarter-mile. Trained Quarter Horses are the fastest horses in the world, covering the quarter-mile in little over 20 seconds from a standing start, and accelerating so quickly that in races jockeys must grip the mane to stay aboard. The breed's speed and hardiness proved useful to American cattle ranchers. The horse is sturdy enough to carry cowhands all day over rough terrain and, because it still has the mustangs' strong herding instinct, it possesses a special "cow sense." It can fix a particular steer with a hypnotic stare and keep it away from the herd by blocking every move. For the pleasure rider, its gentle nature and willingness to learn make the Quarter Horse a treasured companion.

When Dutchman's Trail turns left into Miners Canyon, point your horse onto Coffee Flat Trail (#108) and continue east. The junction of Fraser and Randolph Canyons is a special place of smooth, reddish bedrock and shallow pools of seasonal water. You might like to get off your horse and stretch your legs before continuing up Fraser Canyon to the JF Ranch, a working cattle ranch just outside the wilderness boundary, started by pioneer cattleman Jack Fraser in the 1890s.

At the JF, you need to connect with Woodbury Trail (#114) at the ranch corral. Ride east on the Woodbury and turn north on JF Trail (#106). You'll cross the Randolph Canyon wash twice, then follow the west bank of Randolph Canyon and ride along a hillside dotted with mountain mahogany, sugar sumac, redberry buckthorn, and honey mesquite. After crossing the bed of Randolph Canyon, the trail heads uphill across the ridge through saguaro, ocotillo, prickly pear, and mesquite. At Tortilla Pass continue north on Rogers Canyon Trail (#110).

Rogers Canyon Cliff Dwellings

Plan to spend the night at Angel Basin and walk to the Rogers Canyon Cliff Dwellings, built around A.D. 1300 in a cave about 100 feet above the canyon floor. Around A.D. 700, hunting-gathering groups came from nearby river

THE DUTCHMAN'S GOLD

Much talk in the Superstition Mountains revolves around gold, though no new mining claims can be filed within wilderness boundaries. Rumor says the world's most famous lost mine, the Lost Dutchman, is located inside the Superstition Wilderness, maybe close to where you'll be riding. An estimated 100,000 serious seekers have come to the Superstitions, and the lure of the mountains' riches continues to stir the imagination of gold-hunters from around the world. Some have died while search-ing—meeting foul play, falling into canyons, dying of thirst under a hot summer sun. Others gave up in old age, or because of ill-ness or financial problems, just when they felt near the elusive find. Some claimed to have discovered the mine; many say it never existed.

The story begins with a Jesuit priest, Padre Eusebio Kino, who late in the 1600s founded Arizona's first missions. Legend says the Pima Indians led him to the Superstitions and showed him Coronado's Seven Cities of Gold. After many twists and turns the story arrives at the "Dutchman" for whom the mine and the Dutchman's Trail are named. Jacob Waltz, born in Germany (Deutschland) in 1810, is said to have trained as a mining engineer at Heidelberg University. By 1848 he lived in Mississippi, but hurried west with California's Gold Rush. Living in Arizona by 1864, one story is that he fell in love with a young Apache girl named Ken-tee, who led him to the mine and was killed by her tribe for betraying the secret.

After Waltz started working the mine, he supposedly shot eight men, including one-time partner Jacob Weiser, a fellow German. Others say Waltz allowed the gossip to spread to dis-courage people from following him. In 1875 tax records valued his property at $275, which did not make him a wealthy man. He moved to Phoenix and lived a frugal, quiet life. He befriended a neighbor, Julia (Helena) Thomas, who ran an ice-cream parlor. In 1891—he was now 81—a flash flood swept through Phoenix. The waters washed through Waltz's house, and a night of exposure gave him pneumonia. On his deathbed, legend says, he dictated the mine's map to Julia Thomas and her foster son. In 1893 Julia married and began to sell duplicates of the "deathbed map." And so the story continues.

valleys to the Superstition's high country. Later the Hohokam people established agricultural villages. The Salados occupied several areas within today's wilderness from A.D. 1200 to 1400, but the rugged terrain and lack of water kept their villages and cliff dwellings small. It is unclear whether the Salado migrated from the north and mingled with the Hohokam, or whether they evolved within the Hohokam. The Salado built thick-walled, multistoried houses. Hohokam buildings, before the Salado influence, were thin-walled and single-storied.

After raids in the desert, the Apaches retreated into the Superstition's mountain fortresses. The high bluffs were easily defended; the rugged canyons were excellent hiding places. But in the 1850s U.S. Army cavalry units began threatening the mountain stronghold. Fort McDowell, on the Verde River north of present-day Phoenix, was established to protect settlers from Apache attacks, and Phoenix was settled in 1870 to provide hay for Fort McDowell. Those who lived near the Apaches said that one could not find more reliable and generous friends, or less-forgiving enemies. Today the Western Apaches live on the Fort Apache and San Carlos Reservations in the White Mountains just east of the Superstition Wilderness.

From Angel Basin take Frog Tanks Trail (#112) north along Rogers Canyon, pleasantly shaded by a canopy of sycamores and oaks. The trail is hard to find in places, so be on the lookout and consult your forest service instructions and topographic maps. When pretty Fish Creek enters from the east, follow it until the trail leaves it. Past an abandoned corral you'll head uphill. At the saddle, watch for the outline of an old Indian ruin a few yards off the trail. Point your horse east on Reavis Ranch Trail (#109), and follow it to Reavis Ranch.

Reavis Ranch

Several ranches were established in and around the Superstition Mountains to supply beef to the military and to the mining towns of Pinal and Silver King. Inside today's wilderness two parcels of land were homesteaded—Miles Ranch in the Superstition's southeast corner, patented in 1921, and Reavis Ranch, patented in 1917. Reavis Ranch is named for Elisha M. Reavis, known locally as the "Hermit of the Superstitions," who arrived around 1874. He established a farm and once or twice a month packed his vegetables on burros into Phoenix, Tempe, Mesa, and Florence. Reavis died in 1896; his grave is along the Reavis Trail, not far from Rogers Canyon. Jack Fraser of the JF Ranch acquired the property and used it as a pack and hunting trip destination named Bloomerville. In 1910 the land became a summer resort called Mountain Air, later Pineair.

In 1908 the Superstition Mountains were set aside as part of a forest

HOMESTEADING

The Supersition's Reavis Ranch is a good place to consider the U.S. homestead movement, which developed gradually after 1785. Initially it combined two goals: to generate revenue for the federal government through public land sales, and to enable each American family to own a home or farm. The fulfillment of the first goal resulted in the sale of large blocks of public land and benefited speculators. By 1835 the sales had covered the federal debt.

The second goal's legislative wording caused conflict for many years. While Eastern business interests were eager to preserve high rents and inexpensive labor, Western farmers wanted easy land expansion. The Homestead Act was passed by Congress in 1862. Any person willing to occupy and cultivate land for five years received 160 acres free of charge, but the most fertile land was already in private hands and no longer in the public domain. By 1890 only one in three homesteaders had the five-year residency to gain full title. By the 1950s the U.S. government had approved patents for about 50 million acres of public domain. But much of the land had made its way to large landholders.

reserve. They became the Superstition Primitive Area in 1939, and were upgraded to wilderness status in 1940, one of the 54 original wilderness areas officially recognized by Congress' Wilderness Act of 1964. The federal government purchased Reavis Ranch in 1966 and incorporated it into the wilderness the following year.

Reavis' wooden cabin is long gone, and so is the resort. The skeleton of a later sandstone-and-adobe structure is all that remains. You'll find pleasant, shady campsites among pines and cottonwoods; it's a good place to spend two nights. If you're here in the fall, you'll enjoy fruit from the resort's 600 apple trees. You can day ride to 196-foot Reavis Falls, a few miles north on Reavis Creek, and to Mound Mountain and its Circlestone ruin, a 3-foot-wide sandstone wall built around A.D. 1250–1300 and believed to be celestially oriented.

When it's time to leave Reavis Ranch, retrace your route to the Peralta Trailhead, or ride south on Reavis Ranch Trail (#109) to the Rogers Trough Trailhead. From the trailhead follow Forest Service Road 172A west until it connects with Woodbury Trail (#114). You're now on familiar ground. At the JF Ranch corral, cross over onto Coffee Flat Trail (#108) and point your horse west until Dutchman's Trail (#104) reaches the Peralta Trailhead.

TRAVEL TIPS
Superstition Wilderness

Prime Horseback Season: March and April, October and November

Horse Outfitters: Don Donnelly Stables, Weminuche & Superstition Adventures

Stewardship Agency: Tonto National Forest, Supervisor's Office, P.O. Box 5348, Phoenix, AZ 85010; (602) 225-5200

General Tourist Information: Arizona Department of Tourism, (800) 842-8257

CAPITOL REEF NATIONAL PARK

"All the scenic features of this canyon land are on a giant scale, strange and weird. Every river entering the Colorado has cut a canyon; every lateral creek has cut a canyon; every rill, born of a shower and living only during these showers, has cut a canyon."

John Wesley Powell (1834–1902)

Just One Dip

Capitol Reef National Park offers some of the most exquisite high-desert country on the Colorado Plateau and protects 75 miles of the Waterpocket Fold monocline—a fold in the Earth's surface that bends in one direction only. The Waterpocket was formed during a Colorado Plateau uplift when horizontal layers of sandstone sank along a fault line and left a solitary, gigantic bump. No other monocline in North America is as visible or rises as dramatically.

Out of the original fold millions of years of erosion have carved a stunningly beautiful labyrinth of colorful canyons, ridges, cliffs, buttes, dunes, and monoliths that are home to many desert plants and animals. Massive arches and natural bridges frame exciting landscapes. Geologist Clarence E. Dutton recorded his impressions in 1880. "The colors are such that no pigment can portray," he wrote. "They are deep, rich and variegated; and so luminous are they, that light seems to flow or shine out of the rock rather than to be reflected from it."

Near the Fremont River an especially rugged and spectacular segment of the Waterpocket Fold reminded early travelers of the domes of capitol buildings. The name Capitol Reef was adopted in 1937 for the Capitol Reef National Monument, and the name was adopted for the 241,904-acre (97,896-ha) Capitol Reef National Park in 1971. Capitol Reef currently has the highest concentration of threatened or endangered plants within Utah's national parks. Altogether 896 plant species live within the park's boundaries. You can see many of these species, especially wildflowers, as they blossom in spring. Capitol Reef National Park is adjacent to the Glen Canyon National Recreation Area on its south. From here you have access to Lake Powell and to the Colorado River just before it enters the Grand Canyon.

M.R. Mudge/U.S. Geological Survey

The Waterpocket Fold extends 100 miles southeastward from Fishlake National Forest's Thousand Lake Mountain to the Colorado River.

A Wrinkle to Ride Over, Through, and Behind

As Utah developed around the Waterpocket Fold, the fold's eroded terrain was its savior. Grazing and farming were mostly impractical. The land was so remote that the nearby Henry Mountains were the last unmapped and unnamed mountains in the lower 48 states. No paved roads came close until Highway 24 was completed in 1962, traversing the park east to west. Even today most visitors stay close to the highway and do not venture out; they visit for less than a day, then are off toward their next destination. Only 2 percent enter the Waterpocket Fold's southern district and just 1 percent, the northern section—and the others don't know what they are missing. You, however, will have most of the park to yourself and can take full advantage of its beauty. Before you lies a land worth exploring many days at a time. Even after return visits you will not tire of it and will always cherish your special memories of the Waterpocket Fold, of the people you rode with, and of the horse who was your good companion.

Horseback rides that are recommended by the park take you along the South Draw, the South Desert, and the Old Wagon Trail. From the Post south through the Halls Creek drainage is sanctioned as well, except for Halls Creek Narrows. Unpaved four-wheel-drive roads lead to remote areas, once of interest only to cowboys, sheepherders, miners, and geologists. Trails

THE OUTSIDE WORLD APPROACHES

Fur trappers long searched for an easy passage through the Rocky Mountains. Credit for the discovery of "South Pass," in southwestern Wyoming, is generally given to American fur trapper Jim Bridger, who found it in 1824. But even so, in 1840 few Americans lived in today's western U.S. Barely 100 Americans were in the Pacific Northwest, fewer than that in today's California, and a mere handful in the Southwest, including present-day Utah. California and the Southwest belonged to Spain, later Mexico; the Northwest was loosely claimed by the British. Then, in 1841, after the beaver fur trade had come to an end, Thomas "Broken Hand" Fitzpatrick, an Irish trapper, led the first emigrant wagon train through the pass, and the famous Oregon Trail was born. Throngs of settlers traveled along it for the next 20 years. They changed the West and they changed Utah, and the changes affected the country surrounding the Waterpocket Fold.

In 1847 Mormon leader Brigham Young traveled with an advance party along the Oregon Trail. After South Pass the group turned into present-day Utah and selected the future Salt Lake City as a gathering place for the church's members. In 1849 the Mormons established the provisional state of Deseret, with Young as governor. The next year the land became the Territory of Utah.

Mark Twain (1835–1910) was one of the trail's later travelers. Abraham Lincoln had appointed Twain's brother secretary to the Nevada Territory, and together the brothers traveled to the assignment in 1861. Near South Pass their stagecoach overtook an emigrant train of 33 wagons. "Tramping wearily along and driving their herd of loose cows," Twain reported, "were dozens of coarse-clad and sad-looking men, women and children, who had walked as they were walking now, day after day for eight lingering weeks, and in that time had compassed the distance our stage had come in *eight days and three hours*—seven hundred and ninety-eight miles! They were dusty and uncombed, hatless, bonnetless and ragged, and they did look so tired!"

and cross-country routes radiate from there. If you're traveling without a professional outfitter, it's best to keep to the trails. Much of the park is pure rock, and cross-country routes are difficult to follow. What begins as a promising canyon can become so narrow you'll have to turn back. Reliable water is scarce, heat can be extreme, and help—should you need it—is remote. Thunderstorms can send dangerous flash floods down canyons with little or no warning.

Riding from Pleasant Creek to Grover

Of the many riding choices in Capitol Reef National Park, let's take an out-fitted five-day, cross-country pack trip that cuts east to west across the Waterpocket Fold, then day rides from a base camp among the welcome shade of Dixie National Forest's ponderosa pines. On the first morning the outfitter drives riders south on the partially paved Notom-Bullfrog Road, off Highway 24 along the east side of the park. The road climbs steeply from Fremont River Canyon, then runs between the Waterpocket Fold and the Henry Mountains. At Notom the horses are unloaded. While your group heads west, one of the wranglers drives to the camp site on the other side of the park and drops off your food, water, and gear, and hay for the horses.

You'll ride toward the Waterpocket Fold until you meet Pleasant Creek, then follow the creek south on its spectacular way toward the park. Golden eagles soar in the desert sky above you, and solitary stone monoliths tower over sandy desert plains. At the park boundary you'll join Pleasant Creek Trail and wind through beautiful, steep-walled Pleasant Creek Canyon across the Waterpocket Fold. Each bend in the trail, each climb or descent, brings new sights and impressions. By afternoon you emerge on the park's west and set up camp. You'll use this site for your entire stay, returning to it every afternoon, tired, and satisfied.

The next morning you're off to Jorgensen Flats, circling Lower Bowns Reservoir, trekking above beautiful Oak Creek Canyon, looking down from steep cliffs. Day three finds you riding along Tantalus Creek and over to Sheets Gulch, one of the most spectacular canyons inside the park. Day four is up for grabs. You can ride to Spring Gulch, along Tantalus Creek, or wherever you fancy. On day five you'll guide your horse west up Sulphur Creek to the town of Grover, where your ride comes to an end.

Footsteps Through Time

Dinosaur fossils have been found in the park, and a thick layer of ancient mammoth dung was excavated in a cave near Glen Canyon. Mammoths, slightly larger than modern elephants, died out around 9000 B.C., at the end of the Great Ice Age. As the climate warmed, the mammoths' environment

MORE OF THE OUTSIDE WORLD

In 1848 the Gold Rush belonged to those living in or near California. It was only after President Polk officially reported on the richness of the gold fields on December 5, 1848, that prospectors flocked west.

Easterners had three choices to reach the golden land: by hazardous sea voyage around the tip of South America; by sea through the Caribbean to Panama, overland through malaria-infested jungle, then by ship to San Francisco Bay; or overland through the U.S., a route few if any Easterners tried. But for the young men of the Midwest, the path to the gold lay straight across the plains. After South Pass many cut south through Salt Lake City on what was now a branch of the California Trail. For three years some 15,000 argonauts passed annually through Utah, boosting the territory's economy.

The notion of a railroad across the U.S. seemed a fantasy in the 1850s. The rails would have to pass through many climates and terrains and thorugh hostile Indian territory. What skeptics overlooked, and entrepreneurs realized, was that with the help of federal loans and land grants, the job could be accomplished, and that towns to service the railroad and "civilize" the West would surely follow. The entrepreneurs were right. Within the span of a single generation Congress and state governments granted more than 116 million acres of public domain to Western railroads—free land twice the size of Utah—and advanced $64 million in bonds. Two railroads would be built: the Central Pacific from Sacramento, California, and the Union Pacific from Omaha, Nebraska. Promontory Summit, Utah, 90 miles northwest of Salt Lake City, was to be the meeting point.

On May 10, 1869, the two trains faced each other, the tracks ready to touch. Throngs of workmen, soldiers, and guests waited for the ceremony to begin. Central Pacific's Leland Stanford, the highest-ranking official present, swung a hammer at a ceremonial spike ingeniously wired so that each blow would be telegraphed across the land. He missed. Nevertheless, the alert telegrapher flashed, "Dot. Dot. Dot . . . Done." Celebratory guns boomed in the East, San Franciscans danced in the streets, and, in Salt Lake City, the Mormons prayed.

shrank. Near the Waterpocket Fold the plant foods they favored now grew only in the Henry Mountains' cooler and wetter regions. Some mammoths probably migrated north with the retreating ice and survived for a while. The rest were hunted by Native Americans to local extinction. Upstream along the Colorado, near Canyonlands National Park, mammoth remains were found close to petroglyphs of mammoths.

Native Americans whom archaeologists call the Fremont People— believed related to the Four Corners Anasazi—settled near the Waterpocket Fold's rivers around A.D. 700. Sometime after 1250 they left today's park, probably during the Colorado Plateau's extended dry spell from 1276 to 1300. You can still find their rock art on canyon walls, and you may recognize campfire or corn-grinding sites. Worn, faded lines pecked into sandstone are puzzles. Do they represent a snake? A calendar? A map? In a narrow canyon's cool depth, you may spot a small food-storage cist. Hidden in the rock and carefully sealed with red clay, it still shows the maker's fingerprints, pressed into the mud. Circled depressions mark the sites of ancient homes, chips of

SPEAKING IN TONGUES

Utah is named after the Ute Indians (unfortunately, no relation to the author). The Ute language belongs to the 26 Uto-Aztecan language stocks spoken in the western U.S., Mexico, and northern Guatemala.

When Columbus first landed in the New World in 1492, North America had 1.5 million Native Americans speaking about 300 languages. By 1962 about 200 languages had survived, but some still used by only a few elderly tribe members.

In 1891 Grand Canyon explorer Major John Wesley Powell, whose career combined interests in geology and ethnology (a branch of anthropology), undertook the first comprehensive classification of the North American Indian languages. He found nothing primitive about them. The languages draw on the same linguistic resources and display the same regularities and complexities as those of Europe. Of a total of 57 language families, 37 were spoken west of the Rockies. California alone showed more linguistic variety than all of Europe.

flaked stone the making of tools. Nomadic Utes and Paiutes hunted throughout the Waterpocket Fold after the Fremont people left.

On his celebrated 1869 voyage down the Colorado, Major John Wesley
Powell saw the Fremont River. He called it the Dirty Devil River, a name it
still holds in its lower reaches. In the 1870s Mormons settled in the valleys
west of today's park and established the towns of Loa, Fremont, Lyman,
Bicknell, and Torrey. In the early 1880s other Mormons moved closer to the
Waterpocket Fold, along the Fremont River. Fruita was the Waterpocket
Fold's most successful community. Today you can visit its restored one-room
schoolhouse and pioneer blacksmith shop, and in season you're invited to
sample the former community's fruit orchards.

Water Pockets Change the World

The Waterpocket Fold is named for water pockets, shallow depressions eroded into sandstone where rainwater and snowmelt collect. In the winter moisture freezes and thaws, either in joints or between individual grains of porous
rock. Repeated over and over, the process loosens the grains, breaks off rock
flakes, and initiates the rock's breakdown. As depressions deepen, the pockets
hold more water for a longer time. The wind deposits tiny animals' larvae
and small plants' spores and seeds. The little plants and larvae—many visible

Park rangers on horse patrol in Chimney Rock Canyon

Bob Reynolds/Capitol Reef National Park

only under a microscope—develop in the pools and secrete metabolic acids that further dissolve the stone. When the pools dry up, the wind blows away the loose sand and deepens the hollows.

Take a close look. Places where small rock depressions almost touch each other, particularly along joints, not only hold water but begin to guide its flow. Clefts are formed, crevasses, and eventually the deep, enormous canyons that dwarf horse and rider alike. Rainstorms and snowmelts course through the passageways, scouring and smoothing the surface. Swirling violently, the waters grind large holes and carve the park's natural arches. From Halls Creek Overlook, if you scan through your binoculars carefully, you'll see a double arch below you on the far side of the valley.

The water pockets are essential to local desert dwellers: black bears, mountain lions, bobcats, foxes, coyotes, and mule deer range throughout the park. Ringtails are at home in the rocky ridges and cliffs, usually near water, for instance near Fruita and along Pleasant Creek. Beavers live on the Fremont River and Halls Creek. On Chimney Rock Trail you may meet weasels, and mink along the Fremont River. Yellow-bellied marmots are abundant in the Fruita area but sleep from late August until spring. Somewhere among the low desert shrubs rock squirrels dart toward shelter, and porcupines lumber along. You'll see antelope west of the park near Loa, and a wild buffalo herd ranges between the Henry Mountains and the Colorado River.

TRAVEL TIPS
Capitol Reef National Park

Prime Horseback Season: May–September

Horse Outfitters: Hondoo Rivers & Trails, Pleasant Creek Outfitters

Stewardship Agency: Capitol Reef National Park, HC 70 Box 15, Torrey, UT 84775; (801) 425-3791

General Tourist Information: Utah Department of Tourism, (800) 200-1160

ROCKY MOUNTAIN STATES

Pecos Wilderness. EQUUS•USA

Colorado
WEMINUCHE WILDERNESS

*"We were in such an airy elevation above the creeping populations of the earth . . .
it seemed that we could look around and abroad and contemplate the whole great globe."*
Mark Twain (1835–1910)

Rocky Mountain High

Approaching the Rocky Mountains from a distance is one of the great sights
in North America. As you come closer, they loom like a giant, white-capped
wall climbing to the sky. Once you are in them—in the thin, crisp air, the colors intensified until the lines between sunlight and shadow are as sharp as a
razor's edge—they are breathtaking. Ridges, steeples, crags, canyons, rock
slides, battlements, glaciers, snowfields, and peaks unfold in all directions. The
turbulence of the landscape goes on forever. The sky is so blue it seems artificial. Amid such grand perspectives your sense of scale breaks down. Each time
your horse takes you around a rock outcrop, or steps from a forest into the
dazzle of a sun-swept meadow, the scenes shift too quickly. Summits jut across
humbling distances hard to grasp. Your body forgets what size it is.

The Rocky Mountain chain is the longest and largest mountain system
in North America, no matter where you place its beginning or its end. Some
geologists count the Brooks Range in Alaska as its start and the Sierra
Madre Mountains in Mexico as its finish. Others say the Rockies extend
from Alberta and British Columbia in Canada to the southern border of
New Mexico. The common opinion is from Alaska's Brooks Range to Santa
Fe, New Mexico. The width is also under debate. Some include the mountains of Arizona, Nevada, and Utah; others, none of them. Most geologists
include Utah. Figured this way, in the U.S. alone, from north to south, the
Rocky Mountains cover much of Montana, Idaho, Wyoming, Utah,
Colorado, and New Mexico, and dominate their landscape. From Alaska to
New Mexico, the Rockies span 34 degrees of latitude, or almost one-tenth
the circumference of the Earth. South America's Andes are the only mountains to cross more degrees of latitude, but they provide less dramatically
contrasting climates than the Rockies. The Rockies reach from the Arctic's
blizzard-driven snows to the sunshine lands of New Mexico, and offer an
amazing diversity in between.

Under the single name Rocky Mountains we actually lump together
many mountain ranges: the Bitterroots of Idaho and Montana; Wyoming's

Southfork Outfitters

Southfork Outfitters, Colorado: At timberline near the headwaters of the Weminuche's Rock Creek, on the way to the Continental Divide

Southfork Outfitters

Southfork Outfitters, Colorado: The wranglers have set up camp and a scrumptious dinner is waiting.

Tetons; and the San Juan Range of southwestern Colorado. The San Juans are the largest single range outside Alaska, covering more than 6.4 million acres—enough to enclose all of Vermont and a sliver of New Hampshire.

With 488,300 acres (197,610 ha), the Weminuche (pronounced WHEM-uh-nootch) Wilderness, in the San Juans, is Colorado's largest designated wilderness and one of the biggest in the U.S. It protects some of Colorado's most splendid and remote backcountry and offers you 470 miles of trails. The average elevation is 10,000 feet; three peaks in the Weminuche's Needle Mountains reach over 14,000 feet: Mount Eolus soars 14,083 feet; Windom, 14,082 feet; and Sunlight, 14,059 feet. Peaks over 13,000 feet are common. Established in 1975, the Weminuche is named for the Weminuche Indians, a band of the Ute tribe, who lived here. Many of the major trails in today's wilderness were probably developed by the Weminuche Utes.

Dozens of the Southwest's most important streams and rivers rise in the Weminuche, including the Rio Grande, San Juan, Animas, Los Piños, and Piedra. In all, the Weminuche has nearly 200 miles of mountain streams, and you can swim in 63 crystal-clear high mountain lakes, such as Emerald Lake, Colorado's second-largest natural lake.

Continental Divide National Scenic Trail

As you ride in the Weminuche, you may cross a great new long-distance trail that allows horseback riding. The Continental Divide National Scenic Trail (CDT) follows the entire length of the U.S.'s north-south divide in the lower 48 states, all the way from Canada's mountain magic to the Mexican border. The CDT is longer than the Pacific Crest Trail (see Pacific Coast States section), is the most rugged of the national long-distance trails, and offers a full 3,200 miles (5,150 km) for you to discover by horse.

If you ride the CDT from beginning to end, you'll visit many of the best high-mountain areas of the five major Rocky Mountain states: Montana, Idaho, Wyoming, Colorado, and New Mexico. Three stunning national parks—Glacier, Yellowstone, and Rocky Mountain—lie along the route, and you'll ride through three Native American reservations, more than 20 established or proposed wildernesses, and several spectacular national monuments. If you were to ride 15 miles a day without pause, delays, or side excursions, the entire trip would take you 213 days.

But don't saddle your horse just yet. Even though it was officially added in 1978 to the National Trails Act of 1968, only portions of the trail are in place. Projects of this size require decades. Government agencies in cooperation with Native American reservations, private landowners, and volunteer groups are still selecting the precise path in certain areas and improving and marking the route. Future editions of this book will keep you updated on the trail's progress.

Riding the Weminuche's CDT

From Stony Pass to Wolf Creek Pass, 80 completed miles of the CDT pass through the Weminuche, effectively connecting all of the Weminuche's drainages. Loop rides enable you to climb out of one drainage basin and follow the divide to the next. The trail's elevation averages 12,000 feet in the wilderness, and 10,622-foot Weminuche Pass is the lowest point. Your eyes feast on panoramas of regal peaks, long-distance vistas of the Sangre de Cristo and La Plata ranges, and oceans of wildflowers. A wildflower count near the foothills of Colorado yielded 2,989 different varieties. As you pause on top of the Divide, one stirrup aimed at the Pacific Ocean, the other at the Atlantic, think about the long journey of a drop of rain. Or imagine the landscape in the icy cold of deep winter. A snowflake freezes in the shadow of a mountain. In the spring thaw, gravity pulls it down a network of rills, creeks, and rivers until it adds a few molecules' moisture to one of the oceans—provided, of course, it doesn't first evaporate, seep into the ground, or quench the thirst of a pine tree or black bear.

To reach the western beginning of the Weminuche's CDT from Silverton, drive north about 4 miles on Highway 110 to the townsite of Howardsville at the mouth of Cunningham Gulch, then turn right on Forest Service Road 589 up Cunningham Gulch. Turn left on Forest Service Road 737 and climb 3½ miles to Stony Pass. Unload the horses and saddle up. You are starting over 12,000 feet high and will stay above timberline for most of the trip. To your left, the Rio Grande River is born.

Your horse takes you south past Cunningham Gulch Trail. A little later an unmaintained trail comes in from Highland Mary Lakes. Just past the junction with Elk Creek Trail, you'll ride past 12,504-foot-high Lake Eldorado, with 13,627-foot White Dome looming behind. At Hunchback Mountain, the CDT suddenly turns left and descends to 12,100-foot-high Kite Lake. At the lake an old mining cabin still stands and you'll see a couple of mine shafts, reminders of the area's mining fever. Look for bighorn sheep, mule deer, and elk as you continue along the wildflower-lined trail. Try identifying Colorado's state flower, the blue columbine, and Indian paintbrush, pink moss campion, and yellow cinquefoil. Your horse carries you up Hunchback Pass, then descends a straight barren valley and crosses Vallecito Creek Trail. To your right are the Grenadier Range and the northern end of the granitic Needle Mountains.

If you have time, consider a side trip to the western end of the Weminuche Wilderness. The Vallecito Creek Trail can take you south along the Needle Mountains, then west on Columbine Pass Trail. From here you can admire the Weminuche's three Fourteeners (14,000-plus-foot peaks). Beneath the Needle Mountains the Animas River Canyon cuts through the land.

MESA VERDE NATIONAL PARK

Thirty-six miles west of Durango is the highway turnoff for Mesa Verde National Park—a great sightseeing destination before or after your ride in the Weminuche. Driving toward the park you'll leave the Rockies behind and head into the open expanses of the Four Corners. Mesa Verde is a 15-by-20-mile tabletop mountain rising 2,000 feet above the surrounding land. Because of its abundant juniper and piñon trees the Spanish called it *Mesa Verde*, "green table." Millennia of rain, snow, and wind have carved canyons into the tabletop, and the upper canyon walls are dotted with caves.

A group of Anasazi (Navajo for "The Ancient Ones") moved to Mesa Verde about A.D. 550, when, formerly a nomadic people, they began a more settled life. Agriculture supplemented hunting and gathering, and they built pit houses sunk a few feet into the ground. The pit houses were clustered into small villages on top of the mesa and occasionally in the recesses of the mesa's cliffs.

The times were prosperous, and the tribe's population multiplied. About A.D. 750 they began to build houses above the ground in long, curving rows, often with a ceremonial pit house or two in front. By 1000 they had become skilled stone- masons. Thick stone walls rose two and three stories high and were joined into complexes of 50 or more rooms and round towers. Their pottery gained sophistication, and they cleared more mesatop land for agriculture.

Less than 100 years after moving into their cliff homes, the Anasazi left. By 1300 Mesa Verde was deserted. For almost 600 years it lay forgotten, or at least not known to non-Indian until, in 1859, geologists surveying the area discovered some of the dwellings. In 1874 the famous photographer William H. Jackson took pictures of Two Story House in Mancos Canyon and showed the ruins to the world.

Nearly 600 cliff dwellings grace Mesa Verde National Park's canyon system, ranging from one-room houses to clusters of more than 200 rooms. Cliff Palace is the largest cliff house in North America, with 217 rooms and 23 kivas. It housed 200 to 250 people. Spruce Tree House is the best-preserved Mesa Verde site. Balcony House is well-known for its defensive design.

As you look down on the small blue band of the river, you might hear the clacking of railroad cars above the river's roar. Each summer thousands of eager tourists marvel at the area's beauty from a narrow-gauge steam train that winds its way slowly from Durango to Silverton, clinging precipitously to the narrow canyon's walls with the river directly below. The river's full title is Río de las Animas Perdidas, Spanish for "River of Lost Souls." Long before the railroad was built Spanish adventurers from Santa Fe snooped about the San Juan foothills. Legend has it that five of the king's soldiers wandered up the Animas and never returned.

Back on the CDT, at Nebo Pass, look for a lake with a tremendous chunk of rock in it. Mount Nebo's spectacular cliffs are just beyond. To your left, over the Ute Creek drainage, you see the purplish Ute Ridge, the Rio Grande Pyramid, and the Spanish Window—a cliff edge bisected by a rectangular cut so perfectly symmetrical it could have been shaped by a stonemason. Nearby, it is said, lies a rich lost Spanish gold mine from the 1750s. You'll descend to West Ute Lake, then ride along Middle Ute Lake. In several areas of the Weminuche, as at Twin Lakes, you may see mountain goats.

In 1964 the Colorado Game and Fish Department introduced the goats around several of Colorado's summits, and their descendants appear to be doing well. Their life among the crags and chasms of these high peaks depends on agility, a head for heights, and the ability to leap fearlessly. The animals are so sure-footed that they can jump onto an icy, narrow ledge 25 feet below their

The years 1276 to 1300 saw intense drought in much of the Southwest, probably causing these spectacular Mesa Verde cliff dwellings to become a ghost town.

ARA Mesa Verde

SILVERTON'S SILVER AND GOLD

In 1858 a prospector returning overland from California's gold rush dipped his pan in a creek near present-day Denver and found gold. For the next 40 years everyone who could get his hands on a shovel and pack mule tromped through the Rockies looking for pay dirt. Mining camps sprang up all over the mountains, and if you missed the gold, silver would do—or copper, or lead. Otherwise, you could raise cattle and feed the camps. But ores eventually play out and metal prices drop, and by 1900 most camps had been abandoned to the wind or turned into logging camps for the next free harvest.

In 1871, while someone found gold near Silverton, someone else found silver, and miners hacked them from the mountainsides. The only way to Silverton was a 50-mile haul over Stony Pass, the same route you are following on the Continental Divide National Scenic Trail. Snow blocked Stony Pass from November to April, and for six months Silverton saw no new faces, received no mail, no outside medical care, and no law enforcement. The arrival of the spring's first pack train was the year's wildest excitement. In 1876 the pack mules arrived on May 2, and Silverton just about lost its head. "Somebody gave a shout," the Silverton newspaper reported, "'turn out, the jacks are coming,' and sure enough there were the patient homely little fellows filing down the trail. Cheer after cheer was given, gladness prevailed all around, and the national flag was run up at the post office."

Civilization approached in 1882 with the arrival of the Denver and Rio Grande Western Railroad from Durango, the same scenic-route train visitors ride today. The train stops in the canyon to let off backpackers and their gear, just as it did years ago for prospectors and their supplies. "Puff-chug" goes the coal-burning engine and has to stop every 15 miles for water for its boilers.

The area's mining prosperity soon attracted the interest of the West's most notorious criminals. Utah's Butch Cassidy (1866–unknown) began his bank-robbing career in 1889 with the stickup of Telluride's silver-rich San Miguel County Bank. To oppose the increasing crime and violence, Silverton imported the infamous Bat Masterson from Dodge City.

takeoff point as they work their way back down a mountain. Mountain goats live only in North America and only in the western mountains, originally from southern Alaska to the northern latitudes of the lower 48 states. They are one of the few animals who remain white all year.

When you have sufficiently admired these high-mountain acrobats, follow the CDT as it turns east and leaves the western Weminuche. As your horse plunges deeper into the wilderness, the San Juan Mountains heave and toss with every conceivable land formation: uplifted sedimentary rock, volcanic remnants, fragile sandstone layers, metamorphic rock irrevocably changed during long intervals in the Earth's bowels, and breakneck river gorges cut by patient streams.

Gunsight Pass provides a break in the light-colored crumbling sandstone that encircles half of the Rincon La Osa's basin. When the trail descends into Rincon La Vaca through slopes covered with alpine sunflowers, Weminuche Pass—the Weminuche CDT's lowest point—appears far down the canyon as a small patch of green meadow. Then the Spanish Window and the Rio Grande Pyramid come into close view. At Weminuche Pass your horse takes you to timberline. The trail winds around a ridge into the Pine River's North Fork, then ascends steeply. The meadow along the North Fork widens and the grade lessens, until you cross the stream and the trail begins to climb again. When the CDT descends to the head of Grouse Rincon, watch for the large elk herd that summers here.

At Piedra Pass, consider another side excursion. Riding south on West Fork Trail takes you along volcanic cliffs, shimmering waterfalls, and inviting hot springs. Hop in—that's what it's all about! Red-winged blackbirds warble from nearby roosts, wearing their wings' bright red markings as proudly as a general's epaulets and defending their homes as vigorously. Several stands of old-growth forest live in the Weminuche, some individual trees more than 3 feet in diameter and 450 years old. Outside the wilderness boundary, the Piedra area has the most significant old-growth forests in Colorado. So far they have escaped logging because of their inaccessibility.

Back on the CDT, you begin your home stretch to Wolf Creek Pass, rounding 12,000-foot summits and descending switchbacks with a look into wild Beaver Creek Canyon. From here to 11,680-foot Archuleta Lake the trail is a series of humps and ridges. Your horse is constantly climbing or descending. Five miles before your trip's end you reach the meadows at the head of the Rio Grande's South Fork, and your horse climbs cautiously through a sliderock slope abundant with marmots and pikas. You'll dismount just north of Wolf Creek Pass at Lobo Overlook, where Forest Service Road 402 and Highway 160 return you to "civilization." The Continental Divide National Scenic Trail continues across Wolf Creek Pass toward New Mexico and Mexico.

TRAVEL TIPS
Weminuche Wilderness

Prime Horseback Season: July and August

Horse Outfitters: Over The Hill Outfitters, Rapp Guides & Packers, Ron-D-View Outfitting, Southfork Outfitters, Weminuche & Superstition Adventures

Stewardship Agencies: San Juan National Forest, Supervisor's Office, 701 Camino del Rio, Room 301, Durango, CO 81301; (970) 247-4874. Rio Grande National Forest, Supervisor's Office, 1803 W. Hwy. 160, Monte Vista, CO 81144; (719) 852-5941.

General Tourist Information: Colorado Department of Tourism, (800) 433-2656

Bob Marshall
Wilderness Complex
(BOB MARSHALL, GREAT BEAR, AND SCAPEGOAT WILDERNESSES)

*"For me, and for thousands with similar inclinations, the most important passion
of life is the overpowering desire to escape periodically from the clutches of a
mechanistic civilization. To us the enjoyment of solitude, complete independence,
and beauty of undefiled panoramas is absolutely essential to happiness."*

Bob Marshall (1901–1939)

Wilderness Supreme

The Bob Marshall Wilderness is 1,009,356 acres huge. If you add the Great
Bear Wilderness on its northwest, and the Scapegoat Wilderness on its
southeast, the combined wilderness complex protects 1,535,063 acres
(621,225 ha) of the Rocky Mountains. Together with Glacier National Park
adjacent to the Great Bear Wilderness, and Canada's Waterton Provincial
Park adjacent to Glacier, the area is one of the largest protected high-mountain environments in North America.

Alpine peaks, windswept prairie, bottomless canyons, towering cliffs,
dense forests, wild rivers, and lush meadows keep your senses spinning, trying to take it all in. And the land is just the beginning. The wealth of wildlife
is renowned. The lower 48's largest populations of grizzly bear, bighorn
sheep, and wolverine live in the Bob Marshall–GreatBear–Scapegoat
Wilderness Complex ("The Bob"), and you'll admire mountain goats and
huge herds of elk. Moose browse in willow thickets near rivers, and occasionally you'll hear a gray wolf's distant howl. Except for buffalo and caribou,
every mammal indigenous to this land still lives here.

Saddlin' Up

An astonishing total of 1,941 miles of trails allow you access to The Bob's
remotest corners. Elevations range from 4,000 feet along the river valleys to
the Bob Marshall's 9,392-foot Rocky Mountain Peak and the Scapegoat's
9,411-foot Red Mountain. Several rivers are born in the wilderness—the
Flathead and the Sun are the largest. The most prominent branch, the
Flathead's South Fork, runs through the Bob Marshall for 65 miles. Broad
expanses of lush grass and parklike meadows stretch before you. As you ride

into the valleys, your horse will think it's walked into heaven. Big Salmon Lake at 4½ miles long is the wilderness complex's biggest lake.

One great way to experience The Bob is by horse/raft combo. The Flathead's Middle Fork offers whitewater rafting; on the Flathead's North Fork you can enjoy a scenic float. Both jaunts take you from the Great Bear Wilderness along the border of Glacier National Park. After admiring the country for several days on horseback, you'll enjoy seeing it for a few days from a river perspective.

Riding the Chinese Wall

The Chinese Wall, a 1,000-foot-high limestone scarp that stretches unbroken for a dozen miles, is The Bob's best-known and most popular destination and a dramatic manifestation of North America's Continental Divide. One of the several outstanding trails that lead to the Chinese Wall enters the wilderness by following the Sun River's South and West Forks, between the jagged peaks of the front range and the Continental Divide's sheer walls. For much of this ride you'll be inside The Bob's Sun River Game Reserve, set aside in 1913 to rebuild animal populations depleted by hunting.

From the town of Augusta, take Benchmark Road west. Turn left on Willow Creek Road and follow it as it enters the mountains, bends north,

BOB MARSHALL

The Bob Marshall Wilderness is named for Bob Marshall, an early-day forester with the U.S. Forest Service who believed in preserving true wilderness within the national forest system. In the 1920s and 1930s Marshall, a devoted hiker, made long treks into the mountains of Montana and Idaho. Rarely was a day hike less than 40 miles, most totaled 50 miles or more, and several exceeded 70 miles. In 1939, when he was only 38, he died of a sudden heart attack. In his memory the Bob Marshall Wilderness was created in 1941, pieced together from three sections of national forest. The Scapegoat was protected as a wilderness in 1972; the Great Bear, in 1978.

and ends near the South Fork Sun River Trailhead. From here your horse takes you north on South Fork Sun River Trail over the bridge that spans the river. For the first mile the wide path is through lodgepole pine benchlands above the river, then it turns inland. You'll cross Deer Creek, slog through boggy terrain for a while, then return to a drier lodgepole forest after crossing the wilderness boundary. Near the junction with Bighead Creek Trail, point your horse left on West Fork Sun River Trail. The trail descends and rounds the corner of Deadman Hill. Once you reach the north bank of the West Fork, West Fork Trail turns westward and crosses the rolling prairies bordering the riverbank.

You'll catch your first glimpse of Nineteen Ridge's sharp spires as the trail mounts a shoulder of Prairie Reef. You cross Reef Creek, and your horse climbs onto the grassy slopes of Prairie Reef, giving you views of Red Butte to the far west. The trail passes Prairie Reef Lookout Trail, then descends across grassy benches into Indian Point Meadows. You'll have ridden almost 11 miles by now and might want to look for a campsite nearby.

If you stay in camp another night, you can day ride the next morning to Pearl Basin, noted for its spectacular beauty. On your third day you'll continue on West Fork Trail to the Chinese Wall. Past Indian Point Cabin you'll gradually climb through a forest of lodgepole pine. After passing the White River Pass junction, the climb is steeper. At Black Bear Creek you'll

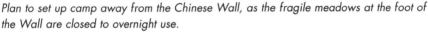

Plan to set up camp away from the Chinese Wall, as the fragile meadows at the foot of the Wall are closed to overnight use.

M.R. Mudge/U.S. Geological Survey

see the ragged peaks of Red Butte across the valley, and you'll climb to a high meadow that gives even greater views. Just below Pine Creek is your first glimpse of the Chinese Wall's southern slopes. Later, when your horse brings you to a high saddle at the foot of Cliff Mountain, one of the tallest bastions along the Chinese Wall, you'll have a commanding view of the seemingly endless scarp stretching along the Continental Divide. To the southeast you'll see Prairie Reef, back toward the start of your journey.

The trail descends steadily through a young stand of whitebark pine and passes a pond, the source of Moose Creek. As you ride by, look for enchanting reflections of the Chinese Wall. This part of the wall is lower than its northern reaches, but the turrets and crenellations are inspiring. The cliffs are home to mountain goats who climb the dizzying heights in search of their favorite foods, the mosses and lichens growing on the faces and in the crevices of high rocks. The goats generally forage in the morning and evening, but on moonlit nights they continue long after dark, then sleep in shallow depressions at the base of high mountain cliffs. On warm days they sun themselves, balancing on narrow precipices. They're actually not goats at all but goat-antelopes related to the chamois of the European Alps and to the Himalayan serow.

Watch for elk and mule deer grazing in the alpine meadows, particularly at dawn and dusk. Ground squirrels busily go about their business, and marmots and pikas live among boulder fields. At times you ride through odd terrain that looks like a giant broke a mountain peak and hurled fragments in all directions. When the trail passes the junction with Moose Creek Trail you'll ascend among house-sized boulders. At the foot of Salt Mountain the trail crests the next drainage. On these saddles get out your binoculars. Swallows build their nests in the Chinese Wall and can be spotted performing aerial ballets in their quest for airborne insects.

When dismounting your horse, step carefully and look closely. In many of The Bob's oldest rocks you are walking on fossils of blue-green algae, the Earth's first green plants. Most often you'll find the algae as inconspicuous and paper-thin laminations. These were scummy growths that covered mud surfaces, then were buried beneath additional mud. In more favorable growing conditions, the algae formed structures called stromatolites, which look like fossilized cabbages. You are peering a long time into the past.

Consider camping a night or two in the wider territory of the Chinese Wall to explore the country nearby. When you're ready to leave, you can either retrace your route or continue farther into the wilderness. A popular one-way trek takes you from here north along the Chinese Wall to Larch Hill Pass, the wall's northern terminus. You'll then pass My Lake, follow Spotted River Trail, and reach Spotted Bear Road 22 miles from Larch Hill Pass, some 46 miles from the South Fork Sun River Trailhead.

LIMESTONE, LIMESTONE EVERYWHERE

Much of The Bob is limestone country, and a few places even reveal fossil coral, some shaped like honeycombs. The mighty Chinese Wall is an ancient limestone reef and so are the even taller Wall Creek Cliffs. Prairie Reef and Slategoat Mountain are prominent limestone landmarks on the east side, and Limestone Wall lies in the west along the Spotted Bear River. The White River's North Fork flows through porous limestone, alternates flowing above and below ground, then emerges in force downstream at Needle Falls. In many places erosion has created caves in the river's limestone. One cave system, on the north side of Silvertip Mountain, has more than 5 miles of lateral tunnels.

A small percentage of limestone is formed without the intervention of life, but most comes from calcite (calcium carbonate) used by plants or animals—for example, by marine molluscs in making elegant shells that serve both as armor to protect vital organs and as a house to live in. After a mollusc dies, its shell is often claimed by another creature.

If you climb to the top of the Chinese Wall, watch for seashells, evidence of ancient oceans. Only 250 years ago the rational and skeptical Voltaire (1694–1778), one of the great French writers of the 1700s, and a friend, the scientist Comte de Buffon (1707–1788), argued about seashells embedded high in the French Alps. Buffon reasoned they belonged to sea creatures who had lived where the mountains now stood. Nonsense, said Voltaire. Early travelers to the high country brought the shells along. The friends argued heatedly and their friendship cooled.

When more open-minded, Voltaire was an ardent crusader against tyranny, bigotry, and cruelty, and his satires of the royal court and liberal religious opinions caused offense. He was imprisoned in the Bastille, then driven into exile. In 1754 he settled in Switzerland. Surrounded daily by the upthrusting and eroding evidence of the Swiss Alps, he pondered Buffon's arguments. Eventually he accepted Buffon's ideas, and they again became friends.

Old Buffalo Trail

This route was used by the Flathead Indians to get to their annual buffalo hunts on the high plains. It gives you a great 53-mile one-way ride across The Bob's width, and includes the beautiful Danaher and Pearl Basins.

You begin this trek on The Bob's west, on Holland Lake's north shore. From here your horse takes you over Gordon Pass and along Gordon Creek's wooded valley. When you reach the Flathead River's South Fork, point your horse south and follow the trail to Youngs Creek Ford. Turn southeast here, up the Danaher Valley as far as Danaher Basin. You'll reach an old battleground where in 1840 the Flatheads and Blackfeet skirmished. Turn northeast up the valley of Camp Creek.

Your horse climbs over Camp Creek Pass, crosses the spectacular Pearl Basin, and descends the wooded valley of Ahorn Creek to Indian Point Meadows. You'll now follow the Chinese Wall route in reverse—riding south on West Fork Trail, then south on South Fork Trail until you reach the South Fork Sun River Trailhead.

Peace and solitude pervade the backcountry.

Ray Mills

BEAVER FUR

You'll come across old fur-trapper cabins in The Bob, strung out about 3 or 4 miles apart along nearby creeks. The cabins were part of a trap-lines network usually worked by one person. Before the Lewis and Clark expedition reached St. Louis in September 1806, one of its members, John Colter, turned right around and went back up the Missouri with two fur traders. He had seen a wild country teeming with beaver and was willing to guide the merchants.

At the height of the beaver fur trade, about 3,000 "mountain men" made their living killing the animals. Some worked for a set annual fee; others, the elite of the profession, traveled at will with their own horses and traps and sold their furs on the open market. Some did their own trapping; most talked Native Americans into doing the work and bringing the pelts to their company's trading posts in exchange for trinkets, guns, and whiskey. With their long hair and greasy buckskins decorated Indian-style, the trappers were picturesque. Many married Native American women, but usually they left their Native wives when they left the mountains. They used bear grease on their hair and skin, and also fried their food and greased their equipment with it. The distinctive odor of the bear grease was made more pungent by the trappers' lack of contact with water.

The Rocky Mountain Fur Company used a new approach. Rather than establish trading posts, it employed white trappers to gather the furs and turn them over to agents at an annual meeting, or "rendezvous." This eliminated the expensive construction of vulnerable forts and gave new mobility to follow the beaver. The rendezvous became an annual event. Trappers traveling alone or in small groups gathered at such places as Wyoming's Jackson Hole or Green River Valley, where wide meadows provided forage for their horses. As many as 1,500 trappers gathered for their once-a-year taste of civilization. In the mid-1830s, the fur trade's heyday came to an end. World fashions changed, and the beaver was saved from extinction—barely. The last rendezvous took place in 1840. The fur trade continued at a trickle, and with a growing emphasis on buffalo hides.

Continental Divide National Scenic Trail

The Continental Divide enters the U.S. from the north at the Canada–U.S. border in Glacier National Park, leaves the park on its south at Marias Pass, and continues through most of the Bob Marshall Wilderness Complex, cutting it roughly in half. Along the divide, you can ride the Continental Divide National Scenic Trail from the Canadian border all the way to Mexico (see Weminuche Wilderness section). Most of the northern portion of the trail is completed and, in the wilderness complex alone, you can follow it for 168 miles. Riding 15 miles a day gives you 11 wonderful days you will always cherish. With rest days and side excursions, you can have a first-class three-week vacation.

Indians and Explorers

Native Americans have used The Bob for thousands of years. Archaeological sites were found along the Flathead's South Fork and are common along the lower forks of the Sun. Passing Indians bathed in Medicine Springs west of Gibson Lake. The Great North Trail, an ancient buffalo and Native American trail, runs east of The Bob's Rocky Mountain Front and is thought to extend north as far as Alaska and south to Mexico. Along it the faint tracks of Indian travois (A-shaped carrying platforms pulled by dogs) can still be seen by air.

On July 3, 1806, on its return voyage, the Lewis and Clark expedition separated after entering Montana. Lewis and nine men headed down the Bitterroot River to explore that part of the country. Clark, with 50 horses, 20 men, and Sacajewea and her baby, headed up the Bitterroot to find the boats and supplies hidden the year before. A few days later, west of today's Scapegoat Wilderness, Lewis' group followed a trail that he identified as a Hidatsa warpath. The party passed the remains of Native American lodges, and later crossed the Continental Divide at present-day Lewis and Clark Pass on the southeastern boundary of the Scapegoat. They reached the Sun River east of today's Augusta.

Occasionally you'll see reminders of early settlers in The Bob. Rusted farm machinery and ruined buildings bear witness to unlucky homesteading attempts. The elevations in this area proved too high, the climate too harsh, and the market too far. So the people packed up and sadly said good-bye, moving on to try their luck elsewhere. Danaher Meadow on the Flathead's upper South Fork and Gates Park on the Sun's North Fork are pioneer sites, as are Biggs and Two Shacks Flats. Early mineral prospecting was unsuccessful, and railroad surveyors failed to find the low mountain pass they hoped for. Too difficult for anything else, the land remained wild.

TRAVEL TIPS
Bob Marshall Wilderness Complex

Prime Horseback Season: July and August

Horse Outfitters: Eastern Bob Marshall: A Lazy H Outfitters, Bear Creek Guest Ranch, JJJ Wilderness Ranch, Montana Safaris, Seven Lazy P Guest Ranch, Wilderness Connection.Western Bob Marshall: Monture Outfitters, White Tail Ranch Outfitters.

Stewardship Agencies: Flathead National Forest, Supervisor's Office, 1935 Third Ave. E., Kalispell, MT 59901; (406) 758-5251. Lewis & Clark National Forest, Supervisor's Office, P.O. Box 869, Great Falls, MT 59403; (406) 791-7700. Lolo National Forest, Supervisor's Office, Building 24 Fort Missoula, Missoula, MT 59801; (406) 329-3750.

General Tourist Information: Montana Department of Tourism, (800) 544-1800

YELLOWSTONE NATIONAL PARK

(NORTHEAST, NORTH, AND WEST ENTRANCES)

"From the forest and wilderness come the tonics and barks
which brace mankind . . . in Wildness is the preservation of the World."
Henry David Thoreau (1817–1862)

Decisions, Decisions

Yellowstone National Park extends into three states: Idaho, Montana, and
Wyoming. Since the bulk of the park is in Wyoming, I have placed the
Yellowstone description there. Of the park's five entrances, Wyoming has
two, Montana three. Here you'll find a brief overview of the Montana entry
points, and of the Montana horse outfitters. All of Yellowstone's entrances
take you into spectacular country, with lots of opportunities to ride.

West Entrance

Coming into Yellowstone from West Yellowstone, Montana, gives you access
to the trails of the park's northwest and southwest. The northwest corner is
an up-and-down place and the views are inspiring. Chances of seeing wildlife
are good any time of the year. Deer and elk live on the high ridges in summer and along the low river valleys in spring and fall. Moose are abundant
along willow-lined streams; bighorn sheep live near Sheep Mountain and
Bighorn Peak.

The northern portion of Yellowstone's southwest corner holds the valley
of the Firehole River, the location of Yellowstone's most famous thermal
areas. The backcountry trails here lead you not only to thermal areas, but to
waterfalls, lakes, and lush meadows. Buffalo and elk herds spend the entire
year in the valley, wintering near the thermal basins, grazing in the summer
in places like Little Firehole Meadows and Buffalo Meadows.

North Entrance

Yellowstone's northern entrance, at Gardiner, Montana, was the railroad
entry used by early Yellowstone visitors. You can still see Roosevelt Arch, the
gateway dedicated in 1904 by President Theodore Roosevelt. At Gardiner

Beartooth Plateau Outfitters

Beartooth Plateau Outfitters, Montana: Outfitter Ronnie Wright, Barb, and Sandi Sue on the trail to the Beartooth Plateau

Beartooth Plateau Outfitters

Beartooth Plateau Outfitters, Montana: Ronnie and Rock 'n Roll, his horse, lead a pack string deep inside Yellowstone.

you are just 5 miles from Yellowstone's famous Mammoth Hot Springs, and have a direct drive to the park's other great thermal features.

The trails on the west take you into Yellowstone's northwest corner (see West Entrance); the trails east of Mammoth Hot Springs, into the Lower Yellowstone River Area. While most of Yellowstone National Park lies 7,000 to 8,000 feet above sea level, the Lower Yellowstone ranges between 5,000 and 6,000 feet. Summer comes early here and winter late, and you'll ride through aspen, cottonwood, Douglas fir, limber pine, and Rocky Mountain juniper instead of the vast, dense lodgepole pine forests of the park's higher elevations. The gneiss and schist rock formations are some of the oldest rocks in the park and differ from the predominantly volcanic material you'll ride through in the rest of Yellowstone.

Northeast Entrance

The northeast entrance is at Silver Gate, Montana, just past Cooke City. Glaciers containing preserved grasshoppers and pink snow ("watermelon snow"), found in only a few places in the world, are visible at a short hiking or riding distance. Beartooth Highway from Red Lodge to Silver Gate, open only during summer, is considered the most scenic drive in the U.S. Reaching heights of 10,947 feet, the 69-mile stretch shows you snowcapped peaks, glaciers, alpine lakes, and vast plateaus. And that's before you enter Yellowstone.

Once inside the park, you'll ride through wide, open Slough Creek Valley, the forested Pebble Creek Valley, and the rugged 10,000-foot mountains that surround the two. Pebble Creek Trail starts from the Warm Creek Picnic Area, about a mile from the northeast entrance. The 5½ miles to the junction with Bliss Pass Trail give you some of Yellowstone's best mountain scenery. Bliss Pass Trail can take you to Slough Creek Trail, and Slough Creek Trail to Buffalo Plateau Trail, which winds north out of the park, then back into it to connect you with a whole new set of outstanding trail choices.

From Cooke City you can ride across Republic Pass and descend along the Cache Creek Trail into Yellowstone National Park. This route, in reverse, is described in Wyoming's Yellowstone section.

TRAVEL TIPS
Yellowstone National Park

Prime Horseback Season: July and August

Horse Outfitters: Northeast Entrance: Beartooth Plateau Outfitters, Skyline Guide Service. North Entrance: Bear Paw Outfitters, Rendevouz Outfitters, R.K. Miller's Wilderness Pack Trips, Wilderness Connection. West Entrance: Jake's Horses.

Stewardship Agency: Yellowstone National Park, P.O. Box168, Yellowstone National Park, WY 82190; general information, (307) 344-7381; lodging (307) 344-7311.

General Tourist Information: Montana Department of Tourism, (800) 541-1447

GILA WILDERNESS COMPLEX

(GILA AND ALDO LEOPOLD WILDERNESSES)

*"In the country which lies around the headwaters of the Gila River I was reared.
This range was our fatherland; among these mountains our wigwams were hidden;
the scattered valleys contained our fields; the boundless prairies, stretching away
on every side, were our pastures; the rocky caverns were our burying places."*

Geronimo (1829–1909)

A Taste of Mexico

In 1924 the Gila (HEE-lah) Wilderness became the world's first designated
wilderness area, when 558,065 acres were protected under the leadership of
forester Aldo Leopold. A portion of the wilderness originally proposed by
Leopold was later protected as the 202,016-acre Aldo Leopold Wilderness. It
lies east of the Gila Wilderness, separated from it by a rough gravel road.
Together the two form the 760,081-acre (307,597-ha) Gila Wilderness
Complex, or Gila for short. The complex is located in the Gila National
Forest, the largest national forest in New Mexico and one of the biggest in
the U.S. The world's largest continuous virgin ponderosa pine stands are
found in the Gila National Forest, as well as more than 20 species of deciduous trees—more than anywhere else in the West. The 533-acre Gila Cliff
Dwellings National Monument, established in 1907, lies adjacent to the
wilderness complex on the south.

The Gila is north of the Sonoran Desert, only 80-some miles from
Mexico. Here the Chihuahua pine reaches its northern limit, and so do
Apache pine, Arizona cypress, Arizona walnut, Arizona madrone, Arizona
sycamore, point-leaf manzanita, alligator juniper, Emory oak, and Schott's
yucca. Exotic animals occasionally visit from south of the border. Jaguars,
coatimundis (ringtail cats), and javelinas have been sighted in the Gila.
Pronghorn antelope—among the fastest animals on Earth—live here, as do
mule deer, elk, black bears, and mountain lions.

The jaguar is the largest cat native to the Americas. A huge yellow feline
with black spots, it resembles the leopard of Africa and Asia but is larger and
more heavily built. Together with the lion of Africa and India and the tiger of
Asia, the jaguar is one of the "big cats." Unlike the other big cats, it doesn't
roar. Jaguars are determined fighters when cornered, and are swift and agile,

Author (front) and friends Judy, Tyler, and Caroline heading into the Gila

but they are shy and normally do not approach humans. The most northerly sightings, long ago, were at the Grand Canyon and at Santa Fe, but the animal is rare now in its northern range, after having been hunted ferociously for its beautiful fur.

Several other unusual flora and fauna species are found in the Gila, including 11 species of orchids. Females of a whip-tailed lizard subspecies found here are capable of self-reproduction by cloning themselves from unfertilized gametes (reproductive cells). The Gila monster, one of two species of venomous lizards in the world, grows to about 20 inches and has a sturdy body with black beadlike scales and pink blotches or bands. It feeds at night on small mammals, birds, and eggs. Fat stored in the tail and abdomen is consumed in winter. The animal is shy and sluggish, and fatalities to humans are rare. A number of rare birds also live in the Gila, including the osprey and the scissor-tailed flycatcher.

Up and Down Riding

The Gila's trails offer 650 miles of outstanding backcountry riding. Elevations range from 4,800 feet in the river valleys to 10,892 feet on Whitewater Baldy in the Gila Wilderness. The trails on the south and west begin at the lower elevations and climb steadily. In a single day you can ride from canyons and foothills in the Upper Sonoran life zone—dominated by cholla, agave, prickly-pear cactus, and sycamore—to a subalpine forest indistinguishable from those in Canada's far north. Past lava pinnacles and steep cliffs you'll ride, through piñon and juniper woodlands and large stands of ponderosa pine, until you arrive on the high peaks covered with spruce-fir forests, meadows, and aspen glades. If you're starting your ride on the north, for example from the Willow Creek or Snow Lake areas, the country is already high. The Mogollon (MOGO-yown) Mountains of the Gila Wilderness and the Black Range of the Aldo Leopold are the Gila's most prominent ranges. Unlike most high mountains in the American West, the Gila's peaks were never glaciated; as a result they're as wild as they were before the Ice Age.

Once the Continental Divide National Scenic Trail is complete (see Weminuche Wilderness section), you'll be able to ride 3,200 miles from Canada to Mexico, including the Gila's stretch of the Divide through the Aldo Leopold Wilderness.

Aldo Leopold once reminisced about a trip in the Gila. "[In the] back of the camp we saw 30 antelope feeding on the mesa to the south. The whole immensity of the Gila basin lay spread before us in a sunset so quiet you could hear a cricket chirp. It was a sight worth the whole trip."

Middle Fork Trail

The Gila River rises in the wilderness complex as three separate forks that join near the national monument. The 41-mile Middle Fork Trail (U.S. Forest Service Trail 157) follows the Gila River's Middle Fork and is the longest continuous trail in the Gila and one of the longest and most beautiful in the Southwest. For almost its entire length, Middle Fork Trail remains on the bottom of Middle Fork Canyon—the canyon's intricate cliffs looming up to 1,000 feet above you. Because you'll cross the river more than 100 times, the trail is ridden only when the river is low. Beware of quicksand in wet areas along the bank. On a one-way trek you can push along the trail in four days, but five days will give you a more leisurely vacation, and additional days allow layovers, side excursions, or a wide return loop.

Riding north-to-south takes you from Gilita Campground to the national monument. You'll pass remnant cliff dwellings along the way and come upon intriguing side trails, canyons to explore, and lovely meadows to rest in for a while. Two miles from the national monument you can immerse yourself in the same hot springs that were used by the Gila's native tribes. After a wonderful day in the saddle, what could be finer than splashing in a warm pool, surrounded by beautiful scenery? As you relax, look up at the bright blue sky, listen lazily to the gurgling of the nearby stream, and wonder about the ways of the universe.

Coming to Gila Cliff Dwellings National Monument from the wilderness

ALDO LEOPOLD

In 1912 Aldo Rand Leopold (1886–1948) became supervisor of the Carson National Forest in northern New Mexico. With a growing interest in wildlife issues, he switched careers in 1917 to become assistant district forester in charge of game, fish, and recreation. His plan for protecting valued game species was to eliminate their predators. Wolves, bears, and mountain lions had to be exterminated. Gradually, he realized that predators play a vital role in maintaining the health of natural regions.

By 1919 Leopold began advocating the preservation of wilderness for recreational and aesthetic values. His ideas bore fruit in 1924 with the establishment of the Gila Wilderness. As the Gila's status as the world's first designated wilderness gained public attention, Leopold saw that people appreciated wilderness areas for more than just recreational use. He came to see wilderness as a symbol of society's capacity for self-restraint in growth and development. At stake was the quality of people's lives. He also recognized wilderness as a reservoir of the frontier environment, of the "America that was." The American character had been shaped in the wilderness, and here it could be sustained in an increasingly urbanized future.

Leopold was appointed professor of wildlife management at the University of Wisconsin in 1933, the first position of its kind in the country, created especially for him. His wildlife management ideas, adopted by a succession of talented students, quickly dominated the profession. Basic to their philosophy was a land ethic that included animals, plants, soils, and waters, or, collectively, "the land." "An action is right," Leopold said, "when it tends to preserve the integrity, stability, and beauty of the biotic community." He and his students considered the environment not a commodity for humans to exploit, but rather a community to which humans belong.

In 1933 he wrote a textbook on game management that drew heavily on earlier studies of animal ecology by Charles Sutherland Elton in England. In 1935 Leopold and Bob Marshall founded the Wilderness Society to support the establishment of additional wilderness areas. Leopold wrote a number of essays on conservation, published in the classic *A Sand County Almanac* (1949) and *Round River* (1953).

after days of riding in the wild is fun. You'll step out of the woods and confront the modern world while in the same instance encountering the ancient ruins. You're caught in the middle: half natural being of the woods, awed by the homes of the Mogollon Indians who lived and breathed wilderness survival; half urban citizen urgently needing to ask car travelers for the latest international news.

A pit house from around A.D. 100 to 400 is the monument's earliest ruin. The Mogollon grew corn and beans, hunted, and gathered wild plants. They made plain brown pottery and undoubtedly other products that have since perished. Nets, snares, baskets, and wooden tools last only a short time when not protected. Later the people built rectangular masonry houses, set above ground. In the late 1200s they moved into the beautiful cliff dwellings of today's monument. Most of the ruin timbers are original, and tree-ring analysis dates them in the late 1270s to 1280s. The people farmed on the mesatops and along the Gila River. Excellent weavers and skilled potters, they made handsome brown bowls with black interiors, and also black-on-white vessels. The most beautiful black-on-white pottery comes from the Mogollon's Mimbres period, displaying bold geometric designs of animals, humans, and composite shapes. Through trade, the Mogollon obtained cotton, obsidian for arrow points, and seashells for ornaments. Only one generation lived in the cliff dwellings; then they left, perhaps to move closer to the Rio Grande.

Whitewater Canyon–Whitewater Baldy Loop

Whitewater Creek is born in the Gila and flows west into the San Francisco River near Glenwood, New Mexico, cutting a magnificent canyon in the process. A challenging five-day pack trip takes you from the heart of that canyon to Whitewater Baldy, the Gila's highest mountain—a climb of some 5,800 feet, the greatest in the Gila. Near Glenwood the canyon is too narrow for horses, so you mount your horse at the Gold Dust Trailhead on Whitewater Mesa off Highway 159 between Alma, a few miles north of Glenwood, and the old mining town of Mogollon. Here, from the rim of Whitewater Canyon, you'll make a long, steep descent on the hair-raising Gold Dust Trail (U.S. Forest Service Trail 41).

As you descend you'll have plenty of time to ponder who was here before you. After an 1879 Apache raid at Alma, a group of miners lay in wait for the Apaches at Whitewater Canyon, a known Apache entry point into the mountains. The miners tied a horse to a tree as bait, then hid. When the Apaches took the horse, the miners opened fire and killed several Indians. Among the dead was Terribio, a son-in-law of Chief Victorio. Old records indicate it was Terribio's death that set off Victorio's campaign of terror, which didn't end until years later when Victorio was killed by Mexican soldiers.

The outlaw Wild Bunch, led by Butch Cassidy, worked at the

APACHES

The Chiricahua (cheer-uh-COW-uh) Apaches ranged through southwestern New Mexico, southeastern Arizona, and the northern parts of the Mexican states of Sonora and Chihuahua. The Spanish who first met the Chiricahuas described them as a peaceful, nomadic people pursuing a hunting-gathering way of life. Shortly after 1600, Spanish documents begin mentioning Chiricahua depredations. From this point forward the Chiricahuas and other Apaches actively resisted the colonization of the Southwest. When the Chiricahuas acquired horses, probably by the late 1600s, their mobility and the extent of their raiding increased. By 1700 the Chiricahuas were well-organized from a military standpoint. Geronimo joined the resistance when he was admitted to the warriors' council in 1846, at age 17. Geronimo became embittered by the death of his mother, wife, and children at Mexican hands in 1858.

In 1874 some 4,000 Apaches, composed of several Apache groups, were forcibly moved to a reservation at San Carlos, a barren wasteland in southeastern Arizona, where they were required to adopt Christianity and agriculture. Under a disastrous management, the Apaches were kept on short rations and denied traditional tribal rights. Malnourished, homesick, and frustrated, some left the reservation and began intermittent raids under the leadership of Geronimo, Victorio, and Nana.

Geronimo surrendered in September 1886 and was put to hard labor in Florida. He did not see his family again until May 1887, at the Mount Vernon Barracks in Alabama. In 1894 he was moved to Oklahoma's Fort Sill, where he died in 1908 after 22 years of incarceration.

As you ride in the Gila, you'll come upon Apache sites. Lookout Mountain, across Mogollon Creek from Shelley Peak, was used by Geronimo as a sanctuary; teepee rings could still be seen in the early 1900s. Teepee Canyon, in the same area and running into Mogollon Creek, is believed to have been Geronimo's refuge in the winter of 1885.

Mark Nohl/New Mexico Magazine

Gila Cliff Dwellings National Monument's most impressive structures are in "Triple Cave," a cave as long as a football field and 50 feet into the rock.

WS Ranch near Alma around 1899. The robbers terrorized the country as far north as Wyoming. On one outing the Wild Bunch carelessly let Pinkerton detectives trail them home. The gang hid in Whitewater Canyon and escaped.

Farther down Gold Dust Trail you'll see Catwalk National Recreation Trail far below you, reminding you of the days when Whitewater Canyon was central to the Gila mining development. The town of Graham, also called Whitewater, grew up around an ore mill built in 1893 by John T. Graham. When it was discovered that the stream frequently dried up at the mill but ran almost continuously in the mountains near the mines, the mill installed 3 miles of pipeline. Despite this large investment, the Graham mill failed. It closed in 1913, just 10 years after opening. Most of the construction materials, including the pipelines, were salvaged and sold, but some of the old track, affectionately called the Catwalk by miners, stayed in place. In 1978 it became a National Recreation Site.

When South Fork Whitewater Trail (#212) comes into the canyon, point your horse south, then follow Whitewater Creek's East Fork (Trail #213). Near 10,135-foot Grouse Mountain, a piece of Deloche Trail (#179) connects you to Holt–Apache Trail (#181). When you reach 10,535-foot Center Baldy, head north on Crest Trail (#182) and follow it to beautiful Whitewater Baldy, then to Hummingbird Saddle. At Hummingbird Saddle you'll begin your return route, riding west on Whitewater Trail (#207). Gold Dust Trail returns you to your starting point.

Plan to walk along the Catwalk after your ride. Just ahead of the Catwalk, you'll see part of the Graham mill still clinging to the west side of Whitewater Canyon. Mr. and Mrs. William Antrim, parents of Billy the Kid (William Bonney, 1860–1881), were residents of Graham. Mr. Antrim, Billy's stepfather, was the town's blacksmith. In a newspaper interview of the time, Sheriff Harvey H. Whitehill said the boy William Bonney received only a scolding for his first offense of stealing several pounds of butter. Billy next stole $70 from a Chinese merchant in Silver City. The Kid was jailed but escaped through a chimney. After a spree of violent crime, he was dead at age 21.

TRAVEL TIPS
Gila Wilderness Complex

Prime Horseback Season: May–September

Horse Outfitters: Entire Gila: New Mexico Outdoors. Northern Gila (Willow Creek/Snow Lake): N Bar Ranch, San Francisco River Outfitters, U Trail Outfitters. Southern Gila (Silver City): Copper Country Outfitters, Wilderness Guides & Outfitter. Western Gila (Glenwood): San Francisco River Outfitters, U Trail Outfitters.

Stewardship Agency: Gila National Forest, Supervisor's Office, 3005 E. Camino del Bosque, Silver City, NM 88061; (505) 388-8201

General Tourist Information: New Mexico Department of Tourism, (800) 545-2040

PECOS WILDERNESS

"Deer walk upon our mountains, and the quail
Whistle about us their spontaneous cries;
Sweet berries ripen in the wilderness . . . "
Wallace Stevens (1879–1955)

The Southernmost Rockies

The 223,667-acre (90,516-ha) Pecos Wilderness is one of the most beautiful wilderness areas in the American Southwest, but with a classic Rocky Mountain look. A gigantic high-mountain country and 13,000-foot peaks lure with an alpine beauty that visitors to the adjacent Santa Fe high-desert plateau can hardly imagine. Thirty perennial streams and 15 high-mountain lakes are yours to explore, and with luck you may see bighorn sheep, elk, mule deer, black bears, mountain lions, coyotes, foxes, beavers, and a wealth of birds, including wild turkeys. Wildflowers abound all summer long.

The Pecos Wilderness belongs to the Sangre de Cristo Range of the Rocky Mountains—considered by many the Rockies' southern terminus. The Sangre de Cristos extend 200 miles between Salida, Colorado, and Santa Fe, New Mexico, and hold the highest, largest, and most imposing mountains in New Mexico.

The wilderness is named for the Pecos River, born in the "Pecos Horseshoe," a beautiful alpine basin below the Santa Barbara Divide. The river flows south from here and leaves New Mexico near Carlsbad National Park's majestic caverns. Perhaps you recall the song lyric, "She's a mile wide and an inch deep and she flows uphill from Texas"? Not very long ago "west of the Pecos" was presumed to be beyond the outer limit of the civilized world. The river's headwaters were protected in 1933 as the Pecos Primitive Area and, enlarged, became the Pecos Wilderness in 1955.

More than 440 miles of trails explore the Pecos Wilderness. You can enter on the north near Peñasco; on the east, near Las Vegas, New Mexico; on the west from the Santa Fe Ski Basin; and on the south from beyond the town of Pecos. Elevations in the Pecos rise from 8,400 feet in the river valleys to 13,102 feet atop South Truchas Peak, New Mexico's second-highest mountain.

Hamilton Mesa Trail

If you enter the southern Pecos Wilderness from Irongate Campground, Hamilton Mesa Trail (U.S. Forest Service Trail 249) takes you through a

EQUUS•USA

North across Hamilton Mesa, with the Santa Fe Range on your left

dense forest for 2 miles. Suddenly the forest stops and you enter the splendor of Hamilton Mesa, a 5-mile-long alpine meadow offering views of the Pecos' major peaks in one breathtaking sweep: Lake Peak, Santa Fe Baldy, Round Mountain, Pecos Baldy, the Truchas. Find an especially pretty spot (easy to do here), get off your horse, sink into an ocean of wildflowers, and take it all in. You have arrived.

Halfway across Hamilton Mesa you have a choice. You can either ride the rest of Hamilton Mesa and continue to Pecos Falls, or turn left to Beatty's Cabin. Around 1870 pioneer prospector George Beatty built a two-room log cabin on a flat spot near the Pecos River. Nothing remains of the cabin, but the Forest Service has erected a plaque near the site and a number of trails intersect in the area. The best approach to the Truchas Lakes starts here, ascending Rio del Padre. Rumors persist that the Lost Padre Mine, said to have been rich in gold, is nearby. Native Americans, the story goes, worked the mine for a Spanish padre from Chimayo until it was covered by a rock slide.

Half a mile south of Beatty's Cabin, two newer cabins are field stations for the U.S. Forest Service and the New Mexico Department of Game and Fish. One mile south of Beatty's, 400-foot cliffs drop into Pecos Canyon.

As you travel deep within the wilderness, look down: your horse may be clip-clopping on limestone deposited in oceans 300 million years ago. Perhaps you'll spot a fossil shell. If you stop at Pecos Falls—the only high waterfall in the Pecos Wilderness—you'll see a yet-older piece of Earth history. The falls plunge 50 feet over quartzite that was sea-bottom sand more than 570 million years ago, when most living things were still only one cell. Or look up at the high Truchas Peaks, where 570-million-year old layers were lifted skyward by the growing Rockies.

Skyline Trail

The 50-mile Skyline Trail (U.S. Forest Service Trail 251) is the longest continuous trail in the Pecos Wilderness and arcs around the entire upper Pecos River drainage basin. The trail is occasionally quite steep, but gives you incomparable mountain-scenery panoramas and an outstanding overview of the wilderness. If you ride 10 miles a day, you'll need at least five days for a one-way trek. With side trips you can spend weeks.

To ride Skyline Trail east to west, drive north from the town of Pecos past Tererro, then take the jeep road to 11,600-foot Elk Mountain south of the

SANTA FE

Most likely you'll stay in Santa Fe for a few nights surrounding your Pecos Wilderness adventure. Founded in 1610 as the capital of a vast Spanish colonial frontier, Santa Fe is the oldest continuously occupied government seat in the U.S. At an elevation of 6,996 feet, it is also the highest.

The city was established on the site of an old Indian pueblo and developed around a central plaza, quickly becoming the center for Spanish missionary work and exploration. After the Pueblo Indians' revolt in 1680, Santa Fe was abandoned, but was reclaimed in 1692 by Don Diego de Vargas. His conquest is celebrated to this day by the annual Santa Fe Fiesta at the beginning of September.

U.S. interest in Santa Fe was aroused by a report from Lieutenant Zebulon M. Pike, who was imprisoned there by Spanish authorities during his 1806 explorations. Today Santa Fe—a vibrant center for art and architecture—is still the heart of the Southwest.

wilderness boundary. You'll pass the abandoned Pecos Mine, once one of the leading zinc–lead–copper mines of the Southwest. From Elk Mountain you'll ride north on Skyline Trail along the East Range and cross into the wilderness.

Until you emerge at the Santa Fe Ski Area's Aspen Basin, you'll be immersed in the splendor of the Sangre de Cristos. On your left you're riding high above canyons carved by the Mora and Valdez Rivers. On your right, you enjoy superb views across the broad, green expanse of the Rociada Valley far below, and of the granite mass of Hermit's Peak, named for Giovanni Maria de Augustino, who arrived in Las Vegas, New Mexico, in 1863 after walking the Santa Fe Trail from Council Grove, Kansas. He stayed in a cave near Romeroville and began ministering to the poor and sick. Later he moved to a cave 250 feet below the rim, where he remained until 1868.

After Skyline Trail crosses Trail 237 from Mora Flats, you'll find Hamilton Mesa on your left. You'll ride parallel to the great meadow for its entire length, with spectacular views of the peaks you will soon visit. Steller's jay and Clark's nutcracker, members of the crow family, may follow you along the trail, commenting on your progress from high above. After Hamilton ends, Gascon Trail, a livestock route from the eastern valleys, crosses your trail and continues to Pecos Falls. The Skyline arcs west and skirts Rincon Bonito. From 12,641-foot Santa Barbara Peak you'll see the Truchas Peaks to the west, the Taos mountains far to the north, and the Great Plains on the horizon to the east.

The Santa Barbara Divide is a local watershed and the boundary between the Santa Fe and Carson National Forests. Even the saddles of the Santa Barbara are over 12,000 feet. From here you look northward down into the deep valleys of the upper Santa Barbara drainage, toward the town of Peñasco. In the lush basin to the south are the headwaters of the Pecos River.

Near the southwest base of Chimayosos Peak you are at the only vantage point in the wilderness where all three of the lofty Truchas Peaks can be seen at close range. At the two Truchas Lakes, 11,900 feet in elevation, you'll have another excellent but more limited view. Middle Truchas Peak can be climbed from the lakes, but South Truchas Peak is best climbed farther south. On the summit of South Truchas you stand 13,102 feet above sea level. Only Wheeler Peak north of Taos exceeds this in New Mexico, but by only 59 feet. You're on top of the world.

Your mount now takes you south along the Santa Fe Range. Between South Truchas Peak and Pecos Baldy Lake you'll ride the crest of Trailriders Wall, with superb views of the East Range, and the great country in between. Pecos Baldy Lake is the largest lake in the Pecos Wilderness and one of its most beautiful, nestled in a steep glacial cirque directly below 12,529-foot East Pecos Baldy. A good trail leads from lake to summit, offering magnificent views back to the Truchas. West Pecos Baldy is slightly lower at 12,500 feet.

SANTA FE TRAIL

Your route from Santa Fe to the southern Pecos Wilderness will, roughly speaking, follow the Santa Fe Trail along Interstate 25. For hundreds of years Spanish settlers, priests, and military personnel in New Mexico and California were surrounded by wild country and dependent on Spain for supplies. California received regular shipments by sea, but in New Mexico, the Camino Real between Santa Fe and Mexico City was the umbilical cord to the civilized Spanish world.

In the 1700s French traders tried to establish commerce with Santa Fe, but New Mexicans were forbidden to trade with non-Spanish merchants. The French were thrown in jail and their trade goods confiscated. In 1792 New Mexico's governor Concha sent French trapper Pierre (Pedro) Vial east to map a trade route to St. Louis in Spanish Louisiana. Although that route was not officially used, the Santa Fe Trail subsequently ran close to Vial's path. When Mexico won independence from Spain in 1821, trade was opened to outsiders.

Santa Fe Trail merchants led enormous caravans of oxen-drawn wagons across what are now Missouri, Kansas, Colorado, and New Mexico. On Santa Fe's plaza the Santa Fe Trail met the Camino Real. In the 1830s tension between the U.S. and Mexico developed, spurred by Texas' independence from Mexico in 1836 and its annexation to the U.S. in 1845. When the Mexican War erupted in 1846, the Camino Real was the U.S. invasion route into Mexico. Today on the 1,203-mile Santa Fe National Historic Trail, more than 200 miles of wagon ruts remain visible, some 30 miles protected on federal lands.

If you leave Interstate 25 at Glorieta on your way to the southern Pecos, you'll pass the Civil War's Glorieta Battlefield. In 1862, Confederate forces, which had come up the Rio Grande from Texas and had won a series of victories over Union troops, met a combined force of Colorado Volunteers and New Mexico Union soldiers here. In a decisive contest for control of the American West, the union troops won.

In the old days, only Spanish fur trappers were allowed into these mountains; non-Spanish trappers were arrested. With the restrictions lifted in 1821, when Mexico won independence from Spain and inherited New Mexico, trappers swarmed everywhere. Early travelers on the Santa Fe Trail still found the forests filled with deer and bear and the plains and canyons full of antelope and buffalo. Beavers were plentiful, and wolves were so numerous that human graves had to be covered with thick layers of rock. But as the settlers' numbers increased, so did hunting. Everyone hunted at will, and hide hunters roamed the mountains.

In 1866 gold was found in Moreno Valley, and thousands of prospectors arrived the following year. Animal species began to disappear, including grizzlies, wolves, native elk, and Rocky Mountain bighorn sheep. In 1895 Professor L.L. Dyche of the University of Kansas visited the Pecos to collect specimens in danger of extinction and still found a few grizzlies. Elk were reintroduced into the Pecos in 1911 and 1915; Rocky Mountain bighorn sheep in 1965 and 1966. Beavers, nearly extinct in 1830, have managed their own slow comeback.

From Pecos Baldy Lake it's about 6 miles to Horsethief Meadows. As you descend into Horsethief, the trail becomes steep; you may want to dismount and lead your horse. Legend has it that these meadows harbored horses stolen from ranches to the east and south. The horses were rebranded here, then taken west and sold in the Rio Grande valley.

The Sangre de Cristo Mountains were Apache and Comanche hunting grounds. Obsidian artifacts have been found at Horsethief Meadows, and broken shards of pottery dated about A.D. 1500 were found between Horsethief Creek and Panchuela West. Early Spaniards ventured into the mountains only in groups, heavily armed. The first Spanish expedition was in pursuit of fleeing Picuris Indians in 1696. Don Diego de Vargas and his men overtook the Indians. Their return trip, by way of the Mora Valley, began in a blinding blizzard and turned into disaster. Over immense snowdrifts, the journey through today's wilderness took ten long days; 200 horses and five mules were lost.

Lake Katherine is a blue-green mountain jewel set among high cliffs, just below 12,622-foot Santa Fe Baldy. The lake is named for Katherine Chavez Kavanagh, who lived on a nearby ranch and, in the early 1900s, blazed and cleared the trail. Although Santa Fe Baldy's summit is a full 1,000 feet above the lake, you should not miss climbing it. The easiest route is over the grassy slope above the lake's north shore. The memory of having reached the goal will always be with you, and you'll be proud of having stood so high and seen so far.

If you arranged to be collected at the Santa Fe Ski Area, then Lake Katherine and Santa Fe Baldy will be your last two major stops on Skyline Trail. From here the trail descends, taking you into Puerto Nambé with great views of the Rio Grande cutting through the desert below. Penitente Peak, Lake Peak, and Santa Fe Lake guide you to the trail's end.

Pecos National Historic Park's Spanish mission ruins. The Pueblo Indians, including the Pecos tribe, are believed to be descendants of the Anasazi.

Pecos National Historic Park

On your last day in the southern Pecos Wilderness try to get back to your car by 2:00 p.m. so you can visit the ruins of the once-great Pecos Pueblo, situated near Glorieta Pass between the Rocky Mountains and the Great Plains. When Coronado's expedition visited the area in 1541 in search of the Seven Cities of Gold, Pecos Pueblo was the largest, most successful of all New Mexico's pueblos, with an estimated 2,000 residents. The pueblo prospered until about 1720, but by 1750 the population had dwindled from sickness and Comanche raids. In 1768 a smallpox epidemic left only 180 survivors. The few remaining inhabitants emigrated in 1838 to Jemez Pueblo, where the same language was spoken. The abandoned pueblo rapidly fell into decay—a process aided by travelers on the Santa Fe Trail who tore out pueblo beams for firewood. Today the ruins are preserved as the Pecos National Historic Park. The most prominent feature is the tall ruin of a Spanish mission erected in the early 1600s to convert the Indians. The park also encompasses the lands of the former Forked Lightning Ranch of the late actress Greer Garson and her husband, Texas oilman E.E. "Buddy" Fogelson.

TRAVEL TIPS
Pecos Wilderness

Prime Riding Season: July and August

Horse Outfitters: Entire Pecos: New Mexico Outdoors. Southern Pecos: Circle S Stables, Tererro General Store & Riding Stables.

Stewardship Agencies: Santa Fe National Forest, Supervisor's Office, P.O. Box 1689, Santa Fe, NM 87504; (505) 988-6940. Carson National Forest, Supervisor's Office, P.O. Box 558, Taos, NM 87571; (505) 758-6200.

General Tourist Information: New Mexico Department of Tourism, (800) 545-2040

YELLOWSTONE
NATIONAL PARK

*"A vast column of steam issues from a cavern in the side of the hill,
with an opening about 5 feet in diameter. The roaring of the waters in the
caverns, and the noise of the waters as they surge up to the mouth of the opening,
are like that of the billows lashing the sea-shore. The water is as clear as crystal,
and the steam is so hot that it is only when the breeze wafts it aside for
a moment one can venture to take a look at the opening."*

Dr. Ferdinand Vandeveer Hayden (1829–1887)

Hydrothermal Paradise

Yellowstone was the world's first national park, and today is the largest national
park in the lower 48 states. Its 2.2 million acres (890,000 ha), larger than
Rhode Island and Delaware combined, are a wonderland of spouting geysers,
boiling hot springs, and sputtering mud volcanoes. Concentrated geyser activity is found in only two other places in the world, Iceland and New Zealand.
Yellowstone has 150 to 200 geysers—more geysers than the rest of the world
combined. Each has a constantly changing pattern of activity, and altogether
you can admire a staggering total of 10,000 hydrothermal features.

The world's tallest active geyser, Steamboat Geyser, is at Yellowstone, its
periodic eruptions reaching as high as 400 feet. The water spouts in two phases:
a short water phase, and a longer steam phase lasting up to 12 hours. The
world's greatest geyser discharge—990,000 gallons—was given off by Yellowstone's Giant Geyser, which presently lies dormant. Old Faithful is the park's, if
not the world's, most famous geyser. Unlike other jet streams, it is highly
dependable. The spectacle has never failed since first described in 1870.
Currently, once every 70 minutes or so Old Faithful's pressures mount, its interior begins to boil, and thousands of gallons of hot water shoot into the air.
Most of Yellowstone's geysers are located in the geyser basins between Norris
Junction and West Thumb, along the western side of the park. Norris Geyser
Basin should not be missed. Old Faithful is in the Upper Geyser Basin.

When hot waters rise under less pressure, they form hot springs instead
of geysers. Mammoth Hot Springs, a few miles south of the Gardiner,
Montana, park entrance, is Yellowstone's most dramatic hot spring and a
"must see." Over the past 8,000 years nearly 100 individual hot springs have

Yellowstone National Park

Beehive Geyser. Photo tip: geysers are spectacular in early morning light when crisp air billows steam. Afternoons give clear view of water patterns, unobscured by steam.

created a massive network of graceful, steplike stone terraces, many beautifully colored by bacteria and algae living in the warm pools. When the hot waters shift to another place, the abandoned sections turn stunningly snow-white. The 370-foot-diameter Grand Prismatic Spring, in Midway Geyser Basin, is Yellowstone's largest hot spring. Morning Glory Pool along the Firehole River is one of the park's most beautiful hot spring pools.

Twelve miles south of Mammoth Hot Springs you'll come upon 200-foot-high Obsidian Cliff, the most spectacular outcrop of volcanic glass in the country. Native Americans valued Obsidian Cliff as an arsenal to make arrow- and spear heads and sharp, shining knives. The cliff formed during a glacial period when molten magma erupted against glacial ice. Large quantities of molten rock chilled rapidly enough to prevent the growth of crystals; the result was glass. Step up and take a close look. The shiny, swirling patterns you see are the last movements within the molten magma when it suddenly cooled.

Mountain man Jim Bridger (1804–1881) was a teller of tall tales that usually contained a grain of truth. He once looked at Obsidian Cliff, he said, and saw an elk seemingly close on the other side of the glass. "Climbin' to the top what do I see but my elk 25 miles yonder, feedin' as peaceable as you please. That mountain worked just like a magnifyin' glass!"

In Yellowstone, Bridger said, are forests of "peetrified trees a-growin', with peetrified birds on 'em a-singin' peetrified songs." East of Mammoth Hot Springs you'll see Yellowstone's stone forests, the world's most extensive fossil forests, remnants of ancient plants and trees covered by volcanic eruptions and buried for millions of years. Erosion has freed the ancient flora, and you can walk among petrified tree trunks up to 6 feet in diameter and 10 feet high, standing erect with stony roots still gripping the soil. Some of the best vertical stumps are at Specimen Ridge. Sycamore, walnut, magnolia, chestnut, oak, redwood, maple, and dogwood are the most common. The nearest living relatives of many of the trees are now found in the warm-temperate to subtropical forests of the southern and southeastern U.S. The rocks surrounding Specimen Ridge are approximately 50 million years old. A total of 27 layers of alternating plant growth and volcanic blanketing have been counted, indicating 27 separate volcanic eruptions.

Hitting the Trails

Every year about 3 million people visit Yellowstone National Park. Most stay only a short while and travel close to the roads, driving for a day or two along the Grand Loop, a 142-mile narrow and winding figure-eight road that leads to many of the park's major sights. But the roads and developed areas cover less than 3 percent of the park. Just beyond the highway, a few feet off the parking lots, is wilderness. For a more intimate look at the park, first spend at least a week riding a portion of the 97 percent that is backcountry.

Each day among the trees and animals sharpens your senses and changes your perspectives. The slightest discovery, encountered by yourself among a few fellow riders, becomes an event; you feel the wonder and astonishment of early explorers. After a few days, your instincts grow strong and you develop an unbreakable bond with the magnificent world around you. Now fully relaxed and curious about everything, spend three to five days by car along the loop.

You have 1,110 miles of trails to choose from, including the Continental Divide National Scenic Trail (see Weminuche Wilderness section). When you ride along the Continental Divide, you'll find a curious phenomenon called Isa Lake. The lake straddles the Divide, and its waters drain in two directions—west to the Pacific Ocean and east to the Atlantic.

What today is Yellowstone National Park was nearly the last unexplored area in the lower 48. It is the largest area in the contiguous U.S. that has never been farmed, fenced, or developed. As a result, here you'll find the richest concentration of wildlife in the U.S. outside Alaska, and hundreds of lakes, streams, mountains, and valleys in their original, virtually undisturbed condition. Riding here you'll sense what the entire continent was once like.

The world's largest number of elk live at Yellowstone; the summer herd is estimated at 30,000 animals. Yellowstone is also one of the grizzly's last remaining strongholds. Buffalo and pronghorn antelope graze in the meadows; moose meander along the lake shores and marshes. Mule deer live in the park, and so do bighorn sheep, black bears, coyotes, mountain lions, and even reintroduced wolves. Animals harassed elsewhere have a home here.

Most of Yellowstone is a broad, level volcanic plateau about 8,000 feet above sea level, surrounded by Rocky Mountain ranges. Snow clogs the mountain passes for a full nine months. Yellowstone's highest summits are in the volcanic Absaroka Range along the park's eastern border. At 11,358 feet, Eagle Peak in the southern Absarokas is Yellowstone's tallest mountain. The Snowy Range hems Yellowstone on the north, the Gallatin Range extends west, the Red Mountains are on the south, and the mighty Tetons of Grand Teton National Park begin near Yellowstone's southern entrance. Forests are extensive, mostly lodgepole pine. Native American tribes favored this tall, straight tree for the frames of their lodges and teepees, hence the name. The landscape you'll ride through, both on the plateau and in the mountains, was modified by glaciers at least three times over the last 300,000 years. The abrasive power of moving ice and running water scoured the peaks. You'll ride through lush, broad valleys widened by ice; Hayden Valley is an Ice Age lake bed.

Thoroughfare Trail to Republic Pass

Of the many, many excellent trail choices in Yellowstone, let's spend a week or more on a one-way trek across the entire eastern side of the park, from

THE FLIGHT OF THE NEZ PERCÉ

When the Lewis & Clark Expedition visited the Nez Percé Indians in Idaho in 1805, they were impressed with the tribe's Appaloosa horses, developed by the Nez Percé from Spanish stock into the first multicolored horse successfully bred in the New World.

By the 1840s white settlers were moving through Nez Percé territory along the Oregon Trail. In 1855 a treaty with the United States created a large Nez Percé reservation that included most of their traditional land. The 1860 discovery of gold on the Salmon and Clearwater Rivers prompted U.S. commissioners to force the treaty's renegotiation. The commissioners fraudulently reduced the size of the reservation by 75 percent. In 1877 the U.S. government compelled the Nez Percé to move to a small reservation. During the journey hostilities broke out and when the U.S. Army was called in some of the bands fled to the east. Those of the Nez Percé who stayed behind lost their horses. It was reasoned that unmounted the Nez Percé would stop wandering and become farmers.

The fleeing Nez Percé, led by several commanders including Chief Joseph, traveled through the Rocky Mountains and Yellowstone National Park and came upon a group of Yellowstone tourists—Mr. and Mrs. George Cowan and friends. The Nez Percé kidnapped the startled tourists and continued their flight. Two of the white men panicked and George Cowan was shot in the thigh and head. Partially paralyzed and left for dead, Cowan dragged himself on his elbows for three days. When he was found by rescuers, he was barely alive.

The Nez Percé quickly released Mrs. Cowan and her friends and continued east. On the Great Plains they turned north, hoping to find refuge in Canada. Just short of the Canadian border most Nez Percé were overtaken by the U.S. Army near the Bearpaw Mountains, Montana. Before they surrendered on October 5, the Nez Percé freed their horses. Today, the five-month flight is commemorated by the 1,170-mile Nez Percé (Nee-MePoo) National Historic Trail. The tribe has resumed breeding Appaloosas.

south to north. The journey begins in one of the jewels of Yellowstone's backcountry, the Thorofare; takes you along the young Yellowstone River and the eastern shore of mighty Yellowstone Lake; shows you the southern edges of wildlife-rich Pelican Valley; and leaves the park along the probable route of Chief Joseph and his fleeing Nez Percé Indians.

In the park's southeastern corner, just south of Thorofare Ranger Station, you'll mount your horse and head north on Thorofare Trail, following the Yellowstone River as it enters the park from its birthplace on Younts Peak a short distance south of here. Among its many attributes, Yellowstone is the source of large and mighty rivers. The Yellowstone River gave the park its name. *Mi tsi a da zi*, "Rock Yellow River," the Minnetaree Indians called it, for the high yellow-rock cliffs along the upper reaches. French fur trappers translated this as "Yellow Rock" or "Yellow Stone." The Snake River, the Columbia River's largest tributary, also rises outside the southern border of the park, then passes through the park west of where you are presently riding.

The Yellowstone River's gravelly banks and lush marshes are home to spotted sandpipers, sandhill cranes, Canada geese, great blue herons, and a variety of ducks. Elk feed in the meadows early and late in the day, but you may see moose just about anywhere at any time. Black bears and grizzlies are numerous, and you'll see their tracks on Thorofare Trail. As you ride past Thorofare Ranger Station the 10,000-foot Trident Range lies to your right; the massive Two Ocean Plateau rises to 10,115 feet on your left. The plateau's high meadows are the summer home for Jackson Hole elk herds who migrate north and up the hillsides as the season progresses, following the growth cycle of tender sprouts. The Continental Divide cuts across the plateau and Two Ocean Creek separates on the divide, forking into Pacific Creek to the west and Atlantic Creek to the east. About 10 miles into your trek Mountain Creek Trail comes in on your right, leading to Eagle Peak, Yellowstone's highest. As you ride this southern portion of Thorofare Trail you'll see fire scars and signs of new forest growth. In 1988 a huge fire swept the park, affecting 36 percent of it to varying degrees. You'll be clear of the fire damage once you reach Yellowstone Lake but return to it toward the end of your ride.

Trail Creek Trail comes in on your left and leads to Heart Lake, but you'll continue north on Thorofare Trail. Your horse takes you across Beaverdam Creek—a favorite place for grizzlies, moose, elk, and sandhill cranes. Just before the creek you'll ride through a stretch of thick willows. It's difficult to see very far in front of you, so make noise to avoid surprising a grizzly.

Shortly after Beaverdam Creek you'll reach Yellowstone Lake. With 110 miles of shoreline and an elevation of 7,731 feet, Yellowstone is one of the world's largest high-country lakes. The lake's winter ice usually does not break until the first or second week in June. You'll ride along most of the lake's eastern edge, sometimes right at the water, most often in the forests next to it. On this stretch of your sojourn you'll have a chance to marvel at some of the rarest and most threatened species of birds, including the trumpeter swan, the most majestic of all waterfowl. White pelicans live in the park in the summer and you'll see them flapping their wings on the lake's surface, forcing fish into dense schools, then scooping them into their pouches. Carrying the fish would make the birds top-heavy for flight, so they quickly drain off the water and swallow their prey.

At Terrace Point the trail cuts through a series of meadows that offer outstanding views of the country you just left—the valley of the Yellowstone River, Colter Peak, and Two Ocean Plateau. For an even better view, leave your horse in the shade and walk up the open slopes for a quarter of a mile. As you ride on, you'll reach Park Point, another excellent spot for beautiful vistas: Dot and Frank Islands, the Promontory, and the lake's south and southeast arms. Watching the sunset from here is one of the trip's highlights.

Thorofare Trail ends 9 miles east of Fishing Bridge on Yellowstone's East Entrance Road, but your journey is far from over. You'll continue north to Pelican Valley to see grazing buffalo herds, moose wading in the creeks, and osprey diving for trout. West of here the Yellowstone River emerges from Yellowstone Lake and farther north enters the 24-mile-long Grand Canyon of the Yellowstone, one of the world's most breathtaking canyons.

Yellowstone is one of the Earth's largest areas to discover on horseback.

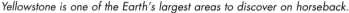

Yellowstone National Park

BUFFALO

With the end of the beaver fur trade in 1840, some beaver trappers became buffalo hunters. The killing of the American buffalo (bison) was already well under way since the animals were competing with settlers' livestock for forage. Some 60 million animals are estimated to have ranged across what are now Canada and the U.S. Although buffalo are primarily grassland inhabitants, they also ranged throughout the eastern woodlands. East Coast settlers first saw buffalo in 1612 near today's Washington, D.C. A buffalo cow and her calf killed in West Virginia in 1825 are the last record of the animal east of the Mississippi. The only traces of the herds' existence were the trails once trampled by their heavy bodies.

In the West the slaughter continued. Millions of buffalo were slain to clear them from western lands, or to prevent damage to railroads. Hundreds of thousands died because buffalo-hide carriage robes became fashionable. Many were killed to furnish a meal of buffalo tongue.

The buffalo was essential to the Plains Indians. The meat was used as food; the hide, for clothing and shelter. Dried buffalo dung was burned for heat. It became clear to the U.S. government that the Native Americans could be more easily subdued if the buffalo were eliminated. With this added impetus, the rate of killing increased. Ironically, many Native Americans joined the slaughter. George Catlin (1796–1872), a lawyer turned artist and author, once saw Indians bring in 1,400 buffalo tongues, which they had cut in one afternoon. White traders paid them with a few gallons of cheap whiskey. "It is not enough," wrote the outraged Catlin, "that we get from the Indian his land, and the very clothes from his back, but the food for his mouth." Much of the hostility between Native Americans and white settlers resulted from the depletion of the buffalo herds.

By 1865 only 15 million buffalo had survived. By 1890 fewer than 1,000 buffalo lived in the U.S. and Canada. By 1900 only two wild herds were known to exist: one in Canada; the other, 21 animals, in Yellowstone National Park. The descendants of the Yellowstone herd usually graze in the Old Faithful and Firehole River thermal basins, and in the Lamar and Hayden Valleys.

Plan to drive to the canyon after your ride and listen to the river sighing and roaring as it cascades 109 feet down the Upper Falls. At Artist Point you'll stand in awe of the magnificent Lower Falls, the Yellowstone River thunderously leaping 308 feet to the canyon below, almost twice the distance of Niagara Falls and one of the longest drops in North America. The 132-foot Tower Fall north of Yellowstone's Grand Canyon is another favored attraction. Altogether, 150 permanent waterfalls grace Yellowstone National Park.

From Pelican Valley, point your horse east on Mist Creek Trail, then north on Lamar River Trail. You're now following the probable route of the fleeing Nez Percé. The Nez Percé entered Yellowstone west of you along the Madison River, slightly north and east of present-day West Yellowstone. At Madison Junction they turned south on the Firehole River, then east along what is now Mary Mountain Trail. They followed the southern edge of Hayden Meadows to Buffalo Ford, where the group crossed the Yellowstone River. Across Pelican Creek they fled into Pelican Valley, and most likely along Mist Creek to the Lamar River—the same way you are riding now. They left the park either at Hondoo Peak, Bootjack Gap, or Republic Pass.

You'll opt for Republic Pass and turn east on Cache Creek Trail. For the first mile your horse carries you through sagebrush, then enters an area of intense burn from the 1988 fires. After 2 miles you'll see Death Gulch and Wahb Springs on the other side of Cache Creek. Death Gulch contains a small thermal area giving off a dangerous gas that has killed everything from sparrows to bears. Wahb Springs is named after the bear in Ernest Thompson Seton's story *Biography of a Grizzly*. When the grizzly Wahb knew his time was up, the huge old bear came to the springs to die.

Near the confluence with South Cache Creek the trail climbs up and away from Cache Creek and follows a tributary. About a mile from Republic Pass the trail leaves the stream and climbs directly to the 10,440-foot pass, where rugged, snow-streaked mountains appear on all sides and grizzlies roam. With a last look back you are leaving Yellowstone National Park. A forest service trail takes you 5 miles down, and the old Irma Mine road connects you with Highway 212 at the east end of Cooke City.

Sheepeaters and Other Travelers

A projectile point found near park headquarters at Mammoth Hot Springs shows that Native Americans hunted in Yellowstone around 9000 B.C. In recent times the only Native Americans living in Yellowstone appear to have been a mixed group of Shoshone and Bannock Indians. In contrast to neighboring bands, this group lacked horses and guns and retreated into the mountains to hunt bighorn sheep. They were known to other tribes as the "Sheepeaters" and, in 1871, were moved to the Wind River Indian

Reservation near Riverton, Wyoming. Old teepee rings and lean-tos are still visible to the discerning eye, and you can follow an ancient Bannock Indian trail from Roosevelt Lodge east of Tower Junction.

After John Colter left the Lewis and Clark expedition in 1806 he worked as a fur trapper and traveled across the American West. Captured by Blackfoot Indians, he was stripped naked, ordered to run for his life, and given a head start. The tribe's swiftest runners followed, armed with spears. After 6 miles Colter outdistanced the Indians and dove into a stream, hiding under a mass of driftwood. When his pursuers left, he walked for seven days in his birthday suit to a fur post on the Big Horn. In 1807, fully clothed, he came into today's park, becoming the area's first white explorer. When he tried to describe Yellowstone three years later in St. Louis, no one believed him. His stories of spouting geysers and gushing hot springs evoked images of fire and brimstone, of the netherworld, and the region became vaguely known as "Colter's Hell."

In 1859 Jim Bridger guided a party of government mapmakers, with Dr. Ferdinand Vandeveer Hayden as head geologist, into Yellowstone, but the expedition encountered deep snow and gave up. In 1869 three Montana miners traveled through Yellowstone as far as Yellowstone Lake. The eruption of Great Fountain Geyser sent them reeling. "We could not contain our enthusiasm," they said. "With one accord we all took off our hats and yelled with all our might." They wrote down their Yellowstone observations and submitted them for publication to various magazines. "Thank you," replied *Lippincott's* magazine in Philadelphia, "but we do not print fiction."

First National Park

In the late summer of 1871 Henry D. Washburn, the surveyor-general of Montana, rode into Yellowstone on horseback with eight other prominent Montana citizens and an Army escort. The party spent 42 days investigating the area and naming many features. "Astonishment and wonder become so firmly impressed upon the mind," wrote Nathaniel P. Langford, a Montana rancher and one of the expedition members, "that belief stands appalled." When they first saw Old Faithful they were entranced; they stayed for nine eruptions. One evening they sat around a campfire and discussed the future of the fantastic region they had explored. Instead of scheming how to make money from it, they felt altruistically that Yellowstone's marvels ought to belong to everyone, and that no part of this wonderland should ever be privately owned.

With the enthusiastic backing of the rest of the group Langford set off for Washington, D.C., where he badgered the government into a federal survey. Dr. Hayden, by then director of the U.S. Geological Survey of the Territories, wanted to return after the failed 1859 attempt. He mounted an official exploration in 1871 that included renowned artist Thomas Moran and famous landscape photographer William Henry Jackson. The combined results—written survey report, photographs, and artist's sketches—were placed on the desk of every senator and congressman, and all reacted the way Langford's group had hoped. The place truly was special. On March 1, 1872, President Ulysses S. Grant signed the bill creating Yellowstone National Park.

TRAVEL TIPS
Yellowstone National Park

Prime Horseback Season: July and August

Horse Outfitters (also see Montana section): Eastern Yellowstone (Cody): Grizzly Ranch Outfitters, Rimrock Ranch Outfitting, Ron Dube's Wilderness Adventures, Sheep Mesa Outfitters, Shoshone Lodge Outfitters, Thorofare-Yellowstone Outfitting. Southern Yellowstone (Jackson Hole): Linn Brothers Outfitting.

Stewardship Agency: Yellowstone National Park, WY 82190; general information, (307) 344-7381; lodging (307) 344-7311

General Tourist Information: Wyoming Department of Tourism, (800) 225-5996

CANADA

Mountain goats. Helen James

JASPER NATIONAL PARK

"National parks are maintained for all the people—for the ill that they may be restored, for the well that they may be fortified and inspired by the sunshine, the fresh air, the beauty, and all the other healing, ennobling and inspiring agencies of Nature. National Parks exist in order that . . . we may absorb the poise and restfulness of the forests; that we may steep our souls in the brilliance of the wild flowers and the sublimity of the mountain peaks . . . that we may be made better, happier and healthier."

James B. Harkin,
First Commissioner of National Parks, Canada, from 1911–1936

Rocky Mountain Majesty and Ice

At over 2.6 million acres (1.1 million ha), Jasper National Park is one of the world's largest national parks. It is in a chain of Rocky Mountain parks and national forests that extends north from Glacier National Park in Montana to Willmore Wilderness Park beyond Jasper, and is a land of massive summits and glaciers, emerald lakes, wild mountain streams, and alpine valleys carpeted with wildflowers. Grizzly and black bears keep you on guard, and coyotes watch you quietly from the forest edge. Mountain lions, lynx, and wolverines have a home here, as have moose, elk, deer, bighorn sheep, and beaver. Over 200 species of birds govern the skies, and a hundred kinds of butterfly glide up on the wind from the prairies.

Traveling from the U.S. you can either drive north and sample the southern Canadian Rockies along the way, or fly into Calgary and rent a car. Either way, try to enter Jasper after a few days in Banff National Park, adjacent to Jasper on the south. Banff was Canada's first national park and is truly magnificent. Then drive for 143 glorious miles on the Icefield Parkway, the most beautiful highway in the world, from Banff's Lake Louise to the town of Jasper inside Jasper National Park. Highlights along the Icefield Parkway are Crowfoot Glacier Viewpoint, Bow Lake, Bow Summit, and the Weeping Wall. Immediately after you enter Jasper National Park, you can visit the Columbia Icefield. If these superlatives haven't yet overwhelmed you, stop at Athabasca Falls, about 12 miles south of the town of Jasper. That will do it.

Fireworks

There you are, at night in Jasper's backcountry in July or August. As you get ready for bed, pleasantly spent and satisfied after a long day in the saddle, you look up to enjoy the vastness of the black, star-studded sky—and what's this? Searchlights from a rescue party on the other side of the ridge? A town lighting up the sky from far, far away? "Look, here," your outfitter shouts from over by the kitchen tent. "Welcome to one of Canada's finest shows. The northern lights, the aurora borealis, have arrived to give you a special night."

You quickly wash up and crawl into your sleeping bag, your head outside the tent. Above you protons and electrons shoot out of the sun's thermonuclear reactions, flinging past our planet at incredible speeds. Some of the charged particles fall into the Earth's magnetic field, accelerate toward the poles, and slam into the thin atmospheric gases. The absorbed energy is given off as light: purple light from molecular nitrogen, greens and reds from atomic oxygen, blue-white in combination. First you see a diffuse ethereal glow on the northeastern horizon, then shafts of light that mark the start of curtainlike shapes. The curtains rise higher and higher until at last the wavy lower edges are clearly seen. Around 2 a.m. or 3 a.m., the aurora is at its best. The lights ripple, flash, and pulsate, catapulting a million amps of electromagnetic energy directly at your camp.

COLUMBIA ICEFIELD

The Columbia Icefield is the Rocky Mountains' largest icefield and one of the most accessible expanses of glacial ice in North America. The ice straddles the Continental Divide and covers some 96,000 acres between the summits of 11,452-foot Mount Athabasca and 12,294-foot Mount Columbia. The Columbia Icefield's meltwaters are the ultimate source of Canada's greatest rivers, including the Athabasca and Columbia. Later, at its end, the mighty Columbia flows into the Pacific Ocean and forms the Oregon–Washington boundary in the U.S.

A short walk takes you right to the ice, or you can tour the icefield's Athabasca Glacier in a park snowmobile. Standing in the summer warmth surrounded by dazzling white, shivering slightly from a glacial breeze, you can imagine what much of North America looked like as late as 8000 B.C. You'll see glacial features normally seen only by mountain climbers and travelers in remote places.

You're about to doze off when you hear howling in the distance. Coyotes? No, wolves. Wolves once lived throughout the northern hemisphere, and in North America still are fairly common from Jasper north. But the animals are shy, and it's unlikely that you will actually see one. If you do, the curious animal may approach to take a closer look but will leave once it smells humans. Wolves are surprisingly tolerant of nonthreatening people, as students of wolves have learned.

Riding Timberline

The next morning you mount your horse and head out. Mountains loom all around you. The Canadian Rockies, though not as high above sea level as other parts of the Rocky Mountains, rise abruptly. Their tops, refined by ice and snow into elegantly sharpened jewels, possess a craggy beauty distinctly their own, and their steepness seems to defy the pull of gravity. In the immensity of the land, space itself becomes palpable and vibrant.

More than 600 miles of trails await you. Over 40 percent of Jasper is above treeline, and as your horse takes you into the highest elevations you'll notice the trees getting increasingly smaller, until finally they are tiny and stunted, barely surviving on this botanical frontier. In New Mexico, at the southern end of the Rocky Mountains, you'll ride into timberline at 12,000 feet. In Banff National Park it starts at 7,500 feet. At Jasper, you're in it at 7,000 feet. Above timberline the mountains become sheer rock walls, gray as slate, relieved only by tundra or glittering white pockets of snow and glacial ice. The park's western edge runs along the crest of the Continental Divide and forms the boundary between British Columbia and Alberta. The highest peak in the Canadian Rockies, 12,972-foot Mount Robson, lies just west of Jasper in British Columbia's Mount Robson Provincial Park. Jasper's highest peak is 11,873-foot Mount Alberta.

With luck you may ride past herds of caribou, another reminder that in Jasper, you're in northern latitudes. You'll enjoy watching mountain goats leaping along cliff faces, up precipices, and over chasms that terrify the bravest and highest-tech-equipped mountain climbers. The unusual wood frog lives at Jasper. In autumn it tugs its back legs under, puts its front legs over its head, and dozes off. Come winter it freezes solid. Yes, solid—no heartbeat, no respiration, no detectable brain activity. In spring the frog thaws and hops away. The wood frog lives as far north as the Arctic Circle and is the most northerly frog in the Western Hemisphere. It lives in damp places and marshes, including above treeline.

In 1923, during his second visit to the park, Sherlock Holmes' creator Sir Arthur Conan Doyle left this entry in the Jasper Park Lodge visitors' book: "A New York man reached Heaven, and as he passed the gate, Peter said, 'I am sure you will like it.' A Pittsburgh man followed, and Peter said,

'It will be a very great change for you.' Finally there came a man from Jasper Park. 'I am afraid,' said Peter, 'that you will be disappointed.'"

Tonquin Valley Horse Trek

Tonquin Valley is one of the grandest places in Jasper National Park and perhaps in the entire Canadian Rockies. A one-way trek through the valley is only 25 miles, but the ride gives you an outstanding experience and can be extended with layover days or by riding back to your starting point, seeing everything afresh in reverse. To reach Maccarib Pass Trail, follow Marmot Basin Road for 4 miles until it crosses Portal Creek. Park in the parking area on the creek's south side, mount your horse, and ascend the narrow canyon of the Portal. Your horse climbs high onto the north side of the valley and carefully traverses the rock slides below Peveril Peak. You have excellent views to the head of the valley and the peaks surrounding Maccarib Pass. Near the pass watch for the caribou for whom the pass is named.

The trail's true reward lies on the western slope of Maccarib Pass. From the first sight of the rugged Rampart Mountains and Moat Pass, each succeeding mile shows you an ever-broadening panorama of the Tonquin Valley and its surrounding peaks. When you reach the beautiful Amethyst Lakes, point your horse east on Astoria River Trail toward Old Horn Mountain.

Unforgettable scenery in Jasper National Park will bring you back again and again.

Scott Rowed/Travel Alberta

LOOKING FOR CARIBOU

Caribou are vegetarians, and you'll see them wander from one tasty lichen patch to the next. But they also feed on grass and shrubs, and the green leaves of birches and willows. The clicking noise you hear as the caribou move is produced by a tendon sliding over a bone in their feet. Caribou are the only deer who congregate in enormous numbers. When still plentiful, up to 200,000 animals migrated together. The land supported such an onslaught because the animals snatch a mouthful and then move on, not depleting their food source; and their hooves splay out, which prevents the soil from turning into a quagmire. On their summer range, caribou break into smaller groups but reassemble in fall to return to the wintering grounds. Caribou numbers have decreased dramatically due to the logging of old-growth forests, human settlement, and human hunters. Of the 500 or so caribou in the Alberta Rockies, 100 to 150 live in Jasper National Park.

Caribou is a New World name. In the Old World, caribou are called reindeer because people put reins on them. Reindeer are ridden routinely by the Arctic peoples of Eurasia, and they pull loaded sleds for days on end. In December 1897 Congress appropriated $200,000 to import 597 Norwegian reindeer along with Lapp handlers to help in the Alaska gold rush, but most of the animals died of hunger for lack of reindeer moss, their staple diet.

Caribou are the only deer species in which the female has horns, though usually smaller and simpler than those of the male. The male sheds his antlers in winter. New antlers grow slowly until warmer weather arrives, then lengthen rapidly. The animals remove the antlers' velvet, or soft covering, by rubbing them against trees. Caribou mate sometime between August and November, depending on location. Mature males fight each other for the control of five to 15 females, roaring mightily from their inflatable throat pouches. Calves are born at the herd's summer range; females lose their antlers after giving birth. Unlike other baby deer, the caribou fawn's coat is not marked with camouflaging spots. A day-old caribou can outrun a human.

You'll switchback down the south slope of Old Horn and continue on the north side of the Astoria River. Through the forest the trail begins the long, gradual climb up Mount Edith Cavell's north slopes and ends at stunning Cavell Lake on Edith Cavell Road.

Skyline Trail

Three special wonders lie in Maligne Valley beyond the town of Jasper: Maligne Canyon, Medicine Lake, and Maligne Lake, at 14 miles the longest natural lake in the Canadian Rockies. Maligne Canyon is an impressive limestone gorge, so narrow in places that squirrels jump across it. Beneath the valley lies a huge limestone cave system. At Medicine Lake the entire Maligne River disappears underground.

You can drive along the Maligne Valley by road, but for a much more satisfying look you can ride portions of the 27-mile Skyline Trail. The best way to see the Skyline is with an outfitter. Private horses aren't permitted between Big Shovel Pass and Maligne Lake, and the trail has no public overnight horse camps. The trail bends far away from the road and stays above treeline half the time. It's one of the most magnificent trails in the Rocky Mountains.

South Boundary Trail

The 108-mile North Boundary Trail and the 103-mile South Boundary Trail are Jasper's longest continuous trails. The South Boundary gives you more serious riding and longer high-country stretches. To ride the South Boundary north to south, drive to Beaver Creek Picnic Area on Maligne Lake Road in the beautiful Maligne Valley and access the South Boundary via the Jacques Lake Trail.

You'll mount your horse at the Jacques Lake Trailhead and begin a gentle 8-mile stretch to Jacques Lake. In this short distance you'll ride through a narrow mountain valley, over a watershed divide, and past four lakes. Your horse crosses the main creek running to Jacques Lake three times, and takes you through several smaller tributaries. Jacques Lake Campground near the lake's outlet is one of the best camping spots along the entire South Boundary route, and even though you haven't ridden very far, you might like to settle down and spend the night.

The next morning, continue on the Jacques Lake Trail as it winds beyond the lake's north end, passes by the Jacques Lake Warden Cabin, and runs northeast down Breccia Creek. For the next miles you are entirely within the forest until your horse takes you down to the rushing waters of the Rocky River at Grizzly Campground. You're now on South Boundary Trail. Twenty-six miles from the Jacques Lake Trailhead you'll reach Rocky Falls,

Crossing one of Jasper's high mountain passes; snow even in summer

Helen James

a waterfall staircase in the Rocky River. You leave the Rocky and follow the Medicine Tent River. A short distance past Medicine Tent Campground, Rocky Pass Trail joins you from the north. Cairn Pass is the highest point of your trek, and the views back down the Medicine Tent River to the Rocky River valley are spectacular. Extensive alpine meadows stretch away from the pass and are dotted with small lakes. Look for the large colony of marmots living at the pass summit.

Beyond Cairn Pass, South Boundary Trail continues in a southeasterly direction and descends through lush meadows for several miles. The low, cone-shaped peak of Southesk Cairn remains visible throughout this stretch. When your horse reaches the mouth of Isaac Creek Canyon, you'll have fine views of the Brazeau Valley and Tarpeian Rock's sheer face. Continuing upvalley you'll alternate between sections of forest and large meadows skirting the Brazeau River. In midsummer the meadows are covered with wood lilies and bluebells. Back into the forest your horse takes you, until you reach Big Springs. Here, large springs gush from the base of a cliff and cascade down to the trail, in the process creating a mini–rain forest in an otherwise semiarid valley.

At the junction with Poboktan Pass Trail consider a short ride to beautiful Brazeau Lake, the largest lake along the South Boundary route. After your excursion, back on South Boundary Trail, you'll continue south past pretty Wolverine South Campground, nestled in a grove of trees beside the Brazeau River. This last leg is one of the most scenic sections of your trek and gives you a fitting climax to South Boundary Trail. At Nigel Pass you cross into Banff National Park and end your trip at the Nigel Pass Trailhead on the Icefields Parkway, near the Columbia Icefield.

TRAVEL TIPS
Jasper National Park

Prime Horseback Season: July and August

Horse Outfitters: Eastern Jasper: Horseback Adventures, Jasper's Backcountry Adventures, Skyline Trail Rides, Tonquin Valley-Amethyst Lakes Wilderness Expeditions. Western Jasper: Borderline Guides, Headwaters Outfitting.

Stewardship Agency: Jasper National Park, P.O. Box 10, Jasper, Alberta T0E 1E0, Canada; (403) 852-6161

General Tourist Information: Alberta Tourism Office, (800) 661-6888 or (403) 427-4321

BEST PLACES TO RIDE:
WORLDWIDE

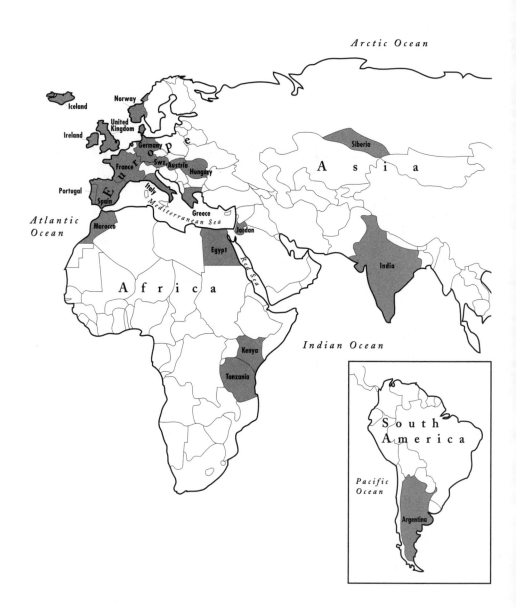

8
BEST PLACES TO RIDE: WORLDWIDE

"Than longen folk to goon on pilgrimages,
And palmers for to seken straunge strondes,
To ferne halwes couthe in sondry londes;
And specially from every shires ende
Of Engelond to Canterbury they wende."
Geoffrey Chaucer (c. 1340–1400),
The Canterbury Tales

Like no other vacation, international riding vacations give you an immediate entry into a foreign country. Horse people the world over feel a special bond and welcome each other's company for riding excursions, for the exchange of horse and riding information, and for companionship. At once you are placed into beautiful countrysides or even onto exclusive private estates. Horses also enable you to travel into vast wilderness regions where vehicles cannot, and your feet might not, take you. There's no better way to see this planet.

Open your world atlas, close your eyes, and point. You've probably landed on a country you can explore on horseback. Hundreds, if not thousands, of horseback rides are available around the globe—more than you can hope to experience in a lifetime.

Riding guides in other countries usually speak at least some English. Your small group of fellow riders will be from all corners of the world, including, perhaps, from North America. The majority tend to come from Europe, where riding vacations have a strong tradition. Most Europeans take mandatory English lessons in school, and English will likely be the common language within the group. The guide and your fellow riders will ease your transition into the host country. If this is your first trip abroad and you feel shy about encountering foreign languages, simply book a trip to an English-speaking country.

Many overseas rides require medium riding skills or better, and are excellent choices for skilled riders seeking a challenge. But some rides are suitable for beginners, and beginners and nonriders are welcome on all stationary programs. Most instructional riding vacations accept riders of all skill levels, from the pure novice to the true expert looking for final refinement. Many overseas vacations use English saddles and tack; some also offer Western.

The costs of these vacations are very reasonable. Most overseas equestrian holidays average from $100 to $200 per person per day—just like in North America—with everything supplied: horses, saddle and tack, riding guides, all meals, camping gear where necessary (except perhaps your own sleeping bag), taxes, and often even airport transfers. The only additional costs are your airfare and gratuities for the riding staff. You can fly to many international destinations for less than $1,000 U.S.

These pages give you an overview of some of the world's most exciting horseback trips. All the vacations are at least a week long; a few give you two weeks or more of adventuresome exploration. Although some international riding vacations involve camping, most are inn-type rides, but don't be misled by the term "inn"—you may stay at a top-of-the-line private estate, a glorious palace, or a fairy-tale castle.

Since it's complicated for the overseas outfitters to book directly with travelers from other countries, the outfitters work through several U.S. booking agents. Their names and addresses are listed at the end of this chapter, including EQUUS★USA, who kindly provided the information for this sec-

One moment Germany's Black Forest awes you, the next you'll ride past a charming village.

Diethard Franz/EQUUS★USA

Diethard Franz/EQUUS•USA

"Bonjour" in France's Auvergne region

tion. The price codes shown in brackets behind each description are based on all-inclusive rates, prime season, per person per day, double occupancy: $ = under $130; $$ = $131–$150; $$$ = $151–$170; $$$$ = $171–$200; $$$$$ = $201 and up.

Africa

Egypt

On purebred Arabian horses you will see Egypt like no other visitors. When the tour buses leave the pyramids in the evening, their splendor is yours to admire from your Berber tent smack next to these world-renowned monuments. As the sun sets and the cooks prepare yet another feast in the kitchen tent, you sit back with a glass of Egyptian red wine and relive the day's experiences. Later, the exotic sound of homemade local music lulls you to sleep, while you hear the gentle stamping of the horses in the desert sand. The next morning you are off again, galloping across the often surprisingly firm desert floor, or making more leisurely progress past farmers tilling their land along the Nile, or groups of women gathered by the river for a communal laundry day. ($–$$)

Kenya

The land of Kenya's Masai is still much as described by Ernest Hemingway and by Karen Blixen in her book *Out of Africa*. The Masai look after their cattle, live in wattle-and-daub huts, hunt lions with nothing but spears, and exude a sense of pride and strength. Their land is home to huge herds of plains game and offers an animal kingdom unrivaled even elsewhere in Africa. When the herds' migration from the Serengeti Plains reaches Masai country in July, up to a million animals are in search of greener pastures. Your drive from Nairobi to the ride start takes you along the Great Rift Valley, then descends 2,000 feet into the plains studded with volcanic mountains. Each day ends with 5 o'clock tea in British-style safari camps. At dinner you can admire the African landscape at sunset and listen to the distant calls of monkeys, lions, and hyenas. ($$$$$)

Morocco

"The Earth is a peacock, and its glorious tail Morocco" is an old saying that describes Morocco's exotic architecture, colorful lifestyles, and general enjoyment of life. Berber villages at the foot of the Atlas Mountains, fanciful adobe castles at the edge of the Sahara, and lush vegetation along the Mediterranean contrast with stern cliffs and rock formations. It's said that the great sultan Mulay Ismael once kept 120,000 horses behind the mighty walls of the city of Fez. Four different rides offer you very different landscapes, from the snow-covered Atlas Mountains to the Sahara Desert sparkling in the sun, or to the beautiful beaches south of Agadirs. Your horse will be a legendary Barb, Arab, or Barb–Arab cross. ($)

Returning to Egypt's Cheops Pyramid after a week in the desert

Diethard Franz/EQUUS-USA

Tanzania

In Tanzania you can experience a true African safari, but on horseback instead of by jeep. No friendly drivers are in radio contact to draw all nearby tourists to a group of sleepy lions. It may take you many hours in the saddle to get the same result, but on horseback you're part of the natural surroundings and can stay far away from the tourist caravans. For five to seven hours a day you ride as fast as the giraffes passing by; or follow alongside herds of zebra, antelope, gazelle, and wildebeest; and from a safe distance watch the "Big Five"—lions, elephants, leopards, water buffalo, and rhinoceri. ($$$$$)

ASIA

India

India offers the exotic charm, colorful architecture, and spectacular landscapes that have lured travelers for thousands of years. Before your ride you can visit attractions such as Delhi, Udaipur, Jaipur, or even the Taj Mahal, but the best way to explore India is on horseback. The villages you visit by horse lie far from the tourist mainstream, but the palaces and castles where you stay at night are fully equipped with all modern comforts. When the distance between guest palaces is more than a day's ride apart, a few overnights are in tents along the way, but even these tents are exceptionally luxurious: high and roomy, with separate sleeping, dressing, and toilet areas. The service is excellent; the food, nothing short of grand. Your horse will likely be a proud Marwari, once regarded a superior war horse, nowadays trained particularly as a polo horse. For a special touch, plan your ride to coincide with a choice of exotic festivals. ($$$–$$$$$)

Russia

Fourteen hundred miles east of Moscow lies a Russia that even Russians hardly know. Its inhabitants may seem poor to us, but they have everything they need for survival and for maintaining an enviable zest for life. Perhaps their ability for happiness is based at least to some extent on the exhilarating scenery of the Altai Mountains. The Altais, also known as "The Mountains of the Yellow Horses," were the last natural habitat for herds of Przewalski's horse, the world's last ancient horse. Horse trails wind through thick forests, across boulder-strewn meadows, over high-mountain passes, and through grasslands with grass so high above your head that it swallows you until you emerge safely on the other side. You might meet Mongolian hunters as they follow their prey into the mountains. Your local hosts still know the true meaning of hospitality, and their food is outstanding. Entire feasts are prepared in the middle of the wilderness, spiced whenever possible with freshly gathered mushrooms and herbs. ($)

EUROPE

Austria

Millions of tourists every year have brought about an infrastructure that makes Austria a perfect country for visitors. Austria has everything: world-renowned scenery; hospitable, charming people; beautiful villages, cities, and towns; interesting cultural events; fascinating landmarks; excellent accommodations; great food and world-famous desserts; an efficient transportation network; and a firm environmental preservation policy. Far from the usual summer crowds, horseback riders enjoy the best vacations of all. One ride takes you for eight fabulous days high into the Alps between the world-famous ski resort of Kitzbühel and the spectacular Hohe Tauern alpine national park.

Another choice takes you from Austria's Mühlviertel to southern Bohemia in the former Czechoslovakia. This is the former border region where, over the past 50 years, no towns or villages were allowed to exist. You'll gallop faster than the waves of the Moldau River, then plunge into a shallow spot for a communal swim of horses and riders. Once dry, you're off across gentle hills to a hearty lunch of Bohemian specialties or freshly caught trout at a former convent or fine country inn. ($)

England

England's Exmoor region is prime horse country. Highlands and moors await you, lovely valleys strewn with lakes, and charming villages with straw-covered roofs—and of course, it's never far from tea time. Another great ride takes you to Wales. Who can resist the land of the wild Welsh, with its dramatic coastline, green hills, fertile valleys, lovely lakes, and steep Black Mountains? During the inn rides you overnight at friendly guest farms and country hotels. If you choose a stationary vacation, you'll stay at a farm nestled in lush green hills. Your cozy room, decorated with antique English furniture, looks down on your hostess' carefully groomed rose garden, and beyond into the high moors. Each day you'll ride in half-day or full-day increments to the loveliest spots in the region. ($–$$$)

France

In France, the mother country of the *randonnée*, the riding tour as it was first defined, you find riding holidays par excellence. Do I need to mention the meals and breads and wines? Come try for yourself and see why French food makes grown men weep. In the valley of the Loire River and its sister rivers Cher and Indre, your ride is a tour through history, with the Middle Ages and the Renaissance as primary background. The royal house of Valois-Orléans-Angoulême had both the power and the funds to stray from the usual building of castles—designed to protect from enemy attacks—to the luxurious manifestations of more recreation- and pleasure-oriented residences. Nonriders may travel in horse-drawn carriages.

The Provence-Camargue is sun country and one of the most beautiful and historically rich areas in France. Trails lead past deep forests, endless meadows, and golden wheat fields. The Carmargue's black steers and white horses graze in lush pastures. Thyme, rosemary, sage, and lavender—the last, the holy flower of the Provence—grow wild and permeate the countryside with a scent you'll never forget. ($–$$$$$)

The defensive walls of Bonifacio on France's Mediterranean island of Corsica

Diethard Franz/EQUUS•USA

Corsica: To the first-time visitor, Corsica appears as a single white mountain rising straight from the ocean floor. The island is actually made of a large number of peaks, 51 of them over 6,000 feet above sea level, that provide surprisingly different landscapes. No roads lead to the coastline, and your horse provides the best means to visit uncrowded beaches. ($$)

Germany

Germany is a land of many contrasts: of the politically conservative south and the politically progressive north; of ultramodern cities like Frankfurt and beautifully maintained medieval villages that make you think you've stumbled into a time warp; of charming, open hospitality and a cautious approach to new encounters; of a past that gave in to the darker forces in life and a new, earnest attempt to become a leading force of what is good or at least fair; of everyone's learning "high" German and the thousands of regional dialects used in everyday living; of the creation of some of the most modern ways of doing things and the talent for *Gemütlichkeit*, a warm, nurturing expression of relaxation, coziness, and an unhurried way of life; of capitalist greed and the generous provision of a social safety net for all who are less well-off; of a fine sense of humor and a pressing need to be "serious"; of homebodies who seldom move away from their birthplace and world travelers familiar with the remotest corners of the globe. If you have an open mind, this country and its people will fascinate you.

For eight wonderful days you'll ride through the Black Forest's fabled woods and fairy-tale hills. Warm summer evenings find you sitting on a veranda with a stein of good beer or a delicate glass of fine wine, talking over the day's riding adventures until sleep gets the better of you. It's time to turn in, to sink deeply into clouds of down bedding, to take a last whiff of the sun-dried, fresh linen, to dream of tomorrow's ride.

Another treat is to stay at a castle offering dressage and jumping instruction. Special weeks are set aside for beginning adult riders. Scheduled rides into the beautiful, forested countryside complete your riding days, and there is plenty of opportunity to hike, bicycle, and jog along special fitness trails or to explore the area by car—for example, into the nearby Black Forest. ($–$$)

Greece

Henry Miller once wrote, "Marvelous things happen to one in Greece—marvelous good things which can happen nowhere else on Earth." To soak up some of the magic, you can ride from Mount Olympus to Pilion, or visit antiquity at Olympia, Messene, Pylos, and Nestor's palace. The Pilion peninsula is 63 miles long and only 13 miles wide and climbs in less than 6 miles

Ancient amphitheater: the stuff of Greek tragedies and myths

Diethard Franz/EQUUS•USA

from sea level to an elevation of 4,800 feet. It's home to about 20 villages, some plastered on the sides of the slopes, some hidden in narrow valleys, some set high on top as though trying to touch the sky.

On foot you'll enjoy the narrow, winding alleyways where neighbors leisurely exchange the latest gossip. Memories of the vivid scents of basil, geraniums, and gardenias from the hidden courtyards will always stay with you and will bring immediate longings for these wonderful days whenever you encounter the scents again. It's highly appropriate to explore Greece— the home of the centaur—on horseback. ($–$$)

Hungary

The friendly Hungarian people are known for their enjoyment of life. Colorful celebrations and folk dances are ways of expressing this life-affirming attitude, as is the pride manifested in the creation and mainte-nance of beautiful villages and towns. The horse is an integral part of Hungary's past and present. Huge herds of horses still roam the country-side, just as they did at the time of the Hussars. Your horse will be a proud Kisber of the Hussars' ancient bloodlines. One popular ride takes you from the famous wine-growing region of Tokaj into the Hortobagy national park that protects 250,000 acres of Hungarian *puszta*, the immense areas of steppe with which Hungary is almost synonymous. Another wonderful ride is in Hungary's northeastern corner in the Zemplén mountains, a seemingly endless chain of volcanic peaks between the romantic Bodrog and Hernád rivers. You'll discover remote farmhouses nestled in the countryside and imposing castles perched high on mountain slopes. ($$$)

Iceland

Pristine nature, wide-open landscapes, glaciers, geysers, and Iceland's slumbering but nonetheless active volcanoes attract riders to visit many times over. All Icelandic rides take along double or triple the usual number of horses to prevent exhaustion in the rough terrain. The rest of the herd runs freely with the riders, a special treat. Along the way, you'll stay in small guest houses or mountain huts where available, or in school dormito-ries in sleeping bags where not. Iceland is famous for its thermal pools, and you can count on never being more than a few nights away from their warmth and relaxation. From the end of May to the end of August is the time of the Midnight Sun, of never-dark nights.

On the most demanding Iceland ride you travel for 10 great days around Lake Lagarfljót, cross the highlands of western Iceland, and ride within reach of Iceland's largest glacier, Vatnajökull. Wild reindeer herds abound, as do pink-footed wild geese. ($$$)

Ireland

In Ireland, the land is so green that artists are hard-pressed to reproduce its intensity and true hues. In the northwestern corner of the green land, in Ireland's county of Donegal, you'll find endless beaches, gentle hills, deep forests, and high moors. Hitch your horse at the local pub, especially after dinner, when the entire countryside seems drawn by magnet to check in with each other, to lift a few Guinnesses, to break into friendly song, or to challenge each other to a fierce game of darts. Wouldn't you like to join them? ($–$$)

Italy

Sardinia: An old legend explains how Sardinia came into existence. After God had created the Earth, he still had some leftover rocks. He threw them into the middle of the Western Mediterranean and stepped on them with his gigantic foot to secure them to the ocean floor. But he was not satisfied. From each of the continents he took various items and sprinkled them across the island. Thus Sardinia became its own little world, filled with aspects of the rest of the planet.

Today this beautiful island is considered one of Europe's major attractions,

Riding on Italy's island of Sardinia, the Mediterranean and delectable seafood dinners are always just hoofbeats away.

Diethard Franz/EQUUS•USA

but most visitors see only the north coast. The rest of the island offers long beaches, steep cliffs, and fertile agricultural lands that produce rich harvests of wine, olives, almonds, and artichokes. Unforgettable, too, are the aromas of the Mediterranean pine and eucalyptus trees. The highlands of Giara are home to Italy's only herds of wild horses. ($)

Tuscany: A mild climate, rich history, high standards in art and architecture, a lush Mediterranean landscape, and a famous cuisine have attracted visitors for thousands of years to Italy's Tuscany region between Florence and Siena—whether Italians such as Dante and da Vinci, or foreign admirers like Goethe. You'll stay at a beautiful estate that has been carefully upgraded into a fine country inn with all the modern conveniences, and ride each day through gentle hills, along meandering rivers, and through small forests. You'll be driven back to the country inn every evening to enjoy an excellent dinner and the local wines, while the horses spend the night on location. In the morning you're returned to the horses to continue exploring the fine countryside. In the Maremma nature park, you have the choice of returning to the inn that night or camping along the beach, perhaps after a friendly beach party with your fellow riders. ($)

Norway

The Scandinavian countries are justly considered bulwarks of unspoiled nature. Their regions are relatively sparsely populated, and their people have demonstrated wisdom from the start in striking a fine balance between living on the land and not abusing the privilege. In Norway your ride leads from the town of Savalen through some of the country's most breathtaking inland scenery. You travel over rocky highlands where reindeer roam, through dense forests where berries and mushrooms provide tasty meals for elk, and across pristine mountain streams and past clear lakes where you can drink the water without fear. ($)

Portugal

Lusitano is the horse breed the Portuguese are so proud of, and with good reason. Riding the famous Lusitanos is a real treat: the horses are especially beautiful, strong, and sensitive, and Portugal itself provides a superb backdrop to ensure a memorable vacation. At one of Portugal's outstanding riding stables 35 expertly trained horses help beginners as well as advanced riders enhance their dressage skills. Instruction is available to the highest levels. Each lesson is not limited to 45 minutes or an hour, but lasts as long as is necessary for a rider to understand a given task. The program can be extended each day with trail rides into the beautiful surroundings or into the nearby Mafra wildlife refuge. The Silver Coast ride takes you along the

Costa de Prata's wide beaches and imposing cliffs, then through the Mafra wildlife refuge, through fragrant eucalyptus forests, along marshlands and lagoons rich in birdlife, near olive groves and vineyards, and past white windmills into romantic villages for the evening. ($$$)

Spain

Andalusía: Spain's romantic Andalusía region is one of Europe's most popular equestrian destinations, with broad pampas, colorful canyons, extensive olive groves, Mediterranean pine forests, endless beaches, towering ocean cliffs, and Moorish villages and towns with narrow alleys and delightful inner courtyards. You ride from Jimena on the Mediterranean coast of Gibraltar to the beaches at Zahara. Only 19 miles from Seville, a classic Andalusían estate returns you to a time you might have thought forgotten. Here, among olive groves and foothills, riders of all skill levels choose either a riding instruction package, a trail package, or a combination.

On Spain's famous Sun Coast, the Costa del Sol, in the mountains less than 4 miles out of Fuengirolo is an excellent breeding and training center for Andalusían horses. If you've never ridden before, you might like to stay ten days. Within a week you'll join the daily rides into the surrounding countryside. The more advanced riders head out each day for up to five hours of exploration, and you can choose a two-day ride to Alhaurin el Grande.

Spain is hardly imaginable without its colorful festivals and celebrations. Although usually based at least in part on religious rituals, none of the celebrations lacks any of the ingredients of a truly "good time"—and the festivities rarely lack horses, an integral part of what Spaniards deem important in life. The local horsefolk will quickly welcome you into their midst and make you one of the crowd. ($)

Extremadura: Extremadura, in western Spain, extends from the Gredos and Gata mountain ranges to Andalusía, and from Castille to Portugal. The region is rich in particularly attractive landscapes—wide plains as well as snow-covered peaks, fertile valleys, lush pastures ringed with Mediterranean oak, giant wheat fields, dramatic rock formations, and picturesque lakes and rivers. The countryside boasts a wealth of wildlife. Remnants of a varied past are never far away: Celts, Romans, Goths, and Arabs have left their imprints. Medieval palaces, ruins, convents, and chapels sprinkle the countryside.

Extremadura is the home of the conquistadors Cortéz, Pizarro, De Soto, and Balboa, who left here to conquer the New World. You will stay in Spanish *paradores*—luxurious country lodgings that were once castles, convents, or large estates—usually situated in outstanding scenery. Your mount will be a beautiful Spanish horse whose ancestors traveled with the conquistadors to the New World and reintroduced horses to the Americas. ($$)

A picture to send home from a sleepy Spanish town. After lunch you'll head into the Extremadura countryside for another superb horseback adventure.

MIDDLE EAST

Jordan

Lawrence of Arabia is familiar to most people, not the least because of his book *The Seven Pillars of Wisdom* and the epic film based on it. If you've seen the movie, you'll quickly have a feeling for what this ride is all about. Your journey starts at the rock formations of Wadi Rum, sprouting straight out of the desert and attracting mountain climbers from all over the world. You continue through one of the world's most beautiful desert regions to Petra, the "rose-red city half as old as time," cut into living rock, one of the architectural wonders of antiquity. Along the way you'll meet the desert-dwelling Bedouins and will probably be their guest on more than one occasion. The ride ends at Aqaba, a well-known beach and diving resort on the Red Sea. Jordan is a constitutional monarchy, with a parliament freely elected by the population, including the country's women. Seventy percent of the 4 million inhabitants live in cities, but about 80,000 nomads still move their camels, sheep, goats, and chickens in search of sporadic rainfall. The primary religion is Islam, but all other religions are legally protected and are freely practiced without fear of discrimination. ($$$$)

SOUTH AMERICA

Argentina

The splendors of the Argentinean Nahuel Huapi national park, high in the Andes, are yours for 12 glorious days. The 1,850,000-acre park is located on the western edge of the Patagonian Rio Negro province and surrounds the always-snow-covered, 11,660-foot Tronador peak. The land is rich in wildlife and bejeweled with mountain lakes and rivers. At the foot of the Andes you'll ride through thick forests, then start climbing to the heights. ($)

U. S. BOOKING AGENTS
For Worldwide Horseback Vacations

Boojum Expeditions, 14543 Kelly Canyon Rd., Bozeman, MT
    59715; (406) 587-0125; fax (406) 585-3474

Equitour, P.O. Box 807, Dubois, WY 82513; (800) 545-0019;
    (307) 455-3363; fax (307) 455-2354

EQUUS★USA, Route 7 Box 124-MU, Santa Fe, NM 87505;
    (800) 982-6861; (505) 982-6861; fax (505) 984-8119

FITS Equestrian, 685 Lateen Rd., Solvang, CA 93463;
    (800) 666-3487; (805) 688-9494; fax (805) 688-2943

9
OUTFITTER DIRECTORY

This directory lists the addresses and telephone numbers for the North American vacation providers mentioned throughout *Saddle Up!* But the directory's real usefulness is its selection criteria, which allows you to match the "what, where, when, and how long" of your vacation planning (see Chapter 2, Planning Your Riding Vacation) with the companies that offer what you are looking for.

What? Which companies specialize in the type of riding vacation you desire?

Where? Which vacation providers service the state or region where you want to ride?

When and how long? Which outfitters arrange scheduled rides? Which make custom dates?

Sooner or later, most vacation decisions become a question of money. The bracketed price codes shown with each listing are based on all-inclusive rates, prime season, per person per day, double occupancy, for scheduled dates: $ = up to $130; $$ = $131–$150; $$$ = $151–$170; $$$$ = $171–$200; $$$$$ = more than $200. Where only custom dates exist, the prices are per person per day in a group of at least four.

When you have selected the two or three companies who meet your criteria, follow the final selection steps laid out in the Selecting Your Outfitter section of Chapter 2.

All of the listed vacation providers were given the opportunity to check their listings in this book. However, it's always best to confirm prices and other details before making your reservations. Reservations for all of the listed vacations can be placed free of charge through EQUUS★USA (see page 245) or your local travel agent.

A LAZY H OUTFITTERS
P.O. Box 729, Choteau, MT 59422;
(800) 893-1155; (406) 466-5564.
Types: Wilderness Expeditions: Bob
Marshall Wilderness Complex.
Scheduled Dates: Yes [$$$], maximum
guests 8.
Custom Dates: Minimum guests 4,
maximum 8.
**Children's Minimum Age (accompa-
nied):** Varies.
Saddle: Western.
Minimum Skill: Novice. Divides by
Skill? No.
Airport Transfers: Charge from Great
Falls, Montana.
Own Horse: No.

ADRIFT ADVENTURES
P.O. Box 577, Moab Utah 84532;
(800) 874-4483; (801) 259-8594.
Types: Horse/Raft Combos.
Scheduled Dates: Yes [$$–$$$].
Custom Dates: Maximum guests varies.
**Children's Minimum Age (accompa-
nied):** Varies.
Saddle: Western.
Minimum Skill: Novice. Divides by
Skill? No.
Airport Transfers: Free from Moab,
Utah.
Own Horse: No.

ADVENTURE SPECIALISTS
Bear Basin Ranch, Westcliffe, CO
81252; summer, (719) 783-2519; winter,
(719) 630-7687.
Types: Horse/Raft Combos.
Scheduled Dates: Yes [$$$], maximum
guests 8.
Custom Dates: Minimum guests 2,
maximum 40.
**Children's Minimum Age (accompa-

nied): Varies.
Saddle: Western.
Minimum Skill: Novice. Divides by
Skill? Yes.
Airport Transfers: Free from Colorado
Springs.
Own Horse: Yes, by special advance
arrangement.

ADVENTURES ON HORSEBACK
32628 Endeavour Way, Union City, CA
94587; (510) 487-9001.
Types: Inn Rides, Instructional Riding
Vacations.
Scheduled Dates: Yes [$$–$$$$], maxi-
mum guests 6.
Custom Dates: Minimum guests 2,
maximum 6.
**Children's Minimum Age (accompa-
nied):** 12.
Saddle: English and Endurance.
Minimum Skill: Novice. Divides by
Skill? Yes.
Airport Transfers: Free from Oakland,
California (or San Francisco, San Jose).
Own Horse: No.

ALL 'ROUND RANCH
P.O. Box 153, Jensen, UT 84035-0153;
(800) 603-8069; (801) 789-7626.
Types: Instructional Riding Vacations.
Scheduled Dates: Yes [$$$–$$$$], max-
imum guests 12.
Custom Dates: Minimum guests 8,
maximum 12.
**Children's Minimum Age (accompa-
nied):** 12.
Saddle: Western.
Minimum Skill: Novice. Divides by
Skill? Yes.
Airport Transfers: Free from Vernal,
Utah.
Own Horse: No.

ARIZONA RIVER RUNNERS

P.O. Box 47788, Phoenix, AZ 85068-7788; (800) 477-7238; (602) 867-4866.
Types: Horse/Raft Combos.
Scheduled Dates: Yes [$$$$$], maximum guests varies.
Custom Dates: Yes.
Children's Minimum Age (accompanied): Varies.
Saddle: Western.
Minimum Skill: Novice. Divides by Skill? No.
Airport Transfers: Free from Las Vegas, Nevada.
Own Horse: No.

BAR TEN RANCH

P.O. Box 1465, St. George, UT 84771; (800) 582-4139; (801) 628-4010.
Types: Cattle Roundups, Wilderness Expeditions: Grand Canyon National Park.
Scheduled Dates: No.
Custom Dates: Minimum guests 6, maximum varies [$–$$].
Children's Minimum Age (accompanied): Varies.
Saddle: Western.
Minimum Skill: Novice. Divides by Skill? Varies.
Airport Transfers: Charge scenic flight Las Vegas, Nevada (or rental car).
Own Horse: No.

BEAR CREEK GUEST RANCH

P.O. Box 151, East Glacier Park, MT 59434; (800) 445-7379; (406) 226-4489.
Types: Wilderness Expeditions: Bob Marshall Wilderness Complex.
Scheduled Dates: Yes [$$$$], maximum guests 8.
Custom Dates: Minimum guests 2, maximum 8.

Children's Minimum Age (accompanied): 7.
Saddle: Western.
Minimum Skill: Novice. Divides by Skill? No.
Airport Transfers: Free from Kalispell, Montana.
Own Horse: Yes, by special advance arrangement.

BEAR PAW OUTFITTERS

136 Deep Creek Road, Livingston, MT 59047; (406) 222-6642.
Types: Wilderness Expeditions: Yellowstone National Park.
Scheduled Dates: No.
Custom Dates: Minimum guests 4, maximum 17 [$$$$$].
Children's Minimum Age (accompanied): 6.
Saddle: Western.
Minimum Skill: Novice. Divides by Skill? Yes.
Airport Transfers: None. Rental car Bozeman, Montana.
Own Horse: Yes, by special advance arrangement.

BEARTOOTH PLATEAU OUTFITTERS

P.O. Box 1127, Roberts, MT 59070; (800) 253-8545.
Types: Wilderness Expeditions: Yellowstone National Park.
Scheduled Dates: Yes [$$$$$], maximum guests 8.
Custom Dates: Minimum guests 1, maximum 8.
Children's Minimum Age (accompanied): 6.
Saddle: Western.
Minimum Skill: Novice. Divides by Skill? Yes.
Airport Transfers: Free from Billings,

Montana.
Own Horse: No.

BEDELL PACK TRAINS
P.O. Box 61, Three Rivers, CA 93271;
(209) 561-4142; (209) 561-3404.
Types: Horse Drives, Wilderness
Expeditions: Pacific Crest Trail, Sequoia
and Kings Canyon National Parks.
Scheduled Dates: Yes [$–$$$], maximum guests 12.
Custom Dates: Minimum guests 4,
maximum 12.
Children's Minimum Age (accompanied): Varies.
Saddle: Western.
Minimum Skill: Novice. Divides by
Skill? No.
Airport Transfers: None. Rental car:
Fresno, California.
Own Horse: No.

BIG SKY OVERLAND CRUISES
P.O. Box 112, Ovando, MT 59854;
(800) 762-2762; (406) 793-5675.
Types: Wagon Trains.
Scheduled Dates: Yes [$], maximum
guests 10.
Custom Dates: Minimum 2, maximum
10.
Children's Minimum Age (accompanied): All ages welcome.
Saddle: Western.
Minimum Skill: Novice. Divides by
Skill? No.
Airport Transfers: Charge from
Helena or Missoula, Montana.
Own Horse: No.

BORDERLINE GUIDES
P.O. Box 434, Valemount, British
Columbia, Canada V0E 2Z0;
(604) 566-9161.

Types: Wilderness Expeditions: Jasper
National Park.
Scheduled Dates: Yes [$$], maximum
guests 8.
Custom Dates: Minimum guests 2,
maximum 8.
Children's Minimum Age (accompanied): Varies.
Saddle: Western.
Saddle: Novice. Divides by Skill? No.
Airport Transfers: None. Rental car
Edmonton or Calgary, Alberta.
Own Horse: No.

BROKEN SKULL CATTLE COMPANY
P.O. Box 774054, Steamboat Springs,
CO 80477; (970) 879-0090.
Types: Cattle Drives.
Scheduled Dates: Yes [$$–$$$], maximum guests 10.
Custom Dates: No.
Children's Minimum Age (accompanied): Varies.
Saddle: Western.
Minimum Skill: Novice. Divides by
Skill? Yes.
Airport Transfers: Free from
Steamboat Springs, Colorado.
Own Horse: Yes, by special advance
arrangement.

BROKEN SPOKE RANCH
4250 Whitewater Creek Road,
Whitewater, CO 81527; (970) 241-3949.
Types: Cow Camps.
Scheduled Dates: Yes [$$], maximum
guests 10.
Custom Dates: No.
Children's Minimum Age (accompanied): 8.
Saddle: Western.
Minimum Skill: Novice. Divides by

Skill? Yes.
Airport Transfers: Free from Grand Junction, Colorado.
Own Horse: Yes, by special advance arrangement.

CALIFORNIA'S REDWOOD COAST RIDING VACATION

24201 North Highway 1, Fort Bragg, CA 95437; (888) 873-5777; (707) 964-7669. Worldwide Web: http://www.horse-vacation.com.
Types: Inn Rides, Instructional Riding Vacations.
Scheduled Dates: Yes [$$$$–$$$$$], maximum guests 24.
Custom Dates: Minimum guests 1, maximum 30.
Children's Minimum Age (accompanied): 6.
Saddle: English and Western.
Minimum Skill: Novice. Divides by Skill? Yes.
Airport Transfers: Charge from San Francisco, California.
Own Horse: Yes, by special advance arrangement.

CHEYENNE RIVER RANCH

1031 Steinle Road, Douglas, WY 82633; (307) 358-2380.
Types: Cattle Drives, Cattle Roundups.
Scheduled Dates: Yes [$$$$], maximum guests 10.
Custom Dates: No.
Children's Minimum Age (accompanied): 11.
Saddle: Western.
Minimum Skill: Novice. Divides by Skill? Yes.
Airport Transfers: Charge from Casper, Wyoming.
Own Horse: No.

CIRCLE S STABLES

Route 1 Box 3-B, Gloriete, NM 87535; (505) 757-8440; (505) 382-7708.
Types: Wilderness Expeditions: Pecos Wilderness.
Scheduled Dates: No.
Custom Dates: Minimum guests 4, maximum 8 [$$].
Children's Minimum Age (accompanied): 8.
Saddle: Western.
Minimum Skill: Novice. Divides by Skill? No.
Airport Transfers: Charge from Santa Fe, New Mexico.
Own Horse: No.

COLORADO TRAILS RANCH

12161 County Road 240, Durango, CO 81301-6306; (800) 323-3833; (970) 247-5055.
Types: Instructional Riding Vacations.
Scheduled Dates: Yes [$–$$$], maximum guests 75.
Custom Dates: Yes.
Children's Minimum Age (accompanied): All ages welcome.
Saddle: English and Western.
Minimum Skill: Novice. Divides by Skill? No.
Airport Transfers: Free from Durango, Colorado.
Own Horse: No.

COPPER COUNTRY OUTFITTERS

P.O. Box 2333, Silver City, NM 88062; (505) 388-2127.
Types: Wilderness Expeditions: Gila Wilderness Complex.
Scheduled Dates: No.
Custom Dates: Minimum guests 1, maximum varies [$].
**Children's Minimum Age

(accompanied): Varies.
Saddle: Western.
Minimum Skill: Novice. Divides by
Skill? No.
Airport Transfers: Charge from El
Paso, Texas.
Own Horse: No.

DALTON GANG ADVENTURES

P.O. Box 8, Monticello, UT 84535;
(801) 587-2416.
Types: Cow Camps.
Scheduled Dates: Maximum guests 6
[$$].
Custom Dates: No.
**Children's Minimum Age (accompa-
nied):** Varies.
Saddle: Western.
Minimum Skill: Novice. Divides by
Skill? Yes.
Airport Transfers: Free from Cortez,
Colorado, and Moab, Utah.
Own Horse: No.

DON DONNELLY STABLES

6010 S. Kings Ranch Road, Gold
Canyon, AZ 85219; (800) 346-4403;
(602) 982-8895.
Types: Wilderness Expeditions:
Monument Valley, Superstition
Wilderness.
Scheduled Dates: Yes [$$$–$$$$$],
maximum guests varies.
Custom Dates: No.
**Children's Minimum Age (accompa-
nied):** 8.
Saddle: Western.
Minimum Skill: Novice. Divides by
Skill? Yes.
Airport Transfers: MV: free from
Gallup, New Mexico. SW: free from
Phoenix, Arizona.
Own Horse: No.

EARLY WINTERS OUTFITTING

HCR 74 Box B6, Mazama, WA 98833;
(800) 737-8750; (509) 996-2659.
Types: Wilderness Expeditions: Pacific
Crest Trail.
Scheduled Dates: Yes [$$], maximum
guests 8.
Custom Dates: Minimum guests 6,
maximum 8.
**Children's Minimum Age (accompa-
nied):** Varies.
Saddle: Western.
Minimum Skill: Novice. Divides by
Skill? No.
Airport Transfers: Charge from
Wenatchee, Washington.
Own Horse: No.

ED BLACK HORSEBACK TOURS

P.O. Box 310155, Mexican Hat, UT
84531; (801) 739-4285.
Types: Wilderness Expeditions:
Monument Valley.
Scheduled Dates: No.
Custom Dates: Minimum guests 5,
maximum 25 [$].
**Children's Minimum Age (accompa-
nied):** Varies.
Saddle: Western.
Minimum Skill: Novice. Divides by
Skill? No.
Airport Transfers: None. Rental car
Cortez, Colorado.
Own Horse: No.

EKNEL TOURS

34011 North 136th Street, Scottsdale,
AZ 85262; (602) 991-0000; (602)
910-0150.
Types: Wilderness Expeditions:
Monument Valley.
Scheduled Dates: Yes [$$$$], maximum
guests 8.

Custom Dates: Minimum guests 4, maximum 8.
Children's Minimum Age (accompanied): 8.
Saddle: Western.
Minimum Skill: Novice. Divides by Skill? Yes.
Airport Transfers: Free from Phoenix, Arizona.
Own Horse: Yes, by special advance arrangement.

ENCINITOS RANCH

P.O. Box 3309, Alice, TX 78333; (800) 222-3824; (512) 568-3429.
Types: Cattle Roundups.
Scheduled Dates: Yes [$$], maximum guests 10.
Custom Dates: No.
Children's Minimum Age (accompanied): Varies.
Saddle: Western.
Minimum Skill: Novice. Divides by Skill? Yes.
Airport Transfers: Free from McAllen or Harlingen, Texas.
Own Horse: Yes, by special advance arrangement.

EVERETT RANCH

10615 County Road 150, Salida, CO 81201; (719) 539-4097.
Types: Cow Camps.
Scheduled Dates: Yes [$], maximum guests 10.
Custom Dates: No.
Children's Minimum Age (accompanied): Varies.
Saddle: Western.
Minimum Skill: Novice. Divides by Skill? Yes.
Airport Transfers: Charge from Colorado Springs or Denver, Colorado.

Own Horse: Yes, by special advance arrangement.

FIREFLY RANCH

P.O. Box 152, Bristol, VT 05443; (802) 453-2223.
Types: Inn Rides.
Scheduled Dates: Yes [$$$], maximum guests 6.
Custom Dates: Minimum guests 1, maximum 6.
Children's Minimum Age (accompanied): Varies.
Saddle: English and Western.
Minimum Skill: Medium. Divides by Skill? Yes.
Airport Transfers: Charge from Burlington, Vermont.
Own Horse: No.

FOX EQUESTRIAN

2000 County Road 30A, Walden, CO 80480; (800) 391-4735; (970) 723-4325.
Types: Instructional Riding Vacations.
Scheduled Dates: Yes [$$$$$], maximum guests 15.
Children's Minimum Age (accompanied): Able to ride full-sized horses.
Saddle: English (Stuebben).
Minimum Skill: Able to jump 18-inch (0.5 m) fences. Divides by Skill? Yes.
Airport Transfers: None. Rental car Denver, Colorado.
Own Horse: Yes, by special advance arrangement.

FRONTIER PACK TRAIN

2095 Van Loon, Bishop, CA 93514; summer, (619) 648-7701; winter, (619) 873-7971.
Types: Horse Drives, Wilderness Expeditions: Pacific Crest Trail, Yosemite National Park, Wildlife

Safaris: Mustangs.
Scheduled Dates: Yes [$–$$], maximum guests 12.
Custom Dates: Minimum guests 2, maximum 12.
Children's Minimum Age (accompanied): Varies.
Saddle: Western.
Minimum Skill: Varies. Divides by Skill? Varies.
Airport Transfers: Free from Mammoth Lakes, California.
Own Horse: Yes, by special advance arrangement.

GLACIER PACK TRAIN
P.O. Box 321, Big Pine,
CA 93513; (619) 938-2538.
Types: Wilderness Expeditions: Pacific Crest Trail, Sequoia and Kings Canyon National Park.
Scheduled Dates: No.
Custom Dates: Yes [$$$$$].
Children's Minimum Age (accompanied): Varies.
Saddle: Western.
Minimum Skill: Novice. Divides by Skill? No.
Airport Transfers: None. Rental car Reno, Nevada.
Own Horse: No.

GLACIER RAFT COMPANY
P.O. Box 218-D, West Glacier, MT 59936; (800) 332-9995; (406) 888-5454.
Types: Horse/Raft Combos.
Scheduled Dates: Yes [$$–$$$$], maximum guests 12.
Custom Dates: Minimum guests 4, maximum 12.
Children's Minimum Age (accompanied): Varies.
Saddle: Western.

Minimum Skill: Novice. Divides by Skill? No.
Airport Transfers: Charge from Kalispell, Montana.
Own Horse: No.

GRAND CANYON NATIONAL PARK LODGES
Reservations, P.O. Box 699, Grand Canyon, AZ 86023; (303) 297-2757.
Types: Wilderness Expeditions (mules, cabins): Grand Canyon National Park.
Scheduled Dates: Yes [$], minimum 1 year advance reservation (or standby).
Custom Dates: No.
Children's Minimum Height: 4 feet 7 inches (1.38 m).
Saddle: Western.
Minimum Skill: Novice. Divides by Skill? No.
Airport Transfers: None. Rental car/bus Grand Canyon Airport.
Own Horse: No.

GREAT DIVIDE TOURS
336 Focht Road, Lander, WY 82520; (800) 458-1915; (307) 332-3123.
Types: Cattle Drives, Cattle Roundups, Horse Drives, Wagon Trains.
Scheduled Dates: Yes [$$–$$$], maximum guests 12.
Custom Dates: Varies.
Children's Minimum Age (accompanied): Varies; Wagon Trains: all ages welcome.
Saddle: Western.
Minimum Skill: Varies (horse drives for experts only). Divides by Skill? Yes.
Airport Transfers: Free from Riverton, Wyoming.
Own Horse: Yes, by special advance arrangement.

GRIZZLY RANCH OUTFITTERS

North Fork Route, Cody, WY 82414;
(307) 587-3966.
Types: Wilderness Expeditions:
Yellowstone National Park.
Scheduled Dates: No.
Custom Dates: Minimum guests 4,
maximum 10 [$$$$].
Children's Minimum Age (accompanied): Varies.
Saddle: Western.
Minimum Skill: Novice. Divides by
Skill? No.
Airport Transfers: Free from Cody,
Wyoming.
Own Horse: No.

HALF MOON CATTLE COMPANY

P.O. Box 573, El Prado, NM 87529;
(800) 830-0080; (505) 758-8379.
Types: Cow Camps.
Scheduled Dates: Yes [$$$], maximum
guests 6.
Custom Dates: No.
Children's Minimum Age (accompanied): Varies.
Saddle: Western.
Minimum Skill: Novice. Divides by
Skill? Yes.
Airport Transfers: None. Rental car
Albuquerque, New Mexico, or Alamosa,
Colorado.
Own Horse: Yes, by special advance
arrangement.

HALF MOON ENTERPRISES

P.O. Box 172, Lavina, MT 59046;
(800) 526-8786; (206) 255-7367.
Types: Cattle Drives with Wagon
Trains.
Scheduled Dates: Yes [$$$$$], maximum guests 30.
Custom Dates: No.

Children's Minimum Age (accompanied): All ages welcome.
Saddle: Western.
Minimum Skill: Novice. Divides by
Skill? Yes.
Airport Transfers: Free from Billings,
Montana.
Own Horse: Yes, by special advance
arrangement.

HAVASUPAI TOURIST ENTERPRISE

Supai, AZ 86435; (520) 448-2121.
Types: Wilderness Expeditions
(motel/own camping): Grand Canyon
National Park.
Scheduled Dates: No.
Custom Dates: Yes [$].
Children's Minimum Age (accompanied): Varies.
Saddle: Western.
Minimum Skill: Novice. Divides by
Skill? No.
Airport Transfers: None. Rental car
Grand Canyon or Flagstaff, Arizona.
Own Horse: No.

HEADWATERS OUTFITTING

P.O. Box 818, Valemount, British
Columbia, Canada V0E 2Z0;
(604) 566-4718.
Types: Wilderness Expeditions: Jasper
National Park.
Scheduled Dates: No.
Custom Dates: Minimum guests 2,
maximum 6 [$$].
Children's Minimum Age (accompanied): 12.
Saddle: Western.
Minimum Skill: Novice. Divides by
Skill? No.
Airport Transfers: None. Rental car
Edmonton or Calgary, Alberta.
Own Horse: No.

HIGH ISLAND RANCH
P.O. Box 71, Hamilton Dome, WY
82427; (307) 867-2374.
Types: Cattle Roundups.
Scheduled Dates: Yes [$–$$$$], maximum guests 25.
Custom Dates: No.
Children's Minimum Age (accompanied): 12.
Saddle: Western.
Minimum Skill: Novice. Divides by Skill? Yes.
Airport Transfers: Charge from Cody, Wyoming.
Own Horse: Yes, by special advance arrangement.

HONDOO RIVERS AND TRAILS
P.O. Box 750098, Torrey, UT 84775-0098; (800) 332-2696; (801) 425-3519.
Types: Cattle Roundups, Horse/Raft Combos, Wilderness Expeditions: Capitol Reef National Park; Wildlife Safaris: Bighorn, Buffalo, Elk, Mustang.
Scheduled Dates: Yes [$$–$$$], maximum guests 10.
Custom Dates: Minimum guests 1, maximum 8.
Children's Minimum Age (accompanied): 14.
Saddle: Western.
Minimum Skill: Novice. Divides by Skill? Yes.
Airport Transfers: Charge from Grand Junction, Colorado.
Own Horse: Yes, by special advance arrangement.

HORSEBACK ADVENTURES
P.O. Box 73, Brulé, Alberta, Canada
T0E 0C0; (403) 865-4777.
Types: Wilderness Expeditions: Jasper National Park.

Scheduled Dates: Yes [$], maximum guests 14.
Custom Dates: Minimum guests 4, maximum 14.
Children's Minimum Age (accompanied): Varies.
Saddle: Western.
Minimum Skill: Novice. Divides by Skill? No.
Airport Transfers: Charge from Edmonton, Alberta.
Own Horse: No.

JAKE'S HORSES
5645 Ramshorn, Gallatin Gateway, MT
59730; (406) 995-4630.
Types: Wilderness Expeditions: Yellowstone National Park.
Scheduled Dates: No.
Custom Dates: Minimum guests 2, maximum varies [$$].
Children's Minimum Age (accompanied): Varies.
Saddle: Western.
Minimum Skill: Novice. Divides by Skill? No.
Airport Transfers: None. Rental car Bozeman, Montana.
Own Horse: No.

JASPER'S BACKCOUNTRY ADVENTURES
RR#1, Bittern Lake, Alberta, Canada
T0C 0L0; (403) 672-4173.
Types: Wilderness Expeditions: Jasper National Park.
Scheduled Dates: Yes [$], maximum guests 16.
Custom Dates: Minimum guests 6, maximum 16.
Children's Minimum Age (accompanied): Varies.
Saddle: Western.

Minimum Skill: Novice. Divides by
Skill? No.
Airport Transfers: Free from
Edmonton, Alberta.
Own Horse: Yes, by special advance
arrangement.

JJJ WILDERNESS RANCH

P.O. Box 310, Augusta, MT 59410;
(406) 562-3653.
Types: Wilderness Expeditions: Bob
Marshall Wilderness Complex.
Scheduled Dates: Yes [$$$$], maximum
guests varies.
Custom Dates: Yes.
**Children's Minimum Age (accompa-
nied):** Varies.
Saddle: Western.
Minimum Skill: Novice. Divides by
Skill? No.
Airport Transfers: Charge from Great
Falls, Montana.
Own Horse: No.

KEDRON VALLEY STABLES

P.O. Box 368, South Woodstock, VT
05071; (800) 225-6301; (802) 457-1480.
Types: Inn Rides, Instructional Riding
Vacations.
Scheduled Dates: Yes [$$$$–$$$$$],
maximum guests 10.
Custom Dates: Minimum guests 4,
maximum 10.
**Children's Minimum Age (accompa-
nied):** Varies.
Saddle: English.
Minimum Skill: Medium. Divides by
Skill? Yes.
Airport Transfers: Charge from
Lebanon, New Hampshire.
Own Horse: No.

LAJITAS STABLES

Star Route 70 Box 380, Terlingua, TX
79852; (915) 424-3238.
Types: Horse/Raft Combos.
Scheduled Dates: No.
Custom Dates: Minimum guests 4,
maximum varies [$].
**Children's Minimum Age (accompa-
nied):** Varies.
Saddle: Western.
Minimum Skill: Novice. Divides by
Skill? Yes.
Airport Transfers: None. Rental car El
Paso or San Antonio, Texas.
Own Horse: No.

LINN BROTHERS OUTFITTING

P.O. Box 71, Wilson, WY 83014;
(307) 733-2425.
Types: Wilderness Expeditions:
Yellowstone National Park.
Scheduled Dates: No.
Custom Dates: Minimum guests 2,
maximum 12 [$$$$].
**Children's Minimum Age (accompa-
nied):** 8.
Saddle: Western.
Minimum Skill: Novice. Divides by
Skill? No.
Airport Transfers: None. Rental car
Jackson, Wyoming.
Own Horse: No.

LOST VALLEY RANCH

29555 Goose Creek Road, Sedalia, CO
80135-9000; (303) 647-2311.
Types: Instructional Riding Vacations.
Scheduled Dates: Yes [$], maximum
guests varies.
Custom Dates: No.
**Children's Minimum Age (accompa-
nied):** Varies. **Saddle:** Western.
Minimum Skill: Novice. Divides by

Skill? No.
Airport Transfers: Charge from Colorado Springs or Denver, Colorado.
Own Horse: No.

MONTANA HIGH COUNTRY CATTLE DRIVE

669 Flynn Lane, Townsend, MT 59644; (800) 345-9423; (406) 266-3612.
Types: Cattle Drives with Wagon Trains.
Scheduled Dates: Yes [$$$$], maximum guests 35.
Custom Dates: No.
Children's Minimum Age (accompanied): All ages welcome.
Saddle: Western.
Minimum Skill: Novice. Divides by Skill? Yes.
Airport Transfers: Free from Bozeman, Montana.
Own Horse: No.

MONTANA SAFARIS

P.O. Box 1004, Choteau, MT 59422; (800) 959-2004; (406) 466-2004.
Types: Wilderness Expeditions: Bob Marshall Wilderness Complex.
Scheduled Dates: Yes [$$].
Custom Dates: Minimum guests 1, maximum 10.
Children's Minimum Age (accompanied): 6.
Saddle: Western.
Minimum Skill: Novice. Divides by Skill? Yes.
Airport Transfers: Free from Great Falls, Montana.
Own Horse: Yes, by special advance arrangement.

MONTURE OUTFITTERS

P.O. Box 112, Ovando, MT 59854;

(800) 762-2762; (406) 793-5618.
Types: Wilderness Expeditions: Bob Marshall Wilderness Complex.
Scheduled Dates: No.
Custom Dates: Minimum guests 2, maximum 10 [$$$$$].
Children's Minimum Age (accompanied): Varies.
Saddle: Western.
Minimum Skill: Novice. Divides by Skill? No.
Airport Transfers: Charge from Missoula, Montana.
Own Horse: No.

MOUNTAIN TOP INN, MOUNTAIN TOP ROAD

Chittenden, VT 05737; (800) 445-2100; (802) 483-2311.
Types: Inn Rides, Instructional Riding Vacations.
Scheduled Dates: No.
Custom Dates: Minimum guests 1, maximum varies [$$$–$$$$].
Children's Minimum Age (accompanied): 8.
Saddle: English and Western.
Minimum Skill: Novice. Divides by Skill? Yes.
Airport Transfers: Charge from Burlington, Vermont.
Own Horse: Yes, by special advance arrangement.

MW RANCH

19451 195th Ave., Hudson, CO 80642; (303) 536-4206.
Types: Cattle Drives.
Scheduled Dates: Yes [$$], maximum guests 28.
Custom Dates: No.
Children's Minimum Age (accompanied): 18.

Saddle: Western.
Minimum Skill: Novice. Divides by
Skill? Yes.
Airport Transfers: Free from Alamosa,
Colorado.
Own Horse: Yes, by special advance
arrangement. Horse: No.

N BAR RANCH
P.O. Box 409, Reserve, NM 87830;
(800) 616-0434; (505) 533-6253.
Types: Cattle Roundups, Wilderness
Expeditions: Gila Wilderness Complex.
Scheduled Dates: Yes [$], maximum
guests 15.
Custom Dates: Varies.
**Children's Minimum Age (accompa-
nied):** 12.
Saddle: Western.
Minimum Skill: Novice. Divides by
Skill? Yes.
Airport Transfers: Free from
Albuquerque, New Mexico.
Own Horse: Yes, by special advance
arrangement.

NEW MEXICO OUTDOORS
Route 7 Box 124-MU, Santa Fe, NM
87505; (800) 982-6861; (505) 982-6861.
Types: Cattle Roundups, Cow Camps,
Horse/Raft Combos, Inn Rides,
Wilderness Expeditions: Gila
Wilderness, Pecos Wilderness.
Scheduled Dates: Yes, for Gila [$].
Custom Dates: Minimum guests 4,
maximum 12 [$–$$$$$].
**Children's Minimum Age (accompa-
nied):** 5.
Saddle: Western.
Minimum Skill: Novice. Divides by
Skill? Yes.
Airport Transfers: Charge for some;
rest rental cars.

Own Horse: Yes, for Wilderness
Expeditions by special arrangement.

NORTH CASCADE OUTFITTERS
P.O. Box 395, Twisp, WA 98856;
(509) 997-1015.
Types: Wilderness Expeditions: Pacific
Crest Trail.
Scheduled Dates: No.
Custom Dates: Minimum guests 4,
maximum varies [$$].
**Children's Minimum Age (accompa-
nied):** Varies.
Saddle: Western.
Minimum Skill: Novice. Divides by
Skill? No.
Airport Transfers: None. Rental car
Seattle, Washington.
Own Horse: No.

OUTBACK RANCH OUTFITTERS
P.O. Box 269, Joseph, OR 97846; (503)
432-9101.
Types: Horse/Raft Combos.
Scheduled Dates: No.
Custom Dates: Minimum guests 1,
maximum 30 [$$$].
**Children's Minimum Age (accompa-
nied):** Varies.
Saddle: Western.
Minimum Skill: Novice. Divides by
Skill? No.
Airport Transfers: Charge from
Lewiston, Idaho.
Own Horse: No.

OUTDOOR ADVENTURES PLUS
4030 W. Amazon, Eugene, OR 97405;
(503) 344-4499.
Types: Wilderness Expeditions: Pacific
Crest Trail.
Scheduled Dates: No.
Custom Dates: Minimum guests 4,

maximum 6 [$$$$$].
Children's Minimum Age (accompanied): Varies.
Saddle: Western.
Minimum Skill: Novice. Divides by Skill? No.
Airport Transfers: Free from Eugene, Oregon.
Own Horse: No.

OVER THE HILL OUTFITTERS

3624 County Road 203, Durango, CO 81301; summer, (970) 259-2834; winter, (970) 247-9289.
Types: Wilderness Expeditions: Weminuche Wilderness.
Scheduled Dates: No.
Custom Dates: Minimum guests 2, maximum 6 [$$$].
Children's Minimum Age (accompanied): 6.
Saddle: Western.
Minimum Skill: Novice. Divides by Skill? No.
Airport Transfers: Free from Durango, Colorado.
Own Horse: No.

PAVOREAL GUEST RANCH

27475 Ynez Road #289, Temecula, CA 92591; (909) 767-3007.
Types: Instructional Riding Vacations.
Scheduled Dates: Yes [$$$$], maximum guests 12.
Custom Dates: Minimum guests 6, maximum 12.
Children's Minimum Age (accompanied): 10.
Saddle: English and Western.
Minimum Skill: Novice. Divides by Skill? Yes.
Airport Transfers: None. Rental car San Diego, California.
Own Horse: No.

PINE CREEK PACK STATION

P.O. Box 968, Bishop, CA 93515; (800) 962-0775; (619) 387-2797.
Types: Wilderness Expeditions: Pacific Crest Trail, Sequoia and Kings Canyon National Parks.
Scheduled Dates: Yes [$], maximum guests 15.
Custom Dates: Minimum guests 1, maximum 15.
Children's Minimum Age (accompanied): Varies.
Saddle: Western.
Minimum Skill: Novice. Divides by Skill? No.
Airport Transfers: Free from Bishop or Mammoth Lakes, California.
Own Horse: Yes, by special advance arrangement.

PLEASANT CREEK OUTFITTERS

P.O. Box 102, Bicknell, UT 84715; (800) 892-4597; (801) 425-3315.
Types: Wilderness Expeditions: Capitol Reef National Park.
Scheduled Dates: No.
Custom Dates: Minimum guests 2, maximum 10 [$].
Children's Minimum Age (accompanied): 6.
Saddle: Western.
Minimum Skill: Novice. Divides by Skill? No.
Airport Transfers: None. Rental car Grand Junction, Colorado.
Own Horse: No.

POWDER RIVER WAGON TRAINS AND CATTLE DRIVES

P.O. Box 676, Broadus, MT 59317; (800) 492-8835; (406) 436-2404.
Types: Cattle Drives with Wagon Trains.

Scheduled Dates: Yes [$$$$], maximum guests 60.
Custom Dates: No
Children's Minimum Age (accompanied): All ages welcome.
Saddle: Western.
Minimum Skill: Novice. Divides by Skill? Yes.
Airport Transfers: None. Rental car Billings, Montana.
Own Horse: Yes, by special advance arrangement.

RAINBOW PACK STATION

P.O. Box 1791, Bishop, CA 93515; (800) 443-2848; (619) 873-8877.
Types: Wilderness Expeditions: Pacific Crest Trail, Sequoia and Kings Canyon National Parks.
Scheduled Dates: Yes [$], maximum guests 15.
Custom Dates: Minimum guests 1, maximum 15.
Children's Minimum Age (accompanied): Varies.
Saddle: Western.
Minimum Skill: Novice. Divides by Skill? No.
Airport Transfers: Free from Bishop or Mammoth Lakes, California.
Own Horse: No.

RAPP GUIDES AND PACKERS

47 Electra Lake, Durango, CO 81301; (970) 247-8923; (970) 247-8454.
Types: Wilderness Expeditions: Weminuche Wilderness.
Scheduled Dates: Yes [$$$$$], maximum guests 10.
Custom Dates: Minimum guests 4, maximum 10.
Children's Minimum Age (accompanied): 10.

Saddle: Western.
Minimum Skill: Novice. Divides by Skill? Yes.
Airport Transfers: Free from Durango, Colorado.
Own Horse: Yes, by special advance arrangement.

RED ROCK RIDE

P.O. Box 128, Tropic, UT 84776; (801) 679-8665.
Types: Wilderness Expeditions: Grand Canyon National Park.
Scheduled Dates: Yes [$$$$$], maximum guests 25.
Custom Dates: Minimum guests varies, maximum 25.
Children's Minimum Age (accompanied): 12.
Saddle: Western.
Minimum Skill: Advanced beginners. Divides by Skill? Yes.
Airport Transfers: Free from Las Vegas, Nevada.
Own Horse: Yes, by special advance arrangement.

RED'S MEADOW PACK STATION

P.O. Box 395, Mammoth Lakes, CA 93546; (800) 292-7758; summer, (619) 934-2345; winter, (619) 873-3928.
Types: Horse Drives, Wagon Trains, Wilderness Expeditions: Pacific Crest Trail, Yosemite National Park.
Scheduled Dates: Yes [$–$$$], maximum guests varies.
Custom Dates: Yes.
Children's Minimum Age (accompanied): Varies.
Saddle: Western.
Minimum Skill: Novice. Divides by Skill? Varies.
Airport Transfers: Free from

Mammoth Lakes, California.
Own Horse: No.

RENDEZVOUS OUTFITTERS

P.O. Box 447, Gardiner, MT 59030;
(800) 565-7110; (406) 848-7110.
Types: Wilderness Expeditions:
Yellowstone National Park.
Scheduled Dates: No.
Custom Dates: Minimum guests 2,
maximum varies [$$$$$].
Children's Minimum Age (accompanied): Varies.
Saddle: Western.
Minimum Skill: Novice. Divides by
Skill? No.
Airport Transfers: None. Rental car
Bozeman, Montana.
Own Horse: No.

RIMROCK RANCH OUTFITTING

2728 North Fork Route, Cody, WY
82414; (307) 587-3970.
Types: Wilderness Expeditions:
Yellowstone National Park.
Scheduled Dates: No.
Custom Dates: Minimum guests 1,
maximum varies [$$$$].
Children's Minimum Age (accompanied): Varies.
Saddle: Western.
Minimum Skill: Novice. Divides by
Skill? Yes.
Airport Transfers: Free from Cody,
Wyoming.
Own Horse: No.

R.K. MILLER'S WILDERNESS WILDERNESS EXPEDITIONS

P.O. Box 467, Livingston, MT 59047;
(406) 222-7809; (406) 586-6702.
Types: Wilderness Expeditions:
Yellowstone National Park.

Scheduled Dates: Yes [$$$$$], maximum guests 10.
Custom Dates: Minimum guests 4,
maximum 10.
Children's Minimum Age (accompanied): Varies.
Saddle: Western.
Minimum Skill: Novice. Divides by
Skill? No.
Airport Transfers: Free from Bozeman
or Billings, Montana.
Own Horse: No.

ROCK CREEK PACK STATION

P.O. Box 248, Bishop, CA 93515; summer, (619) 935-4493; winter, (619) 872-8331.
Types: Cattle Roundups, Horse Drives,
Wilderness Expeditions: Pacific Crest
Trail, Sequoia and Kings Canyon
National Parks, Yosemite National Park;
Wildlife Safaris: Mustangs.
Scheduled Dates: Yes [$–$$], maximum
guests 12–25.
Custom Dates: Varies.
Children's Minimum Age (accompanied): 6. **Saddle:** Western.
Minimum Skill: Novice. Divides by
Skill? Yes.
Airport Transfers: Free from Bishop or
Mammoth Lakes, California.
Own Horse: Yes, by special advance
arrangement.

RON DUBE'S WILDERNESS ADVENTURES

P.O. Box 167, Cody, WY 82450;
(307) 527-7815.
Types: Wilderness Expeditions:
Yellowstone National Park.
Scheduled Dates: Yes [$$$$–$$$$$],
maximum guests 8.
Custom Dates: Minimum guests 4,

maximum 8.

Children's Minimum Age (accompanied): Varies.

Saddle: Western.

Minimum Skill: Novice. Divides by Skill? No.

Airport Transfers: Free from Cody, Wyoming.

Own Horse: No.

RON-D-VIEW OUTFITTING

1151 Anna Road, Ignacio, CO 81137; (970) 563-9270.

Types: Wilderness Expeditions: Weminuche Wilderness.

Scheduled Dates: Yes [$], maximum guests 6.

Custom Dates: Minimum guests 4, maximum 6.

Children's Minimum Age (accompanied): 6.

Saddle: Western.

Minimum Skill: Novice. Divides by Skill? Yes.

Airport Transfers: Free from Durango, Colorado.

Own Horse: Yes, by special advance arrangement.

ROYAL PALMS TOURS

P.O. Box 60079, Fort Myers, FL 33906; (800) 296-0249; (941) 368-0760.

Types: Inn Rides.

Scheduled Dates: Yes [$$$$$], maximum guests 14.

Custom Dates: Minimum guests 8, maximum 14.

Children's Minimum Age (accompanied): 12.

Saddle: Western.

Minimum Skill: Novice. Divides by Skill? Yes.

Airport Transfers: Free from Fort Myers, Florida.

Own Horse: Yes, by special advance arrangement.

SANFORD RANCHES

P.O. Box 191, Thermopolis, WY 82443; (307) 864-3575.

Types: Cow Camps.

Scheduled Dates: Yes [$], maximum guests 12.

Custom Dates: No.

Children's Minimum Age (accompanied): Varies.

Saddle: Western.

Minimum Skill: Novice. Divides by Skill? Yes.

Airport Transfers: Free from Cody, Wyoming.

Own Horse: No.

SAN FRANCISCO RIVER OUTFITTERS

Route 10 Box 179-C, Glenwood, NM 88039; (505) 539-2517.

Types: Wilderness Expeditions: Gila Wilderness Complex.

Scheduled Dates: No.

Custom Dates: Minimum guests 1, maximum 10 [$].

Children's Minimum Age (accompanied): 7.

Saddle: Western.

Minimum Skill: Novice. Divides by Skill? Yes.

Airport Transfers: Charge from El Paso, Texas.

Own Horse: No.

SAWTOOTH OUTFITTERS

P.O. Box 284, Pateros, WA 98846; (509) 923-2548.

Types: Wilderness Expeditions: Pacific Crest Trail.

Scheduled Dates: No.
Custom Dates: Minimum guests 4, maximum varies [$].
Children's Minimum Age (accompanied): Varies.
Saddle: Western.
Minimum Skill: Novice. Divides by Skill? No.
Airport Transfers: None. Rental car Seattle, Washington.
Own Horse: No.

SCHIVELY RANCH

1062 Road 15, Lovell, WY 82431; (307) 548-6688.
Types: Cattle Drives.
Scheduled Dates: Yes [$], maximum guests 16.
Custom Dates: No.
Children's Minimum Age (accompanied): 12.
Saddle: Western.
Minimum Skill: Novice. Divides by Skill? Yes.
Airport Transfers: Charge from Billings, Montana.
Own Horse: No.

SEVEN LAZY P GUEST RANCH

P.O. Box 178, Choteau, MT 59422; (406) 466-2044.
Types: Wilderness Expeditions: Bob Marshall Wilderness Complex.
Scheduled Dates: Yes [$$$–$$$$], maximum guests varies.
Custom Dates: Yes.
Children's Minimum Age (accompanied): Varies.
Saddle: Western.
Minimum Skill: Novice. Divides by Skill? No.
Airport Transfers: Charge from Great Falls, Montana.

Own Horse: No.

SHEEP MESA OUTFITTERS

P.O. Box 1734, Cody, WY 82414; (307) 587-4305.
Types: Wilderness Expeditions: Yellowstone National Park.
Scheduled Dates: No.
Custom Dates: Minimum guests 1, maximum 15 [$$$$].
Children's Minimum Age (accompanied): Varies.
Saddle: Western.
Minimum Skill: Novice. Divides by Skill? No.
Airport Transfers: Free from Cody, Wyoming.
Own Horse: No.

SHOSHONE LODGE OUTFITTERS

P.O. Box 790, Cody, WY 82414; (307) 587-4044.
Types: Wilderness Expeditions: Yellowstone National Park.
Scheduled Dates: No.
Custom Dates: Minimum guests 2, maximum 10 [$$–$$$].
Children's Minimum Age (accompanied): 5.
Saddle: Western.
Minimum Skill: Novice. Divides by Skill? Yes.
Airport Transfers: Free from Cody, Wyoming.
Own Horse: No.

SKYLINE GUIDE SERVICE

Box 1074, Cooke City, MT 59020; (406) 838-2380; (406) 664-3187.
Types: Wilderness Expeditions: Yellowstone National Park.
Scheduled Dates: No.
Custom Dates: Minimum guests 1,

maximum 15 [$$$$$].
**Children's Minimum Age
(accompanied):** Varies.
Saddle: Western.
Minimum Skill: Novice. Divides by
Skill? No.
Airport Transfers: Free from Billings,
Montana.
Own Horse: No.

SKYLINE TRAIL RIDES

P.O. Box 207, Jasper, Alberta, Canada
T0E 1E0; (403) 852-4215.
Types: Wilderness Expeditions: Jasper
National Park.
Scheduled Dates: Yes [$], maximum
guests 12.
Custom Dates: Minimum guests 8,
maximum 12.
**Children's Minimum Age (accompa-
nied):** 7.
Saddle: Western.
Minimum Skill: Novice. Divides by
Skill? No.
Airport Transfers: None. Rental car
Edmonton or Calgary, Alberta.
Own Horse: No.

SOUTHFORK OUTFITTERS

28481 U.S. Highway 160 East,
Durango, CO 81301; (970) 259-4871.
Types: Cattle Roundups, Wilderness
Expeditions: Weminuche Wilderness.
Scheduled Dates: Yes [$–$$$$$], maxi-
mum guests 10.
Custom Dates: Pack trips minimum
guests 4, maximum 10.
**Children's Minimum Age (accompa-
nied):** Pack trips 6, roundups 16.
Saddle: Western.
Minimum Skill: Novice. Divides by
Skill? Yes.
Airport Transfers: None. Rental car

Durango, Colorado.
Own Horse: Yes, by special advance
arrangement.

SPANISH SPRINGS RANCH

P.O. Box 70, Ravendale, CA 96123;
(800) 272-8282; (916) 234-2050.
Types: Cattle Drives, Cattle Roundups,
Horse Drives.
Scheduled Dates: Yes [$–$$$], maxi-
mum guests varies.
Custom Dates: No.
**Children's Minimum Age (accompa-
nied):** Varies.
Saddle: Western.
Minimum Skill: Varies. Divides by
Skill? Yes.
Airport Transfers: Charge from Reno,
Nevada.
Own Horse: No.

SWIFT LEVEL

Route 2 Box 269-A, Lewisburg, WV
24901; (304) 645-1155.
Types: Inn Rides.
Scheduled Dates: Yes [$$$$$], maxi-
mum guests 8.
Custom Dates: Minimum guests 2.
**Children's Minimum Age (accompa-
nied):** Varies.
Saddle: English (some Western).
Minimum Skill: Medium. Divides by
Skill? Yes.
Aiport Transfers: Free from
Lewisburg, West Virginia.
Own Horse: No.

TERERRO GENERAL STORE AND RIDING STABLES

P.O. Box 12, Tererro, NM 87573;
(505) 757-6193.
Types: Wilderness Expeditions: Pecos
Wilderness.

Scheduled Dates: No.
Custom Dates: Minimum guests 4, maximum 12 [$$].
Children's Minimum Age (accompanied): 5.
Saddle: Western.
Minimum Skill: Novice. Divides by Skill? No.
Airport Transfers: None. Rental car Albuquerque, New Mexico.
Own Horse: Yes, by special advance arrangement.

THOROFARE–YELLOWSTONE OUTFITTING

P.O. Box 604, Cody, WY 82414; (800) 587-5929; (307) 587-5929.
Types: Wilderness Expeditions: Yellowstone National Park.
Scheduled Dates: Yes [$$–$$$], maximum guests 8.
Custom Dates: Minimum guests 7, maximum 8.
Children's Minimum Age (accompanied): Varies.
Saddle: Western.
Minimum Skill: Novice. Divides by Skill? No.
Airport Transfers: Free from Cody, Wyoming.
Own Horse: No.

TONQUIN VALLEY–AMETHYST LAKES WILDERNESS EXPEDITIONS

P.O. Box 23, Brulé, Alberta, Canada T0E 0C0; (403) 865-4417.
Types: Wilderness Expeditions: Jasper National Park.
Scheduled Dates: Yes [$], maximum guests 18.
Custom Dates: Minimum guests 16, maximum 18.
Children's Minimum Age (accompa-nied): Varies.
Saddle: Western.
Minimum Skill: Novice. Divides by Skill? No.
Airport Transfers: None. Rental car Edmonton or Calgary, Alberta.
Own Horse: No.

TRAILS WEST

65 Main Street, South Pass City, WY 82520; (800) 327-4052; (307) 332-7801.
Types: Wagon Trains.
Scheduled Dates: Yes [$$], maximum guests 25.
Custom Dates: Minimum guests 2, maximum 25.
Children's Minimum Age (accompanied): All ages welcome.
Saddle: Western.
Minimum Skill: Novice. Divides by Skill? No.
Airport Transfers: None. Rental car Salt Lake City, Utah.
Own Horse: Yes, by special advance arrangement.

TWO CREEK RANCH

800 Esterbrook Road, Douglas, WY 82633; (307) 358-3467.
Types: Cattle Drives, Cattle Roundups.
Scheduled Dates: Yes [$], maximum guests 15.
Custom Dates: No.
Children's Minimum Age (accompanied): Varies.
Saddle: Western.
Minimum Skill: Novice. Divides by Skill? Yes.
Airport Transfers: Charge from Casper, Wyoming.
Own Horse: No.

TX RANCH,

P.O. Box 453, Lovell, WY 82431;
(406) 484-2583.
Types: Cow Camps.
Scheduled Dates: Yes [$], maximum
guests 30 in separate camps.
Custom Dates: No.
Children's Minimum Age (accompanied): 7.
Saddle: Western.
Minimum Skill: Novice. Divides by
Skill? Yes.
Airport Transfers: Free from Billings,
Montana.
Own Horse: Yes, by special advance
arrangement.

U TRAIL OUTFITTERS

P.O. Box 66, Glenwood, NM 88039;
(800) 887-2453; (505) 539-2424.
Types: Wilderness Expeditions: Gila
Wilderness Complex.
Scheduled Dates: Yes [$], maximum
guests 8.
Custom Dates: Minimum guests 2,
maximum 8.
Children's Minimum Age (accompanied): Varies.
Saddle: Western.
Minimum Skill: Novice. Divides by
Skill? Yes.
Airport Transfers: Charge from El
Paso, Texas.
Own Horse: Yes, by special advance
arrangement.

WAGONS WEST

Afton, WY 83110; (800) 447-4711;
(307) 886-9693.
Types: Wagon Trains.
Scheduled Dates: Yes [$–$$], maximum
guests 50.
Custom Dates: Minimum guests 5,

maximum 50.
Children's Minimum Age (accompanied): All ages welcome.
Saddle: Western.
Saddle: Novice. Divides by Skill? No.
Airport Transfers: Free from Jackson,
Wyoming.
Own Horse: No.

WEMINUCHE AND SUPERSTITION ADVENTURES

1174 W. Manzanita, Apache Junction,
AZ 85220; summer, (970) 884-2555;
winter, (602) 671-3372; (602) 710-7431.
Types: Wilderness Expeditions:
Superstition Wilderness, Weminuche
Wilderness.
Scheduled Dates: Yes [$–$$], maximum
guests 8.
Custom Dates: Minimum guests 4,
maximum 8.
Children's Minimum Age (accompanied): Varies.
Saddle: Western.
Minimum Skill: Novice. Divides by
Skill? No.
Airport Transfers: SW: charge from
Phoenix, Arizona. WW: free from
Durango, Colorado.
Own Horse: No.

WESTERN RIVER EXPEDITIONS

7258 Racquet Club Drive, Salt Lake
City, UT 84121; (800) 453-7450;
(801) 942-6669.
Types: Horse/Raft Combos.
Scheduled Dates: Yes [$$$–$$$$$],
maximum guests 25.
Custom Dates: Minimum guests 18,
maximum 25.
Children's Minimum Age (accompanied): 7.
Saddle: Western.

Minimum Skill: Novice. Divides by Skill? No.
Airport Transfers: Free from Salt Lake City, Utah.
Own Horse: No.

WHITE TAIL RANCH OUTFITTERS

82 White Tail Ranch Road, Ovando, MT 59854; (406) 793-5666.
Types: Wilderness Expeditions: Bob Marshall Wilderness Complex.
Scheduled Dates: Yes [$$$$], maximum guests varies.
Custom Dates: Yes.
Children's Minimum Age (accompanied): Varies.
Saddle: Western.
Minimum Skill: Novice. Divides by Skill? No.
Airport Transfers: Free from Missoula, Montana.
Own Horse: No.

WILDERNESS CONNECTION

21 Shooting Star Trail, Gardiner, MT 59030; (800) 285-5482; (406) 848-7287.
Types: Wilderness Expeditions: Bob Marshall Wilderness Complex, Yellowstone National Park.
Scheduled Dates: Yes [$$$$–$$$$$], maximum guests 12.
Custom Dates: Minimum guests 2, maximum 12.
Children's Minimum Age (accompanied): Varies.
Saddle: Western.
Minimum Skill: Novice. Divides by Skill? No.
Airport Transfers: BM: free from Great Falls, Montana. YS: free from Bozeman, Montana.
Own Horse: No.

WILDERNESS GUIDES AND OUTFITTERS

Route 11, P.O. Box 75, Silver City, NM 88061; (505) 536-2879.
Types: Wilderness Expeditions: Gila Wilderness Complex.
Scheduled Dates: Yes [$], maximum guests 8.
Custom Dates: Minimum guests 1, maximum 8.
Children's Minimum Age (accompanied): 8.
Saddle: Western.
Minimum Skill: Novice. Divides by Skill? Yes.
Airport Transfers: Charge from El Paso, Texas.
Own Horse: Yes, by special advance arrangement.

WORLD WIDE RIVER EXPEDITIONS

153 East 7200 South, Midvale, UT 84047; (800) 231-2769; (801) 566-2662.
Types: Horse/Raft Combos.
Scheduled Dates: Yes [$$$–$$$$], maximum guests varies.
Custom Dates: Yes.
Children's Minimum Age (accompanied): Varies.
Saddle: Western.
Minimum Skill: Novice. Divides by Skill? No.
Airport Transfers: None. Rental car Salt Lake City, Utah.

10
ADDITIONAL U.S. PUBLIC LANDS WITH HORSE TRAILS

"The nation behaves well if it treats the natural resources as assets which it must turn over to the next generation, and not impaired in value."
Theodore Roosevelt (1858–1919)

The U.S. public lands must seem never-ending to an individual entering them for the first time. To an ever-increasing population, however, they are oases in a world of urban development. Aldo Leopold felt that a wilderness experience requires an area large enough to "absorb a two weeks' pack trip." You need time to change gears, slow down, forget your usual responsibilities. Then you need more time to let the rhythms of the wilderness take over: the sun and moon marking the days, changing weather, and the brief glimpses into the lives of wild animals and plants.

The following pages list federally managed public lands. Further lands are held in trust by local communities and states. At some listed areas horse outfitters offer wilderness expeditions, others offer only day rides or no outfitting services at all.

NATIONAL PARKS

ALASKA
Denali National Park, P.O. Box 9, Denali Park, AK 99755

Wrangell–Street Elias National Park, P.O. Box 29, Glennallen, AK 99588

CALIFORNIA
Death Valley National Park, P.O. Box 579, Death Valley, CA 92328

Redwood National & State Parks, 111 Second Street, Crescent City, CA 95531

COLORADO
Rocky Mountain National Park, Estes Park, CO 80517-8397

FLORIDA
Everglades National Park, 40001 State Road 9336, Homestead, FL 33034-6733

HAWAII
Haleakala National Park, P.O. Box 369, Makawao, HI 96768

KENTUCKY
Mammoth Cave National Park, Mammoth Cave, KY 42259-0007

MONTANA
Glacier National Park, West Glacier, MT 59936-0128

NEVADA
Great Basin National Park, Baker, NV 89311-9700

NORTH DAKOTA
Theodore Roosevelt National Park, P.O. Box 7, Medora, ND 58645

SOUTH DAKOTA
Badlands National Park, P.O. Box 6, Interior, SD 57750

TENNESSEE
Great Smoky Mountains National Park, 107 Park Headquarters Road, Gatlinburg, TN 37738

TEXAS
Big Bend National Park, P.O. Box 129, Big Bend National Park, TX 79834

Guadalupe Mountains National Park, HC 60 Box 400, Salt Flat, TX 79847-9400

UTAH
Arches National Park, P.O. Box 907, Moab, UT 84532

Bryce Canyon National Park, Bryce Canyon, UT 84717-0001

Zion National Park, Springdale, UT 84767-1099

VIRGINIA
Shenandoah National Park, Route 4 Box 348, Luray, VA 22835-9051

WASHINGTON
Olympic National Park, 600 E. Park Avenue, Port Angeles, WA 98362-9335

WYOMING
Grand Teton National Park, P.O. Drawer 170, Moose, WY 83012

NATIONAL MONUMENTS AND SITES

ALABAMA
Horseshoe Bend National Military Park, Route 1 Box 103, Daviston, AL 36256-9751

ARIZONA
Canyon de Chelly National Monument, P.O. Box 588, Chinle, AZ 86503

Navajo National Monument, HC 71 Box 3, Tonalea, AZ 86044-9704

ARKANSAS
Buffalo National River, P.O. Box 1173, Harrison, AR 72602

CALIFORNIA
Devils Postpile National Monument, P.O. Box 501, Mammoth Lakes, CA 93546

Golden Gate National Recreation Area, Fort Mason, Bldg. 201, San Francisco, CA 94123-1308

Lava Beds National Monument, P.O. Box 867, Tulelake, CA 96134

Point Reyes National Seashore, Point Reyes, CA 94956-9799

Santa Monica Mountains National Recreation Area, 30401 Agoura Road, Suite 100, Agoura Hills, CA 91301-2085

COLORADO
Colorado National Monument, Fruita, CO 81521-9530

Curecanti National Recreation Area, 102 Elk Creek, Gunnison, CO 81230-9304

FLORIDA
Big Cypress National Preserve, HCR 61 Box 110, Ochopee, FL 33943-9710

Canaveral National Seashore, 308 Julia Street, Titusville, FL 32796-3521

GEORGIA
Chattahoochee River National Recreation Area, 1978 Island Ford Parkway, Dunwoody, GA 30350-3400

Chickamauga & Chattanooga National Military Park, P.O. Box 2128, Fort Oglethorpe, GA 30742

Kennesaw Mountain National Battlefield Park, 900 Kennesaw Mountain Drive, Kennesaw, GA 30144-4854

HAWAII
Kalaupapa National Historical Park, P.O. Box 2222, Kalaupapa, HI 96742

IDAHO
City of Rocks National Reserve, P.O. Box 169, Almo, ID 83312

INDIANA
Indiana Dunes National Lakeshore, 1100 N. Mineral Springs Road, Porter, IN 46304-1299

MARYLAND
Chesapeake & Ohio Canal National Historical Park, P.O. Box 4, Sharpsburg, MD 21782

Greenbelt Park, 6565 Greenbelt Road, Greenbelt, MD 20770-3207

MISSOURI
Wilson's Creek National Battlefield, Route 2 Box 75, Rebulic, MO 65738-9514

NEW JERSEY
Morristown National Historical Park, Washington Place, Morristown, NJ 07960-4299

NEW MEXICO
Petroglyph National Monument, 4735 Unser Bouelva Road NW, Albuquerque, NM 87120-2033

White Sands National Monument, P.O. Box 1086, Holloman AFB, NM 88330

NEW YORK
Gateway National Recreation Area, Floyd Bennett Field, Bldg. 69, Brooklyn, NY 11234-7097

Saratoga National Historical Park, 648 Route 32, Stillwater, NY 12170-1604

NORTH CAROLINA
Blue Ridge Parkway, 200 BB&T Bldg., Asheville, NC 28801-3412

Cape Hatteras National Seashore, Route 1 Box 675, Manteo, NC 27954-2708

Kings Mountain National Military Park, P.O. Box 40, Kings Mountain, NC 28086

OHIO
Cuyahoga Valley National Recreation Area, 15610 Vaughn Road, Brecksville, OH 44141-3018

PENNSYLVANIA
Great Egg Harbor Wild & Scenic River, Mid-Atlantic Region, 143 S. 3rd Street, Philadelphia, PA 19106-2818

Valley Forge National Historical Park, P.O. Box 953, Valley Forge, PA 19481

SOUTH CAROLINA
Ninety Six National Historic Site, P.O. Box 496, Ninety Six, SC 29666

TENNESSEE
Big Southfork National River & Recreation Area, Route 3 Box 401, Oneida, TN 37841-9544

TEXAS
Big Thicket National Preserve, 3785 Milam, Beaumont, TX 77701-4724

Lake Meredith National Recreation Area, P.O. Box 1460, Fritch, TX 79036

VIRGINIA
Manassas National Battlefield Park, 12521 Lee Highway, Manassas, VA 22110-2005

Petersburg National Battlefield, P.O. Box 549, Petersburg, VA 23804

WASHINGTON
Lake Chelan National Recreation Area, 2105 Highway 20, Sedro Woolley, WA 98284-9314

WEST VIRGINIA
New River Gorge National River, P.O. Box 246, Glen Jean, WV 25846

NATIONAL TRAILS

Lewis & Clark National Historic Trail, National Park Service, Lewis & Clark National Historic Trail, 700 Rayovac Drive, Suite 100, Madison, WI 53711

Mormon Pioneer National Historic Trail, National Park Service, Rocky Mountain Region, Planning & Compliance Division, 12795 W. Alameda Parkway, Lakewood, CO 80225

Natchez Trace National Scenic Trail, National Park Service, Natchez Trace Parkway, RR 1 NT 143, Tupelo, MS 38801

Nez Perce (Nee–Me–Poo) National Historic Trail, U.S. Forest Service, Northern Region, P.O. Box 7669, Missoula, MT 59807

North Country National Scenic Trail, National Park Service, North Country National Scenic Trail, 700 Rayovac Drive, Suite 100, Madison, WI 53711

Oregon National Historic Trail: National Park Service, Pacific Northwest Region, Oregon National Historic Trail, 83 S. King Street, Suite 212, Seattle, WA 98104

Potomac Heritage National Scenic Trail, C&O Canal National Historical Park, P.O. Box 4, Sharpsburg, MD 21782

Santa Fe National Historic Trail, National Park Service, Southwest Region, Branch of Long Distance Trails, P.O. Box 728, Santa Fe, NM 87504

Trail of Tears National Historic Trail, National Park Service, Southwest Region, Branch of Long Distance Trails, P.O. Box 728, Santa Fe, NM 87504

NATIONAL FORESTS

(Includes National Forest Wilderness Areas)

ALASKA
Chugach National Forest, 201 E. Ninth Avenue, Suite 206, Anchorage, AK 99501-3698

ARIZONA
Apache–Sitgreaves National Forests, P.O. Box 640, Springerville, AZ 85938

Coconino National Forest, 2323 E. Greenlaw Lane, Flagstaff, AZ 76004

Coronado National Forest, 300 W. Congress Street, Sixth Floor, Tucson, AZ 85701

Kaibab National Forest, 800 S. Sixth Street, Williams, AZ 86046

Prescott National Forest, 344 S. Cortez Street, Prescott, AZ 86303

Tonto National Forest, P.O. Box 5348, Phoenix, AZ 85010

ARKANSAS
Ozark–Street Francis National Forests, P.O. Box 1008, Russellville, AR 72801

CALIFORNIA
Angeles National Forest, 701 N. Santa Anita Avenue, Arcadia, CA 91006

Cleveland National Forest, 10845 Rancho Bernardo Road, Suite 200, San Diego, CA 92127

Eldorado National Forest, 3070 Camino Heights Drive, Camino, CA 95709

Inyo National Forest, 873 N. Main Street, Bishop, CA 93514

Klamath National Forest, 1312 Fairlane Road, Yreka, CA 96097

Lassen National Forest, 55 S. Sacramento Street, Susanville, CA 96130

Los Padres National Forest, 6144 Calle Real, Goleta, CA 93117

Mendocino National Forest, 420 E. Laurel Street, Willows, CA 95988

Modoc National Forest, 441 N. Main Street, Alturas, CA 96101

Plumas National Forest, P.O. Box 11500, Quincy, CA 95971

San Bernardino National Forest, 1824 S. Commercenter Circle, San Bernardino, CA 92408-3430

Sequoia National Forest, 900 W. Grand Avenue, Porterville, CA 93257-2035

Shasta–Trinity National Forests, 2400 Washington Avenue, Redding, CA 96001

Sierra National Forest, 1600 Tollhouse Road, Clovis, CA 93611

Six Rivers National Forest, 1330 Bayshore Way, Eureka, CA 95501

Stanislaus National Forest, 19777 Greenley Road, Sonora, CA 95370

Tahoe National Forest, P.O. Box 6003, Nevada City, CA 95959

COLORADO
Arapaho–Roosevelt National Forests, 240 W. Prospect Road, Fort Collins, CO 80526

Grand Mesa–Uncompahgre –Gunnison National Forests, 2250 U.S. Highway 50, Delta, CO 81416

Pike–San Isabel National Forests, 1920 Valley Drive, Pueblo, CO 81008

Rio Grande National Forest, 1803 W. U.S. Highway 160, Monte Vista, CO 81144

Routt National Forest, 29587 W. U.S. Highway 40, Suite 20, Steamboat Springs, CO 80487

San Juan National Forest, 701 Camino del Rio, Room 301, Durango, CO 81301

White River National Forest, P.O. Box 948, Glenwood Springs, CO 81602

GEORGIA
Chattahoochee–Oconee National Forests, 508 Oak Street NW, Gainesville, GA 30501

IDAHO
Boise National Forest, 1750 Front Street, Boise, ID 83702

Caribou National Forest, Federal Bldg., 250 S. Fourth Ave., Suite 282, Pocatello, ID 83201

Challis National Forest, U.S. Highway 93 N., HC 63 Box 1671, Challis, ID 83226

Clearwater National Forest, 12730 Highway 12, Orofino, ID 83544

Coeur d'Alene–Kaniksu–Street Joe National Forests, 1201 Ironwood Drive, Coeur d'Alene, ID 83814

Nez Perce National Forest, P.O. Box 475, Grangeville, ID 83530

Payette National Forest, P.O. Box 1026, McCall, ID 83638

Salmon National Forest, P.O. Box 729, Salmon, ID 83467

Sawtooth National Forest, 2647 Kimberly Road E., Twin Falls, ID 83301-7976

Targhee National Forest, P.O. Box 208, Anthony, ID 83445

ILLINOIS
Shawnee National Forest, 901 S. Commercial Street, Harrisburg, IL 62946

INDIANA
Hoosier National Forest, 811 Constitution Avenue, Bedford, IN 47421

LOUISIANA
Kisatchie National Forest, P.O. Box 5500, Pineville, LA 71361

MICHIGAN
Hiawatha National Forest, 2727 N. Lincoln Road, Escanaba, MI 49829

Huron–Manistee National Forests, 421 S. Mitchell Street, Cadillac, MI 49601

MISSISSIPPI
De Soto–Holly Springs–Homochitto National Forests, 100 W. Capitol Street, Suite 1141, Jackson, MS 39269

MISSOURI
Mark Twain National Forest, 401 Fairgrounds Road, Rolla, MO 65401

MONTANA
Beaverhead National Forest, 420 Barrett Street, Dillon, MT 59725-3572

Bitterroot National Forest, 1801 N. First Street, Hamilton, MT 59840

Custer National Forest, P.O. Box 2556, Billings, MT 59840

Deerlodge National Forest, P.O. Box 400, Butte, MT 59703

Flathead National Forest, 1935 Third Avenue E., Kalispell, MT 59901

Gallatin National Forest, P.O. Box 130, Bozeman, MT 59771

Helena National Forest, 2880 Skyway Drive, Helena, MT 59601

Kootenai National Forest, 506 U.S. Highway 2 W., Libby, MT 59923

Lewis & Clark National Forest, P.O. Box 869, Great Falls, MT 59403

Lolo National Forest, Bldg. 24, Missoula, MT 59801

NEBRASKA
Nebraska National Forest, 270 Pine Street, Chadron, NE 69337

NEVADA
Humboldt National Forest, 976 Mountain City Highway, Elko, NV 89801

Toiyabe National Forest, 1200 Franklin Way, Sparks, NV 89431

NEW MEXICO
Carson National Forest, P.O. Box 558, Taos, NM 87571

Cibola National Forest, 2113 Osuna Road, Suite A, Albuquerque, NM 87713-1001

Gila National Forest, 2610 N. Silver Street, Silver City, NM 88061

Lincoln National Forest, Federal Bldg., 1101 New York Avenue, Alamogordo, NM 88310

Santa Fe National Forest, P.O. Box 1689, Santa Fe, NM 87504

NORTH CAROLINA
Pisgah National Forest, P.O. Box 2750, Asheville, NC 28802

OHIO
Wayne National Forest, 219 Columbus Road, Athens, OH 45701-1399

OREGON
Deschutes National Forest, 1645 U.S. Highway 20 E., Bend, OR 97701

Fremont National Forest, 524 N. G Street, Lakeview, OR 97630

Malheur National Forest, 139 NE Dayton Street, John Day, OR 97845

Mount Hood National Forest, 2955 NW Division Street, Gresham, OR 97030

Ochoco National Forest, P.O. Box 490, Prineville, OR 97754

Rogue River National Forest, P.O. Box 520, Medford, OR 97501

Siskiyou National Forest, P.O. Box 440, Grants Pass, OR 97526

Siuslaw National Forest, 4077 Research Way, Corvallis, OR 97339

Umatilla National Forest, 2517 SW Hailey Avenue, Pendleton, OR 97801

Umpqua National Forest, P.O. Box 1008, Roseburg, OR 97470

Wallowa–Whitman National Forests, P.O. Box 907, Baker City, OR 97814

Willamette National Forest, P.O. Box 10607, Eugene, OR 97440

Winema National Forest, 2819 Dahlia Street, Klamath Falls, OR 97601

PENNSYLVANIA
Allegheny National Forest, P.O. Box 847, Warren, PA 16365

SOUTH CAROLINA
Francis Marion–Sumter National Forests, 1835 Assembly Street, Room 333, Columbia, SC 29201

SOUTH DAKOTA
Black Hills National Forest, Highway 385 N., Route 2 Box 200, Custer, SD 57730

TENNESSEE
Cherokee National Forest, P.O. Box 2010, Cleveland, TN 37320

UTAH
Ashley National Forest, 355 N. Vernal Avenue, Vernal, UT 84078

Dixie National Forest, P.O. Box 580, Cedar City, UT 84721

Fishlake National Forest, 115 E. 900 N., Richfield, UT 84701

Manti–La Sal National Forest, 599 W. Price River Drive, Price, UT 84501

Uinta National Forest, 88 W. 100 N., Provo, UT 84601

Wasatch–Cache National Forests, 8230 Federal Bldg., 125 S. State Street, Salt Lake City, UT 84138

VERMONT
Green Mountain–Finger Lakes National Forests, Federal Bldg., 231 N. Main Street, Rutland, VT 05701

VIRGINIA
Jefferson National Forest, 5162 Valley Pointe Parkway, Roanoke, VA 24091

WASHINGTON
Colville National Forest, 765 S. Main Street, Colville, WA 99114

Gifford Pinchot National Forest, P.O. Box 8944, Vancouver, WA 98668

Mount Baker–Snoqualmie National Forests, 21905 64th Avenue W., Mountlake Terrace, WA 98043

Okanogan National Forest, P.O. Box 950, Okanogan, WA 98840

Olympic National Forest, 1835 Black Lake Boulevard SW, Olympia, WA 98502-5423

Wenatchee National Forest, P.O. Box 811, Wenatchee, WA 98807

WEST VIRGINIA
Monongahela National Forest, 200 Sycamore Street, Elkins, WV 26241

WISCONSIN
Chequamegon National Forest, 1170 4th Ave. S., Park Falls, WI 54552

WYOMING
Bighorn National Forest, 1969 S. Sheridan Avenue, Sheridan, WY 82801

Bridger–Teton National Forests, P.O. Box 1888, Jackson, WY 83001

Medicine Bow National Forest, 2468 Jackson Street, Laramie, WY 82070-6535

Shoshone National Forest, P.O. Box 2140, Cody, WY 82414

BUREAU OF LAND MANAGEMENT (BLM)

Of the 1.8 billion acres (73 million ha) of public land first acquired by the U.S., two-thirds were sold or given to states and private industries and individuals. A portion of the remaining one-third was turned over to the National Park Service, the U.S. Forest Service, and other public purposes. The BLM manages the 272 million acres (110 million ha) left in the public domain, primarily in the western states. These natural areas belong to you, and horseback treks into their hearts make them forever your own.

ARIZONA
Aravaipa Canyon Wilderness, BLM Safford District Office, 711 14th Avenue, Safford, AZ 85546

Black Canyon Trail, BLM Lower Gila Resource Area, 2015 W. Deer Valley Road, Phoenix, AZ 85027

Black Mountains, BLM Kingman Resource Area, 2475 Beverly Avenue, Kingman, AZ 86401

Cactus Plain Wilderness Study Area/East Cactus Plain Wilderness, BLM Havasu Resource Area, 3189 Sweetwater Avenue, Lake Havasu City, AZ 86406

Crossman Peak, BLM Havasu Resource Area, 3189 Sweetwater Avenue, Lake Havasu City, AZ 86406

Dos Cabezas Mountains, BLM Safford District Office, 711 14th Avenue, Safford, AZ 85546

Eagletail Mountains, BLM Yuma Resource Area, 3150 Winsor Avenue, Yuma, AZ 85365

Empire–Cienega Resource Conservation Area, BLM Tucson Resource Area, 12661 E. Broadway, Tucson, AZ 85748

Gila Box Riparian National Conservation Area, BLM Safford District Office, 711 14th Avenue, Safford, AZ 85546

Grand Wash Cliffs Wilderness, BLM Shivwits Resource Area, 225 N. Bluff Street, Street George, UT 84770

Gibraltar Mountain Wilderness, BLM Havasu Resource Area, 3189 Sweetwater Avenue, Lake Havasu City, AZ 86406

Harquahala Mountains, BLM Lower Gila Resource Area, 2015 W. Deer Valley Road, Phoenix, AZ 85027

Javelina Peak, BLM Safford District Office, 711 14th Avenue, Safford, AZ 85546

Paiute Wilderness, BLM Shivwits Resource Area, 225 N. Bluff Street, George, UT 84770

Peloncillo Mountains, BLM Safford District Office, 711 14th Avenue, Safford, AZ 85546

Table Top Mountain Wilderness, BLM Lower Gila Resource Area, 2015 W. Deer Valley Road, Phoenix, AZ 85027

Wabayuma Peak, BLM Kingman Resource Area, 2475 Beverly Avenue, Kingman, AZ 86401

White Canyon Wilderness, BLM Lower Gila Resource Area, 2015 W. Deer Valley Road, Phoenix, AZ 85027

CALIFORNIA

Afton Canyon, BLM Barstow Resource Area, 150 Coolwater Lane, Barstow, CA 92311

Alabama Hills, BLM Bishop Resource Area, 787 N. Main, Suite P, Bishop, CA 93514

American River–South Fork, BLM Folsom Resource Area, 63 Natoma Street, Folsom, CA 95630

Bizz Johnson Trail, BLM Eagle Lake Resource Area, 705 Hall Street, Susanville, CA 96130

Cache Creek, BLM Clear Lake Resource Area, 2550 N. State Street, Ukiah, CA 95482

Carrizo Plain Natural Area, BLM Caliente Resource Area, 3801 Pegasus Drive, Bakersfield, CA 93308-6837

Chimney Peak Recreation Area, BLM Caliente Resource Area, 3801 Pegasus Drive, Bakersfield, CA 93308-6837

Cow Mountain, BLM Clear Lake Resource Area, 2550 N. State Street, Ukiah, CA 95482

Fort Piute Historic Site, BLM Needles Resource Area, 101 W. Spikes Road, Needles, CA 92363

Indian Valley–Walker Ridge, BLM Clear Lake Resource Area, 2550 N. State Street, Ukiah, CA 95482

Jawbone/Dove Springs, BLM Ridgecrest Resource Area, 300 S. Richmond Road, Ridgecrest, CA 93555

Joshua Tree National Park Area, BLM Palm Springs–South Coast Resource Area, P.O. Box 2000, North Palm Springs, CA 92258

**King Range National Conservation
Area**, BLM Arcata Resource Area,1125
16th Street, Room 219, Arcata, CA 95521

McCain Valley Conservation Area,
BLM El Centro Resource Area, 1661 S.
Fourth Street, El Centro, CA 92243

Mecca Hills Recreation Area, BLM
Palm Springs–South Coast Resource
Area, P.O. Box 2000, North Palm
Springs, CA 92258

Merced River, BLM Folsom Resource
Area, 63 Natoma Street, Folsom, CA
95630

Mojave National Preserve Area, BLM
California Desert District Office, 6221
Box Springs Boulevard, Riverside, CA
92507

Owens Peak Wilderness Study Area,
BLM Bakersfield District Office, 3801
Pegasus Drive, Bakersfield, CA 93308-
6837

**Providence Mountains State
Recreation Area**, BLM California
Desert District Office, 6221 Box Springs
Boulevard, Riverside, CA 92507

Rainbow Basin, BLM Barstow
Resource Area, 150 Coolwater Lane,
Barstow, CA 92311

Rand Mountains, BLM Ridgecrest
Resource Area, 300 S. Richmond Road,
Ridgecrest, CA 93555

Sacramento River, BLM Redding
Resource Area, 355 Hemsted Drive,
Redding, CA 96002

Samoa Dunes, BLM Arcata Resource
Area, 1125 16th Street, Room 219,
Arcata, CA 95521

San Joaquin River Squaw Leap Trails,
BLM Folsom Resource Area,
63 Natoma Street, Folsom, CA 95630

Santa Rosa National Scenic Area,
BLM Palm Springs–South Coast
Resource Area, P.O. Box 2000, North
Palm Springs, CA 92258

South Fork Eel River, BLM Arcata
Resource Area, 1125 16th Street, Room
219, Arcata, CA 95521

Spangler Hills, BLM Ridgecrest
Resource Area, 300 S. Richmond Road,
Ridgecrest, CA 93555

Trinity River, BLM Redding Resource
Area, 355 Hemsted Drive, Redding, CA
96002

Trona Pinnacles Recreation Lands,
BLM Ridgecrest Resource Area, 300 S.
Richmond Road, Ridgecrest, CA 93555

Upper Klamath River, BLM Redding
Resource Area, 355 Hemsted Drive,
Redding, CA 96002

COLORADO
Gunnison Gorge, BLM Uncompahgre
Resource Area, 2505 S. Townsend Ave.,
Montrose, CO 81401

Upper Colorado River, BLM White
River Resource Area, P.O. Box 928,
Meeker, CO 81641

IDAHO

Appendicitis Hill, BLM Idaho Falls District Office, 940 Lincoln Road, Idaho Falls, ID 83401

Grandmother Mountain, BLM Coeur d'Alene District, 1808 N. Third Street, Coeur d'Alene, ID 83814

Jacks Creek, BLM Boise District Office, 3948 Development Avenue., Boise, ID 83705

Owyhee Canyonlands, BLM Boise District Office, 3948 Development Avenue, Boise, ID 83705

Salmon Falls Creek & Reservoir, BLM Burley District Office, Route 3 Box 1, Burley, ID 83318

Sawtooth Mountains/Quigley Canyon, BLM Shoshone District Office, P.O. Box 2B, Shoshone, ID 83352

MONTANA

Axolotl Lakes, BLM Headwaters Resource Area, P.O. Box 3388, Butte, MT 59702

Big Hole River, BLM Headwaters Resource Area, P.O. Box 3388, Butte, MT 59702

Centennial Mountains, BLM Dillon Resource Area, P.O. Box 1048, Dillon, MT 59725

Holter Lake Recreation Area, BLM Headwaters Resource Area, P.O. Box 3388, Butte, MT 59702

Little Rocky Mountains Recreation Area, BLM Phillips Resource Area, HC 65 Box 5000, Malta, MT 59538

Pryor Mountain National Wild Horse Refuge, BLM Billings Resource Area, 810 E. Main Street, Billings, MT 59105

Ruby Mountains, BLM Dillon Resource Area, P.O. Box 1048, Dillon, MT 59725

Sleeping Giant Wilderness Study Area, BLM Headwaters Resource Area, P.O. Box 3388, Butte, MT 59702

NEVADA

Antelope Range, BLM Battle Mountain District, P.O. Box 1420, Battle Mountain, NV 89820

Bitter Springs Trail Back Country Byway, BLM Las Vegas District Office, 4765 Vegas Drive, Las Vegas, NV 89107

Black Rock Range, BLM Winnemucca District Office, 705 E. Fourth Street, Winnemucca, NV 89445

Buffalo Hills, BLM Winnemucca District Office, 705 E. Fourth Street, Winnemucca, NV 89445

Calico Mountains, BLM Winnemucca District Office, 705 E. Fourth Street Winnemucca, NV 89445

Clan Alpine Mountains, BLM Carson City District Office, 1535 Hot Springs Road, Suite 300, Carson City, NV 89706

Clover Mountains, BLM Las Vegas District Office, 4765 Vegas Drive, Las Vegas, NV 89107

Condor Canyon, BLM Las Vegas District Office, 4765 Vegas Drive, Las Vegas, NV 89107

Cottonwood Canyon, BLM Red Rock Canyon National Conservation Area, 4765 Vegas Drive, Las Vegas, NV 89107

Desatoya Mountains, BLM Carson City District Office, 1535 Hot Springs Road, Suite 300, Carson City, NV 89706

Fox Range, BLM Winnemucca District Office, 705 E. Fourth Street, Winnemucca, NV 89445

Valley Range, BLM Carson City District Office, 1535 Hot Springs Road, Suite 300, Carson City, NV 89706

Gleason Canyon & The Charcoal Kilns, BLM Las Vegas District Office, 4765 Vegas Drive, Las Vegas, NV 89107

Gold Butte Back Country Byway, BLM Las Vegas District Office, 4765 Vegas Drive, Las Vegas, NV 89107

Goshute Canyon & Goshute Canyon Natural Area, BLM Ely District Office, 702 N. Industrial Way, Box 33500, Ely, NV 89408

Goshute Mountains, BLM Elko District Office, P.O. Box 831, Elko, NV 89803

Grant Range, BLM Battle Mountain District, P.O. Box 1420, Battle Mountain, NV 89820

Jackson Mountains, BLM Winnemucca District Office, 705 E. Fourth Street, Winnemucca, NV 89445

Mathews Canyon Reservoir, BLM Caliente Resource Area, P.O. Box 237, Caliente, NV 89008

Meadow Valley Range & Mormon Mountains, BLM Las Vegas District Office, 4765 Vegas Drive, Las Vegas, NV 89107

Mount Grafton, BLM Ely District Office, 702 N. Industrial Way, Box 33500, Ely, NV 89408

North Fork Little Humboldt River, BLM Winnemucca District Office, 705 E. Fourth Street, Winnemucca, NV 89445

Parsnip Peak, BLM Ely District Office, 702 N. Industrial Way, Box 33500, Ely, NV 89408

Pine Canyon Reservoir, BLM Caliente Resource Area, P.O. Box 237, Caliente, NV 89008

Pine Forest Range, BLM Winnemucca District Office, 705 E. Fourth Street, Winnemucca, NV 89445

Queer Mountains, BLM Battle Mountain District, P.O. Box 1420, Battle Mountain, NV 89820

Rainbow Canyon, BLM Las Vegas District Office, 4765 Vegas Drive, Las Vegas, NV 89107

Red Rock Canyon National Conservation Area, BLM Red Rock Canyon National Conservation Area, 4765 Vegas Drive, Las Vegas, NV 89107

Roberts Creek Mountains, BLM Battle Mountain District Office, P.O. Box 1420, Battle Mountain, NV 89820

South Egan Range, BLM Ely District Office, 702 N. Industrial Way, Box 33500, Ely, NV 89408

South Pahroc Range, BLM Las Vegas District Office, 4765 Vegas Drive, Las Vegas, NV 89107

South Reveille Range, BLM Battle Mountain District, P.O. Box 1420, Battle Mountain, NV 89820

Stillwater Range, BLM Carson City District Office, 1535 Hot Springs Road, Suite 300, Carson City, NV 89706

Virgin Peak, BLM Las Vegas District Office, 4765 Vegas Drive, Las Vegas, NV 89107

NEW MEXICO
Bisti Wilderness, BLM Farmington District Office, 1235 La Plata Highway, Farmington, NM 87401

Cabezon Wilderness Study Area, BLM Rio Puerco Resource Area, 435 Montaño Road NE, Albuquerque, NM 87107

Cebolla Wilderness, BLM Rio Puerco Resource Area, 435 Montaño Road NE, Albuquerque, NM 87107

De–Na–Zin Wilderness, BLM Farmington District Office, 1235 La Plata Highway, Farmington, NM 87401

Fort Stanton Recreation Area, BLM Roswell Resource Area, P.O. Driveawer 1857, Roswell, NM 88202

Horse Mountain Wilderness Study Area, BLM Socorro Resource Area, 198 Neel Ave. NW, Socorro, NM 87801

Ignacio Chavez/Chamisa Wilderness Study Area, 435 Montaño Road NE, Albuquerque, NM 87107

Organ Mountains, BLM Mimbres Resource Area, 1800 Marquess Street, Las Cruces, NM 88005

Sierra De Las Canas & Presilla Wilderness Study Areas, BLM Socorro Resource Area, 198 Neel Ave. NW, Socorro, NM 87801

Sierra Ladriveones Wilderness Study Area, BLM Socorro Resource Area, 198 Neel Ave. NW, Socorro, NM 87801

OREGON
North Umpqua River & Trail, BLM Roseburg District, 777 NW Garden Valley Boulevard, Roseburg, OR 97470

Row River Trail, BLM Eugene District, P.O. Box 10226, Eugene, OR 97440

Table Rock Wilderness Area, BLM Salem District Office, 1717 Fabry Road SE, Salem, OR 97306

UTAH

Canaan Mountain, BLM Dixie Resource Area, 225 N. Bluff Street, Street George, UT 84770

Canyon Rims Recreation Area, BLM Grand Resource Area, P.O. Box 970, Moab, UT 84532

Great Western Trail, BLM Kanab Resource Area, 318 N. First Street, Kanab, UT 84741

Henry Mountains, BLM Henry Mountains Resource Area, P.O. Box 99, Handsville, UT 84734

Pony Express Trail Back Country Byway, BLM Salt Lake District Office, 2370 S. 2300 W., Salt Lake City, UT 84119

Red Cliffs Recreation Site, BLM Dixie Resource Area, 225 N. Bluff Street, Street George, UT 84770

Swasey Mountain, BLM House Range Resource Area, P.O. Box 778, Fillmore, UT 84631

Wah Wah Mountains, BLM Richfield District Office, 150 E. 900 N., Richfield, UT 84701

WASHINGTON

Yakima River Canyon, BLM Spokane District Office, 1103 N. Francher, Spokane, WA 99212

WYOMING

Honeycomb & Oregon Buttes, BLM Green River Resource Area, 1993 Dewar Drive, Rock Springs, WY 82901

Lake Mountain Wilderness Study Area, BLM Pinedale Resource Area, P.O. Box 768, Pinedale, WY 82941

McCullough Peaks, BLM Cody Resource Area, P.O. Box 518, Cody, WY 82414

Medicine Lodge Canyon, BLM Worland District Office, P.O. Box 119, Worland, WY 82401

Middlefork Special Recreation Management Area, BLM Buffalo Resource Area, 189 N. Cedar Street, Buffalo, WY 82834

Oregon/Mormon Pioneer/California/Pony Express National Historic Trails Special Recreation Management Area, BLM Wyoming State Office, P.O. Box 1828, Cheyenne, WY 82003

Raymond Mountain Wilderness Study Area, BLM Kemmerer Resource Area, 312 US 189 N., Kemmerer, WY 83101

Red Desert, BLM Green River Resource Area, 1993 Dewar Drive, Rock Springs, WY 82901

Scab Creek Wilderness Streetudy Area, BLM Pinedale Resource Area, P.O. Box 768, Pinedale, WY 82941

INTERNATIONAL READERS

Converting to Metric

Length
1 inch = 2.54 cm
1 foot = 0.3048 m
1 yard = 0.9144 m
1 mile = 1.6093 km

Area
1 square inch = 6.452 square cm
1 square foot = 0.0929 square m
1 square yard = 0.8361 square m
1 square mile = 2.590 square km (259 ha)
1 acre = 0.4047 ha

Liquids
1 quart = 0.9464 liter
1 gallon = 3.7854 liter

Temperature
Celsius = (Fahrenheit – 32) x 5/9

SADDLE UP! WANTS TO HEAR FROM YOU

The African saying "It takes a village to raise a child" can also be applied to guidebooks. Along with the writer's research, it takes conscientious readers to continually improve the communal pool of knowledge. So I encourage you to write me with your comments, corrections, and what you would like to see in future editions.

Thanks very much. I look forward to hearing from you.

Ute Haker
c/o EQUUS★USA
Route 7 Box 124–MU
Santa Fe, New Mexico 87505 USA

EQUUS★USA

Free & Easy Central Reservations

Saddle Up! provides detailed information for finding riding vacations throughout North America and the rest of the world. I encourage you to read and study the book. If after doing so you still would like assistance, please call us.

In the early 1980s, several riding friends and I found that even though North America has the world's richest selection of equestrian vacations, information is often difficult to find. We began gathering a store of knowledge for our own vacations and the vacations of friends. In 1989 we realized we had become experts and together with professional travel agents founded EQUUS★USA, the only organization worldwide specializing in North American riding vacations. A short time later we added outstanding international equestrian vacations.

Since its inception EQUUS★USA has helped North American and overseas clients have the horseback holidays of their dreams. Families, groups, corporations, and singles regularly rely on our expertise. They either feel overwhelmed by the choices or realize the benefit of one central, free-of-charge service making their travel arrangements. With one call or fax you are in touch with all the vacations listed in the book.

Reservations: (800) 982–6861, or (505) 982–6861
Fax: (505) 984–8119
Mail: Route 7 Box 124–MU, Santa Fe, New Mexico 87505 USA
For readers outside North America it's easiest to contact us by fax.

When you call or fax, please provide the following details:
1. Information about you:
   ★ Your first and last name
   ★ Your daytime telephone number & best times to reach you
   ★ Your fax number (especially for inquiries from outside the U.S.)
   ★ Your address (if outside the U.S., please note country)
   ★ Number of people in your party and ages of children
   ★ Everyone's riding skill (nonrider, novice, beginner, advanced beginner, medium, expert)

2. Information about your vacation:
   ★ Type of riding vacation you wish (consult this book for an overview)
   ★ Where you want to ride (country/state/name of national park or wilderness)
   ★ Your planned riding dates (desired month or exact dates)
   ★ How long a riding vacation you would like (usually a week or more)
   ★ How many hours you want to ride each day

If you have prepared a day-by-day itinerary (see Planning Your Riding Vacation: Making Your Reservations), please fax it along or have it handy when you call. After you have provided this information, one of our associates will contact you.

INDEX

Other Books from John Muir Publications

Rick Steves' Books

Asia Through the Back Door, 400 pp., $17.95

Europe 101: History and Art for the Traveler, 352 pp., $17.95

Mona Winks: Self-Guided Tours of Europe's Top Museums, 432 pp., $18.95

Rick Steves' Baltics & Russia, 160 pp., $9.95

Rick Steves' Europe, 560 pp., $18.95

Rick Steves' France, Belgium & the Netherlands, 304 pp., $15.95

Rick Steves' Germany, Austria & Switzerland, 272 pp., $14.95

Rick Steves' Great Britain & Ireland, 320 pp., $15.95

Rick Steves' Italy, 240 pp., $13.95

Rick Steves' Scandinavia, 208 pp., $13.95

Rick Steves' Spain & Portugal, 240 pp., $13.95

Rick Steves' Europe Through the Back Door, 520 pp., $19.95

Rick Steves' French Phrase Book, 192 pp., $5.95

Rick Steves' German Phrase Book, 192 pp., $5.95

Rick Steves' Italian Phrase Book, 192 pp., $5.95

Rick Steves' Spanish & Portuguese Phrase Book, 336 pp., $7.95

Rick Steves' French/German/Italian Phrase Book, 320 pp., $7.95

A Natural Destination Series

Belize: A Natural Destination, 344 pp., $16.95

Costa Rica: A Natural Destination, 416 pp., $18.95

Guatemala: A Natural Destination, 360 pp., $16.95

City•Smart™ Guidebook Series

City•Smart Guidebook: Cleveland, 208 pp., $14.95

City•Smart Guidebook: Denver, 256 pp., $14.95

City•Smart Guidebook: Minneapolis/St. Paul, 240 pp., $14.95

City•Smart Guidebook: Nashville, 256 pp., $14.95

City•Smart Guidebook: Portland, 232 pp., $14.95

City•Smart Guidebook: Tampa/St. Petersburg, 256 pp., $14.95

Travel•Smart™ Trip Planners

American Southwest Travel•Smart Trip Planner, 256 pp., $14.95

Colorado Travel•Smart Trip Planner, 248 pp., $14.95

Eastern Canada Travel•Smart Trip Planner, 272 pp., $15.95

Florida Gulf Coast Travel•Smart Trip Planner, 240 pp., $14.95

Hawaii Travel•Smart Trip Planner, 256 pp., $14.95

Kentucky/Tennessee Travel•Smart Trip Planner, 248 pp., $14.95

Minnesota/Wisconsin Travel•Smart Trip Planner, 240 pp., $14.95

New England Travel•Smart Trip Planner, 256 pp., $14.95

Northern California Travel•Smart Trip Planner, 272 pp., $15.95

Pacific Northwest Travel•Smart Trip Planner, 240 pp., $14.95

Other Terrific Travel Titles

The 100 Best Small Art Towns in America, 256 pp., $15.95

The Big Book of Adventure Travel, 384 pp., $17.95

Indian America: A Traveler's Companion, 480 pp., $18.95

The People's Guide to Mexico, 608 pp., $19.95

Ranch Vacations: The Complete Guide to Guest and Resort, Fly-Fishing, and Cross-Country Skiing Ranches, 632 pp., $22.95

Understanding Europeans, 272 pp., $14.95

Undiscovered Islands of the Caribbean, 336 pp., $16.95

Watch It Made in the U.S.A.: A Visitor's Guide to the Companies that Make Your Favorite Products, 328 pp., $16.95

The World Awaits, 280 pp., $16.95

The Birder's Guide to Bed and Breakfasts: U.S. and Canada, 416 pp., $17.95

Automotive Titles

The Greaseless Guide to Car Care, 272 pp., $19.95

How to Keep Your Subaru Alive, 480 pp., $21.95

How to Keep Your Toyota Pickup Alive, 392 pp., $21.95

How to Keep Your VW Alive, 464 pp., $25

Ordering Information

Please check your local bookstore for our books, or call **1-800-888-7504** to order direct and to receive a complete catalog. A shipping charge will be added to your order total.

Send all inquiries to:
John Muir Publications
P.O. Box 613
Santa Fe, NM 87504